An Introduction to Spanish for Health Care Workers

An Introduction to Spanish for Health Care Workers

Communication and Culture

THIRD EDITION

Robert O. Chase

Clarisa B. Medina de Chase

YALE UNIVERSITY PRESS NEW HAVEN & LONDON

Publisher: Mary Jane Peluso
Editorial Assistant: Elise Panza
Project Editor: Timothy Shea
Production Editor: Ann-Marie Imbornoni
Production Controller: Karen Stickler

Designed by James J. Johnson and set by
Integrated Publishing Solutions.

Printed in the United States of America.

A catalogue record for this book is available
from the British Library.

This paper meets the requirements of ANSI/
NISO Z39.48-1992 (Permanence of Paper).

10 9 8 7 6 5 4 3

*Library of Congress Cataloging-in-Publication
  Data*

Chase, Robert O. 1955–
  An introduction to Spanish for health care
workers : communication and culture / Robert
O. Chase [and] Clarisa B. Medina de Chase. —
3rd ed.
      p.   cm.
ISBN 978-0-300-12426-2 (pbk. : alk. paper)
1. Spanish language—Conversation and phrase
books (for medical personnel) 2. Spanish
language—Textbooks for foreign speakers—
English. I. Medina de Chase, Clarisa B., 1963–
II. Title.
    PC4120.M3C43   2008
    468.3′42102461—dc22   2008026314

Contents

Scope and Sequence

Preface

Effective communication is essential in health care, and communication is most effective when both parties share a common language. Patients are expected to articulate history, symptoms, and their understanding of diagnosis and treatment recommendations. Health care workers must clarify and comprehend this information, teach patients about treatment options, and obtain informed consent for procedures.

When the patient and the health care provider do not speak the same language, there are many reasons to accommodate the patient. Language accommodation increases health care access for a growing clientele of people with limited proficiency in English. Providers who accommodate the patient's language elicit better information for diagnosis and treatment and inspire patients to follow recommendations, thus reducing delays in seeking care, enhancing quality of care, and improving treatment outcomes. When health care providers are able to include family and community members in communication, patients are more able to make use of these informal supports.

Language accommodation, also called language access services, helps to meet accreditation standards, increases patient satisfaction and retention, and may decrease malpractice claims. Beginning in 2005 the Joint Commission required hospitals and other providers to document each patient's language and communication needs in the medical record. Newer elements of performance require that organizations respect the right and need of patients for effective communication; that written information provided be appropriate to the patient's language; and that organizations provide or assist patients in obtaining interpretation and translation services as necessary. Good practice is the best inoculation against malpractice. Because the angry patient is the most likely to become litigious, then forming satisfying relationships and investing in effective communication may help reduce exposure to judicial intervention.

Working in two languages is satisfying to health care givers as well. More than a competitive edge in the job market, bilingual health care workers gain the ability to directly communicate with patients with whom they otherwise would have required an interpreter. Of course, qualified medical interpreters are essential for complex communication tasks that are beyond the language ability of the practitioner. However, in many common interactions a functionally bilingual professional is able to conduct specific linguistic tasks without an interpreter and to avoid the temptation to inappropriately make use of a family member or non-qualified person as interpreter. Non-native speakers of a second language develop positive attitudes towards the second language and its speakers. They learn to appreciate the challenges and accomplishments of their patients who acquire English as a second language. Bilingual health care workers are more sensitive to cultural nuances that affect communication, relationship styles, and treatment adherence. In addition, studies have shown that bilingualism itself promotes memory and helps postpone age-related cognitive losses.

United States law requires language accommodation. Title VI of the Civil Rights Act of 1964 prohibits the exclusion of individuals from federally funded activities on the basis of race, color, or national origin. Almost ten years later, a group of students of Chinese origin raised its concern that language differences kept the group from having access to federally funded educational programs in San Francisco, California. The United States Supreme Court addressed this (Lau v. Nichols, January 21, 1974) by clarifying that Title VI prohibited conduct that had a disproportionate effect on limited-English-proficiency individuals, because such conduct constituted national origin discrimination.

The Civil Rights Division of the United States Department of Justice enforces laws that require taking reasonable steps to provide meaningful access for limited-English-proficiency (LEP) individuals. LEP individuals do not speak English as their primary language and have a limited ability to read, write, speak, or understand English. Many LEP persons are in the process of learning English and have various levels of proficiency. LEP status may be context-specific. That is, an individual may have sufficient English skills to communicate basic information but not to communicate detailed medical or affective information in English.

In many areas, Latinos suffer disproportionately from preventable diseases, late prenatal care, and hospitalization for chronic conditions such as childhood asthma and adult diabetes. Although poverty and lack of insurance are factors, a lot of Latinos indicate that they have difficulty understanding the treatment provider's language.

Practitioners and health care organizations can take various steps towards becoming linguistically competent and accessible. These include hiring clinically, linguistically, and culturally competent bilingual staff; employing qualified interpreters; and providing target-language written materials. Bilingual staff should be carefully screened for their linguistic proficiency in both languages, rewarded for their important contribution, and given interpreter training. Qualified interpreter agencies are useful when proven bilingual staff is not available, and telephone services should be reserved for emergencies. Professionals who work through interpreters can seek training to learn to use interpreters more effectively.

Taking a course based on *An Introduction to Spanish for Health Care Workers* is a good first step toward acquiring Spanish as a second language for health care workers who are committed to relating directly with patients in specific medical practice areas. Subsequent steps include continued practice with native speakers, further course work, and if possible, immersion in a Spanish-speaking community or country.

Acknowledgments

Friends, students, family, and coworkers enriched this edition with their expertise and encouragement. We are indebted to each person who listened to ideas, revealed lexical needs, read manuscript, tested activities, or play-acted improvisations. We gratefully acknowledge our sister, Professor Myra M. Medina of Miami Dade College, and our colleague and friend Doctor William Fernando Jiménez P. for reviewing the video script. We thank our friends Harry and Elizabeth Hernández and Ruby Sol Herrera de Muldoon for helping with a first trial run of the scenes. Lively groups of medical students from the Yale School of Medicine and the Yale School of Public Health, and a hard-working group of medical residents from the Hospital of Central Connecticut, tested classroom activities and identified lexical needs. Our friend Stephen Lieberman and other students of Tunxis Community College tested *Drama imprevisto* features. Alexandre Carré, M.D. and Norma Wright, R.Ph. of the Whiting Forensic Institute reviewed specific sections of the text and artwork. Mike Zych, who inspires the best in everyone, was an art technology mentor. Graphic artist Frank Dlugoleski has been a committed and central member of our team since the first edition.

The third edition also was improved by criticism, comments, and recommendations submitted by a sample group of professors who have either reviewed or adopted previous editions, and by comments elicited by sales representative Jennifer Matty of Yale University Press. These reviewers included Victor Manuel Duran, University of South Carolina; Sarah Dutton, Johns Hopkins Medical Institutions; John Hays, Tyler Junior College; Katya E. Monge-Hall, Pacific University; Nela Navarro, Rutgers University; Eva Paris-Huesca, University of Nebraska; Sara Scavongelli, University of Virginia; and Mary-Anne Vertterling, Regis College.

We give heartfelt thanks to Doctor Julia Ball of the University of South Carolina, Aiken, School of Nursing, for video location. We send a warm "Hey, all y'all!" with our loving appreciation to a fun and dedicated film production crew from Truth-Function, including Hugo, Tom, Dave, Lamar, and Dan; a rocking group of gaffers, grips, swings, hair, makeup, and wardrobe professionals; and acting talents Daisy, Luisa, Isabella, Luis, and Franco.

Introduction

An Introduction to Spanish for Health Care Workers facilitates better communication between health care providers and the growing Spanish-speaking community in the United States. It is not a phrase book or a translator. It is a first course in Spanish, progressively merging conversation and health care vocabulary in various medical contexts. Although it does not call for a prerequisite knowledge of Spanish, this book is also helpful to people who speak limited Spanish and aspire to apply their Spanish in a medical setting. Topics include building the patient-practitioner relationship, the patient's chief complaint, taking medical history, and defining current symptoms. We progress to injuries, pharmacotherapy, diet and nutrition, tests and procedures, diagnoses, and specialized topics such as hospitalizations, dentistry, mental health, palliative care, maternity, and the promotion of safer sex.

The crucial precepts of the book are context and communication. Vocabulary is organized by specific medical themes, and grammar lessons do not distract from the goal of conversing with patients. While sitting on a Cancún beach during spring break, no thirsty student thinks, "What an ideal place to use a stem-changing verb in the present tense!" Rather, the need to communicate trumps grammar, and the student ventures, "*Quiero una piña colada por favor.*" The message is first, and the student learns correct speech by using language for a purpose. The text is divided into sections that are named for practical communication goals. This highlights the focus on learning functional language that prepares students to deliver health care in a patient's preferred language. Grammar appears in the context of specific communication tasks. For example, command forms are taught in the context of giving medication instructions. This is a guided, learn-by-doing approach in which students acquire language while using it in meaningful interaction.

The third edition has added several additional grammatical structures, including the imperfect mood of the past tense and the informal commands. The imperfect mood is presented in the learning context of talking about former, unhealthy practices while at a cardiac rehabilitation center. In the video program, the protagonists illustrate the imperfect mood by talking about things they miss most from their countries of origin. The third edition teaches formal commands earlier in the text, in chapter 6, which employs the learning context of the pharmacy. Informal commands appear in chapter 12, in the context of labor and delivery. Some of the artwork has been updated, and new illustrations have been added to the third edition. The newer illustrations are linked to communicative activities that cue, prompt, and scaffold conversation. The third-edition lexicon is expanded to more than 1,500 words in each of the glossaries, English to Spanish and Spanish to English.

Recognizing the preeminence of comprehensible input and good lexical models in second-language acquisition, the third edition features a professionally produced, high definition, DVD-format video program. The twenty-four video clips are brief enough to enhance "replay-ability" and not overwhelm the student. Video segments are called *La trama* (the plot) and *Demostración. La trama* is a series of interactions between the Flores family, Dr. Vargas, and Dr. Vargas's nurse, Rosmery. These closely follow the lexicon and structure as they develop in the book. *Demostración* is a segment that demonstrates a specific communication task in health care. For example, in chapter 2, Dr. Vargas and Sr. Flores demonstrate how to evaluate a patient for orientation to person, place, and time. The final two chapters do not have a *Demostración*. Instead, they present an *Atracción especial,* in which the cast performs improvisation exercises from chapters 11 and 12. Spanish subtitles are available.

The third edition has a companion Web site, where you'll now find the Learning Check feature. Self-correcting quizzes test new skills while reinforcing medical vocabulary and related grammar. Students receive feedback about which skills may need further practice and have the opportunity to e-mail results to their instructor. The Web site also provides links to medical and language sites on the World Wide Web and ideas for teachers and learners. These post-communicative activities allow learner autonomy while making use of authentic resources. On the Web site you'll be able to download the video program soundtracks to personal digital audio players. The companion Web site can be found at **www.yalebooks.com/ medicalspanish**.

An Introduction to Spanish for Health Care Workers structures class sessions around exercises that compel students to speak Spanish in the classroom, preparing them for the emotional and linguistic challenges of speaking to native Spanish-speaking patients. The third edition reduces the number of mechanical exercises and increases the number of unscripted interaction activities. We use five icons to differentiate types of class activities.

A bicycle icon denotes *Ejercicios,* or directed mechanical activities that have only one correct response and are intended to promote accuracy. The third edition limits the number of mechanical exercises to those that are needed to clarify grammar instruction. This leaves room for more effective communicative classroom activities that require autonomous (student-directed) language production. There tend to be more *Ejercicios* in the first chapter, where everything may be new to you, and in the chapter about pharmacy, where accuracy is even more essential. At the end of the book you'll find an answer key to the *Ejercicios.*

An icon of two faces identifies communicative *Actividades,* which are interactive and open-ended. They call for students to use Spanish to complete a practical task that is typical to a medical setting. The instructor is available for coaching and consultation, while students practice with partners, play roles, and solve problems.

Two Greek drama masks signal unscripted improvisation activities, called *Drama imprevisto.* Of all the risks you'll take as a novice speaker, improvisation may be the most enjoyable. When you improvise, you encode your own thoughts into words within a defined social and lexical context. You can repeat, videotape, and review your improvisations. This allows you to monitor and correct your own speech. Self correction is considered more effective than instructor-originated correction, which is called recasting. When you improvise, you take responsibility for your speech as you explore the cultural aspects of social interaction. Even an exceptionally shy student may start as an observer or evaluator prior to joining as an actor. Improvisation is a fun way to build confidence, and may be "the new role-play" of the communicative classroom.

A three-arrow recycling icon appears next to *Reciclaje* activities that consolidate learning by showing new uses for previously learned vocabulary and structures. When acquiring a second language, it is not possible to review too much.

Where the DVD icon appears, students are prompted to watch a section of the video and to do activities based on the video program. At times, a student will not understand a video scene upon first viewing, although this will resolve after completing the corresponding chapter and reviewing the video. Each scene illustrates the structure, vocabulary, and communication goals of the chapter in which it appears. These are integrated into the text with activities based on the video. This allows students to observe good models interacting with patients, to check their comprehension, and to practice new skills while being coached by peers and the instructor.

A Cultural Note appears at the end of each chapter. The culture features that we recall from high school Spanish taught us about flags, exports, and capitals. The notes in this book do not focus on specific countries, as Spanish and Hispanic cultures are exceptionally diverse. Instead, they inform you on matters of immigration, acculturation, worldviews, diverse customs, communication styles, and language accommodation to support your development of an even more culturally competent practice.

Note that the medical information and illustrations included in the text are not intended to diagnose or treat illnesses. Although these dialogues, vignettes, and exercises are derived from lexical needs assessments and the authors' experiences interpreting for various practitioners, they are included here for the sole purpose of teaching language.

Chapter 1

«Buenos días, soy el doctor»

By the time you finish this book you will be able to conduct essential medical interviews in Spanish, including patient registration, history-taking and physical examinations, common procedures, instructions for diet and pharmacotherapy, and health education. You will be more aware of some cultural dynamics of the healing relationship. With practice and experience, you will be able to communicate effectively in Spanish in your medical setting. By the end of this chapter, you will be able to greet patients in Spanish, introduce yourself by name and profession, and describe people.

Greet Your Patient and Introduce Yourself

DIÁLOGO

Dr. Vargas:	Buenos días. Soy el doctor Vargas.
Sr. Flores:	Buenos días, doctor. Me llamo Francisco Flores.
Dr. Vargas:	Mucho gusto.
Sr. Flores:	El gusto es mío. ¿Cómo está usted?
Dr. Vargas:	Muy bien, gracias, ¿y usted?
Sr. Flores:	Bien, bien, gracias.

«Mucho gusto.»

Vocabulario: Saludos y despedidas (Greetings and Farewells)

Hola.	Hello.
Buenos días.	Good morning.
Buenas tardes.	Good afternoon.
Buenas noches.	Good evening; good night.
¿Cómo está usted?	How are you?

Estoy bien, gracias.	I am fine, thank you.
Muy bien.	Very well.
Me alegro.	I'm glad.
¿Y usted?	And you?
Estoy mal.	I'm ill.
Lo siento.	I'm sorry.
Mucho gusto.	Pleased to meet you.
Encantado/a.*	Pleased to meet you.
El gusto es mío.	The pleasure is mine.
Igualmente.	Same here
Adiós.	Good-bye.
Hasta luego.	See you later.

Preguntas útiles

¿De dónde es usted?	Where are you from?
¿Cómo se llama usted?	What is your name?

Expresiones útiles

Soy el doctor Vargas.	I am Doctor Vargas.
Me llamo Francisco Flores.	My name is Francisco Flores.
Soy de Puerto Rico.	I am from Puerto Rico.
Soy puertorriqueño.	I am Puerto Rican.
Le presento a la doctora García.	I introduce you to Doctor García.

 ## 1.1 Actividad

Repeat the greetings and farewells after the instructor. After the instructor demonstrates with several students, get up and move around the room, greeting your peers. It is customary to shake hands when you greet someone. Many people consider *hola* too casual for a first meeting. The letter «h» is silent in Spanish, as in *hola* (OH-la) and *hospital* (os-pi-TAL). The letter «ñ», as in the title *señora,* is pronounced like the "ni" in the word "onion". The letters «v» and «b» in Spanish both sound similar to the English "b" but are pronounced more softly. (There are pronunciation notes at the end of each of the first five chapters.)

 ## 1.2 Actividad

From your places, take turns introducing yourselves to your neighbor by name.

---

*If you are female, say *encantada.*

	Example:	Student 1:	Buenas tardes. Me llamo Paul. ¿Cómo se llama usted?
		Student 2:	Buenas tardes. Me llamo Carol.
		Class:	Hola, Carol. ¿Cómo está usted?
		Student 2:	Bien, gracias. (*To student 3*) Buenas tardes. Me llamo Carol. ¿Cómo se llama usted?

Continue in this way until everyone has had a turn.

The nouns *cubano, mexicana,* and *enfermero* can end in *-o* or *-a.* The *-o* denotes the masculine form, and the *-a* denotes the feminine form. These nouns are used in their masculine or feminine form in order to agree with the gender of the person they represent. Words for nationalities are not capitalized in Spanish (*cubano*). Notice that upside-down question marks and exclamation marks are used at the beginning of written questions and exclamations.

Soy enfermera.   Soy enfermero.

Estructura: Los sujetos y el verbo *ser*
(Subject Pronouns and the Verb *Ser*)

- These are the singular subject pronouns.

yo	I
tú	you (*familiar*)
él	he

ella	she
usted (Ud.)	you (*formal*)

- Note that *el* means "the" and *él* means "he." The subject pronouns *tú* and *usted* both mean "you." *Tú* is normally used with someone with whom you are on a first-name basis and with a child. *Usted* is used with all others. Using *usted* where *tú* is normally used may seem overly formal or make more obvious the fact that you are not a native speaker, but it will not offend anyone. (Granted, it would sound silly if used with a child!) Using *tú* where *usted* would be proper may offend. Certain ethnic groups (those from the Caribbean, for example) use the *tú* form more readily than others, but one should always use *usted* when in doubt.

- Here is the verb *ser,* which means "to be." It can be used to tell your name, your occupation, or your national origin, for example. As in English (*I am, you are*), the verb changes its form depending on its subject. Note that with the forms *soy* and *eres,* the pronoun is implied; the form *es* can mean *you, she, he,* or *it is.* In forming questions, the subject and verb can be reversed.

Soy enfermero.	I am a nurse.
¡*Eres* muy amable!	You are very kind!
¿*Es* usted la madre?	Are you the mother?
Él *es* mi papá.	He is my dad.
Ella *es* doctora.	She is a doctor.
El hospital *es* grande.	The hospital is big.

 ## 1.3 Ejercicio

You work in an emergency room. Say whether you would use *tú* or *usted* with the following people.

> Answers to the *Ejercicios* may be found in the Answer Key at the end of the textbook.

- A. The Spanish-speaking nurse who usually works with you.
- B. Your patient, age five.
- C. Your new pediatric patient's mother.
- D. The new resident physician from Guatemala, whom you've not met.
- E. A friend from the Spanish class who meets you for lunch.
- F. Your new patient, age forty-seven.

 ## 1.4 Ejercicio

Fill in the blanks with the missing information.

Soy Juan.	I am Juan.
Soy norteamericano.	_____ North American.
_____ enfermero.	I am a (male) nurse.
¿Es usted estudiante?	Are _____ a student?
Él es el señor Soto.	_____.
_____.	He is North American.
_____.	She is Doctor Jerez.
_____.	She is Mexican.

Note: Spanish does not use the definite article *el* or *la* (the) or the indefinite article *un* or *una* (a, an) after the verb *ser* when stating a profession or nationality. For example, *Soy médico* means "I am a doctor." The definite article is often used with titles, as in the sentence *La doctora es la doctora García.* Such titles as *doctor* and *señor* are capitalized only when abbreviated (*Dr.* and *Sr.*).

Vocabulario: Las profesiones (Professions)

el anestesiólogo (*male*), la anestesióloga (*female*)	anesthesiologist
el asociado médico, la asociada médica	physician's assistant
el audiólogo, la audióloga	audiologist
el/la ayudante de enfermero	nurse's aide
el cardiólogo, la cardióloga	cardiologist
el cirujano, la cirujana	surgeon
el comadrón, la comadrona	midwife
el consejero, la consejera	counselor
el/la dentista, el odontólogo, la odontóloga	dentist
el dermatólogo, la dermatóloga	dermatologist
el/la dietista	dietitian
el doctor, la doctora, el médico, la médica	doctor

el endocrinólogo, la endocrinóloga	endocrinologist
el enfermero, la enfermera	nurse
el/la estudiante de medicina	medical student
el farmacéutico, la farmacéutica	pharmacist
el ginecólogo, la ginecóloga	gynecologist
el/la higienista dental	dental hygienist
el/la médico/a generalista, el/la medico/a de cabecera	general practitioner
el médico internista, la médica internista	internist
el neumólogo, la neumóloga	pulmonologist
el neurólogo, la neuróloga	neurologist
el/la nutricionista	nutritionist
el/la obstetra	obstetrician
el oftalmólogo, la oftalmóloga	ophthalmologist
el oncólogo, la oncóloga	oncologist
el/la ortopedista	orthopedist
el otorrinolaringólogo, la otorrinolaringóloga	ENT doctor
el partero, la partera	midwife
el/la pediatra	pediatrician
el podiólogo, la podióloga	podiatrist
el psicólogo, la psicóloga	psychologist
el/la psiquiatra	psychiatrist
el radiólogo, la radióloga	radiologist
el/la recepcionista	receptionist
el reumatólogo, la reumatóloga	rheumatologist
el secretario, la secretaria	secretary
el técnico de radiografía, la técnica de radiografía	x-ray technician
el/la terapeuta	therapist
el/la terapeuta del habla	speech therapist
el terapeuta físico, la terapeuta física	physical therapist
el terapeuta respiratorio, la terapeuta respiratoria	respiratory therapist
el trabajador social, la trabajadora social	social worker
el urólogo, la uróloga	urologist

Preguntas útiles

¿En qué trabaja usted?	What do you do for work?
¿Cuál es su especialidad?	What is your specialty?

la doctora el doctor

el obstetra

el pediatra

la radióloga

la secretaria

la cirujana

The Spanish translation of "physician's assistant," *asociado médico,* was adopted by the American Academy of Physician Assistants in 1998 and re-affirmed in 2003. Due to its uniqueness to the United States, the special-ization of nurse practitioner does not have a concise counterpart in Span-ish. Depending on state laws, you may say, *un enfermero con licencia para diagnosticar y tratar padecimientos y recetar medicamentos* (a nurse who has a license to diagnose and treat ailments and prescribe medications).

 ## 1.5 Ejercicio

Repeat after the instructor the words in the preceding vocabulary list. You'll notice that many have accents that guide pronunciation. The letter «g» is fricative like the English "h" when it precedes the vowels «e» and «i». It is like the "g" in the English word "go" before the vowels «a», «o», and «u». The word *ginecólogo* contains an example of both. «J» is always pronounced like English "h," as in *cirujano.*

 ## 1.6 Ejercicio

Words that sound similar in two languages and have the same meaning are called "close cognates." Those that have different meanings are called "false cognates," and may lead to misunderstanding. You'll safely guess the meaning of the following close cognates. Listen to the instructor read the following patient chief concerns, and refer him or her to the appropriate discipline, as in the example. There may be more than one correct response.

> Example: Instructor: Sufro de migrañas.
> Class: Usted necesita un neurólogo.

A. Necesito una inyección.
B. Sufro de problemas cardíacos.
C. Sufro de diabetes.
D. Necesito una operación.
E. Sufro de cáncer de los pulmones.
F. Sufro de cataratas.
G. Necesito una dieta especial.
H. Sufro de problemas emocionales.
I. Sufro de artritis.
J. Tengo la clavícula fracturada.
K. Sufro de psoriasis.
L. Mi bebé tiene fiebre.

 ## 1.7 Actividad

Speed dating is here! Find the Spanish name for your own profession. Next, move around the classroom introducing yourself and asking fellow students their occupations, as in the example.

> Example: Student 1:   Buenas tardes. Soy Roberto. Soy
>   enfermero.
>   Student 2:   Mucho gusto, Roberto. Soy Nancy.
>   Student 1:   Encantado. ¿En qué trabaja usted?
>   Student 2:   Soy médica.
>   Student 1:   ¿Cuál es su especialidad?
>   Student 2:   Soy oftalmóloga.

Continue until you have spoken with everyone. When you have finished, take turns reporting your findings to the class. For example, *Ella es Nancy; es oftalmóloga. Él es William; es cirujano.*

 ## 1.8 Drama imprevisto

Review the list of medical professions and find one that you may be able to mime. All students then mingle in the classroom and simultaneously mime their chosen specialties. If you are able, say words, ask questions, or make statements that are associated with the profession that you selected from the list. To finish, try to guess each person's role: *Sarah es odontóloga; Paul es ortopedista,* and so on.

Estructura: El género y número de los nombres y artículos definidos (Gender and Number of Nouns and Definite Articles)

- In Spanish some nouns are masculine, like *el hospital* (the hospital), while others are feminine, like *la cama* (the bed). The singular masculine article is *el,* and the singular feminine article is *la.* With some exceptions, nouns ending in *-o* are masculine, and nouns ending in *-a* are feminine.
- Some nouns that refer to people change the last letter to become masculine or feminine. A male nurse is *el enfermero,* and a female nurse is *la enfermera.* Similarly, nouns indicating origin, such as *norteamericano,* end in either *-o* or *-a* according to the gender of the person to whom they refer. For example,

el enfermero   los enfermeros   la enfermera   las enfermeras

Soy Marco. Soy enfermero. Soy norteamericano.

La doctora García es cirujana. No es chilena, es mexicana.

- Recall that medical professions ending in *-iatra* and *-ista* can be either masculine or feminine. In these cases the definite articles are used to indicate gender. A male pediatrician is *el pediatra,* while a female pediatrician is *la pediatra.*
- When speaking about a third person and using a title with the last name, the definite article is placed before the title, as in *El doctor Robinson es norteamericano.* The definite article is not used when addressing someone, as in *Buenas tardes, doctor Robinson.*
- Nouns or adjectives ending in *-e,* such as *estudiante* and *paciente,* can be either masculine or feminine, depending on the gender of the person. A male student is *el estudiante,* while a female student is *la estudiante.* Words ending in *-ción,* such as *la infección,* are feminine. *Día* is masculine, so we say, *¡Buenos días! Mano* is feminine, so we say, *la mano.* Most words ending in *-ma* or *-pa* are masculine and are of Greek origin: for example, *el mapa, el problema,* and *el sistema.*

- To make nouns plural in Spanish we add -*s* to nouns that end in vowels and -*es* to those ending in consonants. The articles and nouns must always agree in gender and number. The plural masculine article is *los*, and the plural feminine article is *las*.

Singular	*Plural*
el enfermero	los enfermeros
la enfermera	las enfermeras
el doctor	los doctores
la doctora	las doctoras
el hospital	los hospitales

 1.9 Ejercicio

Change the nouns to agree with the gender of the person, as in the example.

Example: El señor Nieves es secretario / La señora Nieves
El señor Nieves es secretario; la señora Nieves
es secretaria.

A. El doctor Colón es neurólogo / La doctora Palma
B. El doctor Aquino es odontólogo / La doctora Valenzuela
C. Ana es trabajadora social / Tomás
D. El señor García es consejero / La señora Marques
E. Leomara es farmacéutica / Alfredo
F. La doctora López es cardióloga / El doctor López
G. La doctora Negrón es dentista / El doctor Losada Gutiérrez

 1.10 Ejercicio

Give the plural of the following nouns and definite articles as in the example.

Example: la trabajadora social / las trabajadoras sociales

A. la clínica   _____ _____

B. la puerta   _____ _____

C. el monitor   _____ _____

D. la cama   _____ _____

E. la sábana   _____ _____

F. la frazada   _____ _____

G. la almohada   _____   _____

H. el doctor   _____   _____

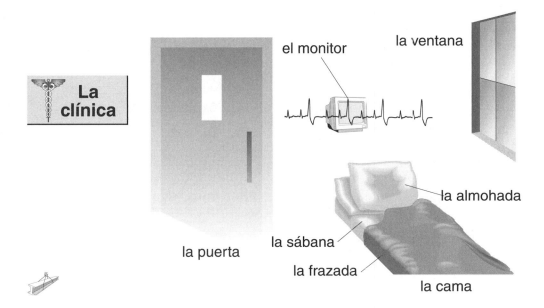

Estructura: Las formas plurales del verbo *ser*
(Plural Forms of the Verb *Ser*)

- Subjects and verbs, of course, have plural forms as well. These are the plural subject pronouns.

nosotros	we (*males or mixed gender*)
nosotras	we (*all females*)
ellos	they (*males or mixed gender*)
ellas	they (*all females*)
ustedes	you (*plural, or "you all"*)

- Note that the masculine forms *nosotros* and *ellos* are used for a group of all males or a mixed group of males and females; the feminine forms *nosotras* and *ellas* are used with groups of all females. Perhaps a linguistic vestige of patriarchy or like the proverbial rotten apple that spoils the barrel, the presence of even one male in a group of females requires the use of the masculine form.

- Here are the plural forms of the verb *ser.*

Nosotros *somos* enfermeros.	We are nurses.
Nosotras *somos* mexicanas.	We (all female) are Mexican.
Ellos *son* estudiantes.	They are students.
Ellas *son* doctoras.	They (all female) are doctors.
Ustedes *son* estudiantes.	You all are students.

1.11 Ejercicio

Subject pronouns can substitute for the name of a person or thing and act as the subject of the verb. Say which Spanish pronouns or subjects are implied by the following, as in the example, and add the appropriate form of the verb *ser*. Note that the Spanish word *y* means "and," and is pronounced like "ee" in the English word "see."

Example: Juan   *él es*

A. El Sr. Romero _____   F. la clase y yo   _____

B. Juan y yo   _____   G. los doctores   _____

C. Sergio y Ana   _____   H. el doctor y el enfermero _____

D. las enfermeras _____   I. la clínica   _____

E. la familia   _____   J. usted, usted y usted   _____

 1.12 Ejercicio

Express the following statements in Spanish. Remember the agreement of gender and number. The first statement has been done for you.

A. Juan and Marco are nurses.   Juan y Marco son enfermeros.

B. Ana and María are doctors.   _____.

C. We are students.   _____.

D. Pablo and I are social workers. _____.

E. Héctor and I are neurologists. _____.

F. The (female) nurses are
    Mexican.   _____.

G. The (mixed gender) nurses are
   Spanish.   _____.

H. Daniel and Patricia are
   psychologists.   _____.

1.13 Actividad

The lines of the following dialogue are out of order. Work in groups of three to put them in the correct order by numbering them in the spaces provided. Then take turns reading your finished product to the class.

_____ Dr. Vargas: Buenos días. Soy el doctor Vargas.

_____ Sr. Flores: Bien, bien, gracias. Doctor, le presento a mi esposa Marisol García de Flores.

_____ Dr. Vargas: Muy bien, gracias, ¿y usted?

_____ Sr. Flores: El gusto es mío. ¿Cómo está usted?

_____ Dr. Vargas: Encantado.

_____ Dr. Vargas: Soy de Puerto Rico.

_____ Sra. Flores: Igualmente. Usted habla español. ¿De dónde es usted?

_____ Dr. Vargas: Mucho gusto.

_____ Sr. Flores: Buenos días, doctor. Soy Francisco Flores.

> *¿dónde?* where?

Vocabulario: Los países y las identidades nacionales
(Countries and Ethnicities)

Región	*País*	*Identidad nacional*
	España	español/española
	los Estados Unidos	estadounidense, norteamericano/a
	México	mexicano/a
El Caribe		
	Cuba	cubano/a
	La República Dominicana	dominicano/a
	Puerto Rico	puertorriqueño/a
América Central		
	Guatemala	guatemalteco/a
	Honduras	hondureño/a
	El Salvador	salvadoreño/a
	Nicaragua	nicaragüense
	Costa Rica	costarricense
	Panamá	panameño/a

América del Sur

Venezuela	venezolano/a
Colombia	colombiano/a
Ecuador	ecuatoriano/a
Perú	peruano/a
Bolivia	boliviano/a
Paraguay	paraguayo/a
Chile	chileno/a
Uruguay	uruguayo/a
Argentina	argentino/a

Preguntas útiles

¿De dónde es usted?	Where are you from?
¿De dónde eres?	Where are you from (*informal*)?

Expresiones útiles

Soy de Colombia.	I am from Colombia.
Soy colombiano.	I am Colombian.
La doctora es uruguaya.	The doctor is Uruguayan.

Puerto Rico has commonwealth status with the United States. Some ethnic groups have popular words for their national identity. For example, Puerto Ricans may call themselves *boricuas* or *borinqueños;* Dominicans, *quisqueyanos;* and Costa Ricans, *ticos.* Immigrants to the United States may add the extension *americano/a* to their national origin when they wish to, as in *colombianoamericano.*

✎ Ask Your Patient's Name

Recall that *¿Cómo se llama usted?* means "What is your name?" Literally, it means, "How do you call yourself?" The letters «ll» are pronounced like the English letter "y." The reflexive pronouns *se* and *te* are discussed in chapter 11. Here are some variations.

¿Cómo se llama usted?	What is your name?
¿Cómo te llamas?*	What is your name?
Me llamo Arturo.	My name is Arturo.
¿Cómo se llama el (la) bebé?	What is the baby's name?
¿Cómo se llama el niño (la niña)?	What is the child's name?
Él se llama Armando.	His name is Armando.
Ella se llama Rosalinda.	Her name is Rosalinda.

*This is the familiar *tú* form, used with acquaintances and children.

1.14 Actividad

With so many new friends from class, it is time to update your Rolodex™. Move around the classroom asking fellow students their name, profession, and national origin. Fill in the Rolodex™ cards that follow.

Nombre: _____

Profesión: _____

Nacionalidad:_____

Nombre: _____

Profesión: _____

Nacionalidad:_____

Nombre: _____

Profesión: _____

Nacionalidad:_____

Nombre: _____

Profesión: _____

Nacionalidad:_____

Nombre: _____

Profesión: _____

Nacionalidad:_____

Nombre: _____

Profesión: _____

Nacionalidad:_____

Nombre: _____

Profesión: _____

Nacionalidad:_____

Nombre: _____

Profesión: _____

Nacionalidad:_____

1.15 Actividad

Role-play a case conference or morning rounds. Designate a classmate to be the patient, and take turns introducing yourself by name, profession, and national origin.

> Example: Hola. Me llamo Cristóbal. Soy dietista. Soy de los Estados Unidos.

When you have finished, test your memory by introducing all of the people in the room. For example, *Ella es Nancy; es trabajadora social. Él es Bill; es cirujano. Bill es estadounidense.* If you forget someone's personal information, ask for it again. You've learned how to ask someone's name, profession or occupation, and national origin.

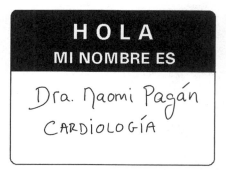

HOLA
MI NOMBRE ES

Dra. Naomi Pagán
CARDIOLOGÍA

 ## 1.16 Drama imprevisto

Circulate in the classroom asking classmates for name, profession, and national origin. This time, fib about all of it, telling the same fib each time you are asked. Practice new words and test your classmates' memory. After everyone has a turn interviewing each classmate, share the information (false as it may be) you have found out with the class.

 ## Video Program: «*Buenos días, soy el doctor Vargas*»

> From the textbook's Web site you can download the audio tracks of the video program to your personal digital audio player.

Watch the *Trama* for chapter 1 and do the activities that follow.

Mi nombre es Elsita. Mi papá se llama Francisco Flores, y mi mamá se llama Marisol García de Flores. Mi muñeca se llama Samantha. Ella está enferma. Le duelen los oídos. Necesita consultar con un otorrinolaringólogo.

Me llamo Francisco Flores. Soy casado. Mi esposa se llama Marisol García de Flores. Tenemos una hija. Ella se llama Elsita.

Soy Marisol García de Flores. Soy dominicana, de Santo Domingo. Mi padre tiene problema con la próstata, pero está bien, gracias a Dios. Vamos a consultar con un urólogo.

Soy el doctor Vargas. Soy de Puerto Rico. Soy médico generalista. No soy especialista. Trabajo con una variedad de problemas médicos.

Sr. Flores:	Doctor, le presento a mi esposa Marisol García de Flores y a nuestra hija, Elsita.
Dr. Vargas:	Encantado.
Sra. Flores:	Igualmente. Usted habla español. ¿De dónde es usted?
Dr. Vargas:	Soy de Puerto Rico.
Sra. Flores:	Ah, usted es puertorriqueño. Soy dominicana, de la capital, Santo Domingo. ¿Cuál es su especialidad, doctor? ¿Es cardiólogo?
Dr. Vargas:	No, no soy cardiólogo. Los cardiólogos trabajan con problemas del corazón. Yo soy un médico generalista. Trabajo con una variedad de problemas médicos.

Sra. Flores:	Doctor, perdón, pero mi padre sufre de la próstata y no tiene doctor. Él necesita un médico, y usted es muy amable.
Dr. Vargas:	Si su padre tiene problema con la próstata, necesita un urólogo. Hay un buen urólogo en la clínica ambulatoria del hospital.
Sra. Flores:	Gracias. Doctor, otra pregunta. Elsita necesita un pediatra. ¿Hay algún pediatra bueno en la clínica también?
Dr. Vargas:	Sí. Los pediatras son especialistas que trabajan con los niños. ¿Cómo estás, Elsita?
Elsita:	Yo estoy bien, gracias, pero mi muñeca no está bien. Está enfermita. Le duelen los oídos. Le duelen mucho los oídos.
Dr. Vargas:	¿Cómo se llama tu muñeca?
Elsita:	Ella se llama Samantha.
Dr. Vargas:	Samantha es un nombre bonito. No te preocupes, Elsita. Samantha va a estar bien. Si le duelen los oídos, tiene que ir a un otorrinolaringólogo. Los otorrinolaringólogos son especialistas con los oídos, la nariz y la garganta.

 1.17 Ejercicio

Complete the following sentences with the correct words from those in parentheses, and read them aloud.

A. La esposa del Sr. Flores se llama (a. Elsita, b. Marisol, c. Francisca).

B. El doctor Vargas es de (a. Puerto Rico, b. La República Dominicana, c. México).

C. La familia Flores es de (a. Puerto Rico, b. La República Dominicana, c. México).

D. El doctor Vargas es (a. cardiólogo, b. urólogo, c. médico generalista).

E. El cardiólogo trabaja con problemas (a. del corazón, b. de los pulmones, c. del esqueleto).

F. Necesitas un urólogo si tienes problema con (a. la nariz, b. la próstata, c. los oídos).

G. Si te duele el oído, necesitas consultar con un (a. otorrinolaringólogo, b. pediatra, c. odontólogo).

1.18 Drama imprevisto

Work in groups of three or four to spontaneously present a skit that is similar to the first meeting of Dr. Vargas and the Flores family. Substitute your own personal information, and don't worry about following the video script. Some group members will speak of imaginary friends or family members who suffer from various ailments, and other members of the group will suggest what medical professional should be consulted.

gordo   bajo   alto y delgado

 Describe People

Vocabulario: Características personales
(Personal Characteristics)

The verb *ser* is used to describe physical characteristics and personality traits. The following words are often used with *ser:*

rubio/a	blonde, fair	moreno/a*	brunette, dark
viejo/a; anciano/a	old	joven	young
grande	big	pequeño/a	small
alto/a	tall	bajo/a	short (height)
largo/a	long	corto/a	short (length)
mediano/a	medium	gordo/a, obeso/a	fat, obese
delgado/a	thin	flaco/a	skinny
bonito/a	pretty	guapo/a	handsome
feo/a	ugly	bueno/a	good
inteligente	intelligent	simpático/a	kind
amable	pleasant	agradable	kind

Preguntas útiles

¿Cómo es Juan?   What is Juan like?

*There is regional variation in the use of the word *moreno/a,* which may be used to refer to people with black hair in Spain, people of African descent, or people with rather dark complexion in Spanish-speaking America.

Doña Gloria es dominicana y es
morena. Sus padres son de Haití.

Don Samuel es rubio y viejito. Sus
padres son de Cuba.

 1.19 Ejercicio

The instructor will ask for the opposite of each of the following words. For example, *¿Cuál es el opuesto de flaco?*
Students respond: *El opuesto de flaco es gordo.*

> ¿cuál? what?
> opuesto opposite

A. alto	D. viejo	G. largo
B. delgado	E. grande	H. feo
C. bajo	F. corto	I. gordo

 ## Estructura: La concordancia de sustantivos, adjetivos y artículos indefinidos
(Agreement of Nouns, Adjectives, and Indefinite Articles)

- Adjectives, like nouns, have gender (*género*) and number (*número*). Adjectives ending in *-o* change to *-a* to become feminine (for example, *alto, alta*). Adjectives ending in a vowel add *-s* to become plural and those ending in a consonant add *-es*.
- When an adjective modifies a noun, it must agree with that noun in gender and number. Therefore, an adjective that describes a feminine singular noun is used in the feminine singular form. An adjective that describes a feminine plural noun is used in the feminine plural form. In Spanish a descriptive adjective normally *follows* the noun.

el coche blanco	the white car
los coches blancos	the white cars
la casa blanca	the white house

las casas blancas	the white houses
El enfermero es alto.	The (*male*) nurse is tall.
La doctora es delgada.	The (*female*) doctor is thin.

- Adjectives ending in -*e* modify both masculine and feminine nouns.

El niño es amable.	The boy is nice.
La niña es inteligente.	The girl is intelligent.

- The indefinite articles, which correspond to "a," "an," and "some" in English, have both gender and number. They are *un, una, unos,* and *unas.* The indefinite article is generally not used after forms of the verb *ser,* unless the object is followed by an adjective. The articles, nouns, and adjectives must agree in both gender and number. When referring to a mixed group of males and females, the male forms are used.

Marco es enfermero.	Marco is a nurse.
Marco es un enfermero nuevo.	Marco is a new nurse.
Ana es médica.	Ana is a doctor.
Ana es una médica buena.	Ana is a good doctor.
Marco y Ana son altos.	Marco and Ana are tall.

 1.20 Ejercicio

Agree with the descriptions of the following people, according to the example. Remember to use the correct indefinite article when the noun is followed by an adjective.

> Example: La profesora es simpática.
>   Sí, es una profesora simpática.

A. La doctora es inteligente.
B. Los estudiantes son interesantes.
C. La enfermera es joven.
D. El profesor es guapo.
E. El médico es alto.
F. Los pacientes son delgados.
G. Los doctores son viejos.
H. El neurólogo es simpático.

 1.21 Ejercicio

To make a statement negative, place the word *no* before the verb. *Juan es alto* becomes *Juan no es alto.* When answering a question, you can use the word *no* twice. *¿Es alto Juan? No, Juan no es alto.* In this exercise, the first sentence tells you something about someone and the second sentence asks about his or her opposite. Notice that the gender also changes in each. Make the adjectives agree with their nouns.

Example: Student 1:   Luis es alto. ¿Cómo es Guillermina?
             Student 2:   Guillermina no es alta. Es baja.

A. Pedro es feo. ¿Cómo es
   Estrella?

B. Marta es gorda. ¿Cómo es
   Juan?

C. Miguel es alto. ¿Cómo es
   Rosa?

D. Ana es baja. ¿Cómo es
   Marco?

E. María es vieja. ¿Cómo es
   José?

F. Carlos es guapo. ¿Cómo es
   Ana?

G. Luis es delgado. ¿Cómo es
   Estrella?

H. Juana es joven. ¿Cómo es
   Timoteo?

 1.22 Actividad

Look at the chart that follows and state the similarities and the differences between the following people. For example, *Cristina Rojas y Samuel Ortiz son enfermeros.* Then, ask questions of classmates. For example, *¿Cómo es el doctor Andino?*

Nombre	Profesión	Nacionalidad	Características físicas
Cristina Rojas	enfermera	mexicana	joven, alta, delgada
Felipe Andino	cirujano	chileno	bajo, guapo
Carmen Machado	cirujana	mexicana	baja
Raquel Droz	obstetra	chilena	alta, delgada
Samuel Ortiz	enfermero	argentino	joven, alto, delgado

 1.23 Actividad

Describe the following people by drawing conclusions from the information presented in the chart. Note that while the titles *señor* and *señora* are used with the last name, the titles *don* and *doña,* which refer to seniors, are used with first names.

Nombre	Estatura (Height)	Peso (Weight)	Edad (Age)
Doña Afortunada	5 pies	200 libras	68 años
Don Amilcar	6 pies, 3 pulgadas	151 libras	72 años
Arturito	40 pulgadas	85 libras	5 años
Aurelina	44 pulgadas	42 libras	5 años

 1.24 Actividad

| pies feet |
| pulgadas inches |

Describe one of your friends or family members to the class. For example, *José es mi mejor amigo. Es bajo, gordito, guapo y muy amable.*

La pronunciación de las vocales (Pronunciation of Vowels)

- For the most part, Spanish is pronounced as it is written. If you can spell it, you can say it. If you hear it spoken, you can write it. Imagine speaking by telephone to a Spanish-speaking receptionist. You leave one message for Guillermina Estelvina Rodríguez Asunción de Torres and another for Bill Jones. Then comes the obvious question, "Jones, how do you spell Jones?" (*¿Cómo se escribe Jones?*) The Spanish alphabet appears in appendix 1.
- Each vowel in Spanish has only one fundamental sound. The vowel sounds do not have exact English counterparts. To learn them, listen to and mimic native speakers, comparing your sounds to theirs. After learning the vowels, practice exercises like *ma - me - mi - mo - mu* and *ta - te - ti - to - tu.*

Vowel	*Like the English . . .*		*Examples from Spanish*	
a	ah	m*a*ma	mano	mamograma
e	eh	w*ay*	vena	cerebro
i	ee	pol*i*ce	crisis	biopsia
o	oh	fl*ow*	droga	social
u	ooh	r*u*de	pulso	músculo

- Two vowels together are pronounced separately unless they form a diphthong. Practice the following: *pie* (pi-E), *idea* (i-DE-a), *fiebre* (fi-E-bre), *luego* (lu-E-go), *heroína* (e-ro-I-na), and *codeína* (co-de-I-na). When unstressed «i» or «u» falls next to another vowel in a syllable, it unites with that vowel to form a diphthong. The vowels still sound the same, but they are pronounced as one syllable. Examples are *aire, seis, oigo,* and *pausa.*
- In spoken Spanish, vowels create linkages across word boundaries. For example, *mucho gusto* sounds like a single word. *¿Es usted la madre?* may sound like *¿esustedlamadre?* Notice the linkages in *los hospitales* and *la clínica.*
- Regressed students might practice this well-known refrain of sassy children: *A, E, I, O, U, ¡más sabe el burro que tú!,* which means, "A, E, I, O, U; a donkey knows more than you!" Courageous students might practice the following *trabalenguas,* or "tongue twisters."

> Mi mamá me mima mucho.
> Como poco coco como, poco coco compro.
> Corto caña, caña corto; corto caña, caña corto; corto caña, caña corto.
> Poquito a poquito Paquito empaca poquitas copitas en pocos paquetes.
> Si Pancha plancha con cuatro planchas, ¿con cuántas planchas plancha Pancha?

Cultural Note: Spanish-Speakers in the United States

According to United States Census 2000, more than 28 million persons over the age of five (one out of ten people) speak Spanish at home (a substantial increase from 17 million in 1990). This makes Spanish the second most spoken language in the United States. More than a quarter of these Spanish-speakers stated they spoke English either not well or not at all. Chinese was the third most spoken language, with more than 2 million speakers.

Some North Americans refer to people whose native language is Spanish as being "Spanish people." Actually, the word "Spanish" refers only to the people and culture of Spain. Persons who originate in other Spanish-speaking countries are called Hispanic, Latino/a, or Spanish-speaking. Some people want to be called Hispanic, and others prefer to be called *Latino/a*. People of Mexican descent who live in the United States are sometimes called *Chicano/a*. Note that most Latinos living in the United States are U.S. citizens, although some are legal resident aliens, and a very small percentage are undocumented. Over two-thirds of Mexican Americans were born in the United States (some of them are descended from people who lived in parts of Mexico that were annexed by the United States).

The terms "Hispanic" and "Latino/a" can be misleading. The term "Hispanic" was adopted during the Nixon administration to replace "Spanish-American." It refers to a combination of ethnicities more than to a "race." The concept of race itself is decaying. In the 2000 U.S. Census, nearly 7 million respondents stated that they were of more than one race. The terms "Latino" and "Hispanic" do not necessarily describe an individual. Nor do they identify a group of people according to common characteristics. They do not say whether a person has a Spanish surname or even whether he or she speaks Spanish. They do not indicate place of birth, national origin, citizenship, or immigrant status, and do nothing to define any specific cultural identity. Neither do these commonly used terms acknowledge the rich pre-Columbian cultures of many Spanish-speakers. (Twenty-seven languages are spoken in Guatemala, and one of those has more than 2 million speakers.)

There is no typical Latino person or country. The Spanish-speaking world is polycultural. It is made up of Spain, Mexico, six Central American countries, nine South American countries (Portuguese is spoken in Brazil), the Caribbean nations of Cuba, the Dominican Republic, and Puerto Rico, and many communities within metropolitan areas of the United States. For example, Los Angeles is the fifth largest Spanish-speaking city in the world. Although their customs and traditions vary, most Spanish-speaking people are proud of their common language.

The first Spanish explorers in the New World arrived before the Pilgrims boarded the *Mayflower*. Christopher Columbus (*Cristóbal Colón*) colonized the island the newcomers named Hispaniola (now the Dominican Republic and Haiti) in 1492. Juan Ponce de León landed on the shores of what is now Florida in 1513. New Spanish-speaking immigrants arrive in the United States every day. No longer concentrated in a few urban areas, they are very widely dispersed. Although most Spanish-speaking immigrant families assimilate by the third generation in the host culture, many still identify highly with their country of origin and strive to pass on ethnic traditions and the Spanish language to their children.

The Caribbean island of Puerto Rico came under United States control in 1898 as a result of the Spanish-American War. Puerto Ricans were granted U.S. citizenship in 1917, and have United States passports. Puerto Ricans can move freely to the mainland United States, and many do so to obtain jobs. On the island, there has been an ongoing struggle among those who favor statehood, those who favor independence, and those who support the status quo as a commonwealth, but with more autonomy and greater economic flexibility. Nonbinding referendums in 1967, 1993, and 1998 rejected statehood, while 5 percent of Puerto Rico's inhabitants supported the Puerto Rican Independence Party. Many voters fear they will lose their culture, language, and flag and will face an undesirable tax system and a loss of business incentives if they become a state.

The United States uses the name "American" for its citizens, but there are other Americas. People from the Caribbean (where America was "discovered"), Central America, and South America have rights to the name as well. People originating in the United States are often called *norteamericanos*, although Canadians and Mexicans also live in North America.

Spanish-speaking countries continue to be a large source of immigration to the United States. Some people flee political oppression. Most of the people who immigrate do so not to sever ties with their beloved homelands but to seek the opportunity to work and send financial support to those who remain behind. In 2000 the population of the United States was 12.5 percent Hispanic (the term used by the census) and 12.3 percent black, making Hispanics the largest minority group there. By the year 2050, the breakdown is projected to be roughly 50 percent white, 25 percent Hispanic, 15 percent black, and 10 percent Asian. The Hispanic population in the United States is growing rapidly because of immigration plus a tendency to have larger families (31 percent of Hispanic households have five or more people).

Chapter 2
«¿Cómo está usted?»

By the end of this chapter you will be able to ask patients how they feel and ask questions to clarify various states of feelings. You will learn how to ask and give information about the location of people and places. You will know the difference between the two verbs that mean "to be" (*ser* and *estar*) and when to use each. You will learn the days of the week in Spanish, begin to talk about weekly schedules, and test whether the patient is oriented to person, place, and time.

Ask How Your Patient Is Feeling

DIÁLOGO

Dr. Vargas: Buenas tardes don Francisco. Buenas tardes doña Marisol. Hola Elsita.

Sr. Flores: Buenas tardes, doctor.

Sra. Flores: ¿Cómo está usted?

Dr. Vargas: Yo estoy bien, gracias a Dios. Y ustedes, ¿cómo están?

¿Qué te pasa, Elsita?

Sr. Flores: Estamos un poco cansados, doctor. Elsita está enfermita.

Dr. Vargas: Lo siento. ¿Qué te pasa, Elsita?

Sometimes in fast-paced North American society we ask, "How are you?" without waiting for an answer. In many cultures it is customary not only to wait for an answer but to ask about family as well. (Family relationships are treated in chapter 5.)

Vocabulario: Los sentimientos (Feelings)

bien	well, good	mal	not well, ill
feliz	happy	triste	sad
regular	okay	así-así	so-so
enfermo/a	ill, sick	cansado/a	tired
mejor	better	peor	worse
igual	the same	más o menos	so-so
nervioso/a	nervous	preocupado/a	worried

Preguntas útiles

¿Cómo está usted?	How are you?
¿Cómo estás?	How are you? (*informal*)
¿Qué tal?	How are you? (*informal*)
¿Cómo está la familia?	How is your family?

Expresiones útiles

Estoy bien, gracias.	I am fine, thank you.
Gracias a Dios.	Thank God.
Me alegro.	I am glad to hear it.
No estoy bien.	I don't feel well.
Lo siento.	I am sorry.
Estoy en la lucha.	I am hanging in there ("in the battle").

Estoy enfermo.

 ## Estructura: El verbo *estar* (To Be)

- The verb *estar,* like the verb *ser,* means "to be." Whereas *ser* is used to express profession, origin, ethnicity, and physical or personal attributes, *estar* is used to express a state of being or condition, including how one feels and where someone or something is located. Thus *estar* is used to ask "How are you?" and "Where are you?"
- These are the forms of the verb *estar* in the present tense.

yo	*Estoy* cansado.
tú	¿*Estás* bien?
él, ella, usted	Ella *está* mejor.
nosotros/nosotras	*Estamos* contentos.
ellos, ellas, ustedes	Los niños *están* enfermos.

2.1 Ejercicio

Recall that answers to the *Ejercicios* are presented at the end of the book.

Fill in the blanks with the Spanish or English words and phrases that are indicated.

_____ enfermo.   I am ill.

¿_____ bien?   Are you (*informal*) well?

Juan está regular.   _____.

Mi bebé está enfermo.   _____.

Rosa y yo _____ enfermos.   Rosa and I are ill.

Los pacientes _____ mejores.   The patients are better.

**El paciente está mejor.
La doctora está contenta.**

 2.2 Actividad

Go around the classroom asking each student how he or she feels. Give appropriate group feedback to each response.

Example: Class: Buenas tardes. ¿Cómo estás?
           Student 1:   Buenas tardes. No estoy bien. Estoy
                        enfermo/a.
           Class: ¿Estás mejor, igual o peor?
           Student 2:   Peor.
           Class: Lo siento (pobre-c-i-i-i-t-o).

 2.3 Actividad

In groups of two or three, ask each other, *¿Cómo está el dolor?* Instruct, *Señale con el dedo,* which means, "Point with your finger." Find out whether the pain is better, worse, or the same as before. Here are some designations:

¿Cómo está el dolor?
Señale el dibujo que corresponda.

| 0 | 1 | 2 | 3 | 4 | 5 | 6 | 7 | 8 | 9 | 10 |
| No duele | | Duele un poco | | | Tolerable | | Duele mucho | | | Intolerable |

No duele.	It doesn't hurt.
Duele un poco.	It hurts a little.
El dolor molesta.	The pain is annoying.
Duele mucho.	It hurts a lot.
No aguanto el dolor.	I can't stand the pain.

 2.4 Drama imprevisto

Choose a "feeling" from the vocabulary list at the beginning of this chapter. The instructor may assign these anonymously by distributing index cards with one of the feeling states written on each. Next, mingle in the classroom, introducing yourself to your peers by name, profession, and so on, and acting—or over-acting—your chosen or assigned emotion. Afterwards, identify each person's affective state. For example, *Bill, estás triste, ¿no?*

Ask Where People and Places Are Located

The verb *estar* is used to ask about where a person, place, or thing is located. For example, *¿Dónde está la clínica?* means "Where is the clinic?" Used in questions, interrogative words have written accents.

 2.5 Ejercicio

Supply the missing information in Spanish or English, as indicated. Notice that the Spanish *en* is usually used for the English "at." (It means "in," "at," and "on.")

¿Dónde _____ usted?   Where are you (*formal*)?

Estoy en casa.   _____ at home.

Estoy en el hospital.   I am at _____.

¿_____ está el cirujano?   Where is the surgeon?

El cirujano _____ en el hospital.   The surgeon is at the hospital.

Estructura: Posesión (Possession)

- English employs an apostrophe and letter *s* to indicate possession, as in "the doctor's office." One way to indicate possession in Spanish is with the formula *de* + noun, as in *el consultorio del doctor.*

La casa de Juan.	Juan's house.
La casa de los padres de Juan.	Juan's parents' house.
El departamento de psiquiatría.	The psychiatry department.

- Spanish also uses possessive adjectives, which we'll review in chapter 5. As in the case of all adjectives, these must agree in gender and number with the nouns that they modify. Also, there are formal and informal adjectives that mean "your." For example,

Mi casa es tu casa.	My house is your (*informal*) house.
Mi casa es su casa.	My house is your (*formal*) house.
Mis padres están vivos.	My parents are alive.
Sus ideas son buenas.	Your ideas are good.

- The formula *de* + noun is the clearest way to express possession, because the terms *su* and *sus* have a surplus of meanings in Spanish. For example,

mi, mis	my
tu, tus	your (*informal*)
su, sus	your (*formal*), his, her, its, their
nuestro/a/os/as	our

2.6 Ejercicio

Read the following statements aloud, saying the appropriate possessive adjective where indicated.

Example: la casa de Miguelito   __su__ casa

A. las sábanas de Elsa   _____ sábanas

B. la cama de usted   _____ cama

C. las frazadas de nosotros   _____ frazadas

D. las camas de José y Rosa   _____ camas

E. la silla de la doctora   _____ silla

Vocabulario: «¿Dónde está?» (Where Is It?)

en el quinto piso	on the fifth floor
a la derecha	on/to the right
a la izquierda	on/to the left
derecho	straight ahead
al final del pasillo	at the end of the hallway

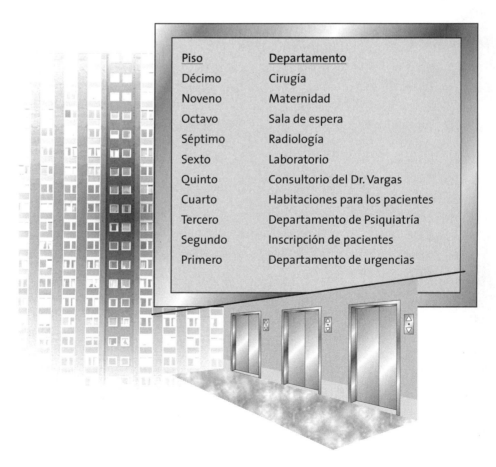

Piso	Departamento
Décimo	Cirugía
Noveno	Maternidad
Octavo	Sala de espera
Séptimo	Radiología
Sexto	Laboratorio
Quinto	Consultorio del Dr. Vargas
Cuarto	Habitaciones para los pacientes
Tercero	Departamento de Psiquiatría
Segundo	Inscripción de pacientes
Primero	Departamento de urgencias

Note that the numbers *primero* and *tercero* drop the final -*o* before a masculine singular noun. For example, *¿Dónde está el departamento de psiquiatría? Está en el tercer piso, a la derecha* (It is on the third floor, to the right). As adjectives, these have gender, as in l*a segunda puerta a la izquierda.*

 ## 2.7 Actividad

Look at the drawing of the hospital elevator and additional vocabulary. In groups of two or three, ask and tell where various areas of the hospital are located.

 ## 2.8 Drama imprevisto

Think about the hospital or clinic with which you are most familiar. Draw the building elevations and a floor plan. Next, in small groups take turns acting unscripted skits asking and giving directions to specific places that are located on the drawings.

Vocabulario: Los días de la semana (Days of the Week)

el lunes	Monday
el martes	Tuesday
el miércoles	Wednesday
el jueves	Thursday
el viernes	Friday
el sábado	Saturday
el domingo	Sunday
el fin de semana	weekend
todos los días	every day
de lunes a viernes	from Monday to Friday
Hoy es lunes.	Today is Monday.
mañana	morning; tomorrow
el lunes que viene	next Monday
el próximo martes	next Tuesday

Preguntas útiles

¿Qué día es hoy?	What day is it today?
¿Dónde estamos?	Where are we?

Notice that the days of the week do not start with a capital letter. Notice, too, that the definite article is omitted with the days of the week when used after the verb *ser*. For example, *Hoy es lunes; mañana es martes.* Note that when the definite article is used, it can be singular or plural depending on the meaning of the sentence. For example,

Estoy en el hospital *el lunes.*   I am at the hospital *this Monday.*
Estoy en el hospital *los lunes.*   I am at the hospital *on Mondays.*

 2.9 Ejercicio

With your instructor, make up drills to practice the days of the week.

Example: Instructor: Si hoy es lunes, ¿qué día es mañana?
               Class: Si hoy es lunes, mañana es martes.

 2.10 Actividad

The terms *abierto* (open) and *cerrado* (closed) are used as adjectives and therefore must agree in gender with the noun they modify. For example, *El consultorio del doctor está abierto los lunes. La clínica está cerrada los sábados.*

With a partner, ask and answer the following questions, as in the example. Answer ad lib.

Example: Student 1:   ¿Está abierta la clínica los lunes?
              Student 2:   No, la clínica está cerrada los lunes, pero el consultorio está abierto los lunes.

A. Ask whether *el laboratorio* is open on Wednesdays.
B. Ask whether *la farmacia* is open on Sundays.
C. Ask whether *el consultorio* is open this Monday.
D. Ask whether *la clínica ambulatoria* is closed on Saturdays.
E. Ask whether *el departamento de radiología* is open this Friday.

 Estructura: Haciendo preguntas (Forming Questions)

- To form a question, place the subject pronoun after the verb.
     ¿Está usted contento?   Are you happy?
     ¿Está el doctor en la clínica?   Is the doctor at the clinic?
- Spanish-speakers also may form a question from a statement by changing intonation.
     ¿Usted está contento?   You are happy?
     ¿El doctor está en la clínica?   The doctor is in the clinic?
- The expressions *¿no?, ¿verdad?,* or *¿No es verdad?* may be placed at the end of a statement to form a question.
     Juan está enfermo, ¿no?   Juan is ill, isn't he?
     Juan está mejor, ¿verdad?   Juan is better, right?

2.11 Actividad

Consult the *Horario del doctor*. Ask your partner where the doctor is on certain days, or when he or she is at the clinic or hospital, as in the example. Make your own questions.

Horario del doctor	
lunes	la clínica
martes	el hospital
miércoles	la clínica
jueves	el hospital
viernes	el consultorio
sábado	libre
domingo	libre

Example: Student 1: ¿Dónde está el doctor los lunes?

Student 2: Los lunes el doctor está en la clínica.

Student 1: ¿Cuándo (when) está en el hospital el doctor?

Student 2: El doctor está en el hospital los martes y los jueves.

 ## 2.12 Actividad

Take turns telling about your schedule for various days of the week. For example,

Estoy en la clínica de lunes a viernes.
Estoy en la clase los jueves.
Estoy en casa los fines de semana.

 ## Estructura: Choosing Between *Ser* and *Estar*

- *Ser* is used when speaking of origins (birthplaces), professions, and nationalities. It is also used with adjectives that describe inherent characteristics, such as tall and intelligent, and to tell the day, date, and time.

Origin:	Soy de Colombia.	I am from Colombia.
Nationality:	Soy norteamericano.	I am North American.
Profession:	Mi esposa es dentista.	My wife is a dentist.
Characteristics:	Ella es alta y delgada.	She is tall and thin.
Telling time:	Mañana es sábado.	Tomorrow is Saturday.

- *Estar* is used in connection with locations of things or people and with adjectives that describe states of being, such as emotions, feelings, health, or conditions such as open, closed, broken, and swollen.

Location:	Estoy en la clínica.	I am at the clinic.
Emotions:	Gloria está deprimida.	Gloria is depressed.
Feelings:	¿Estás enfermo?	Are you ill?
Conditions:	La clínica está abierta.	The clinic is open.

- The adjectives *contento/a* (happy), *cansado/a* (tired), and *pálido/a* (pale) are always used with *estar*. Many adjectives can take on different meanings, depending on whether they are used with *ser* or with *estar*. The use of *ser* implies enduring traits. The use of *estar* implies there has been a recent change. For example,

Ser	*Estar*
Ella es feliz.	Ella está feliz.
(She is always happy.)	(She feels happy now.)
Eres delgado.	Estás delgado.
(You are thin.)	(You've lost weight.)
Yahaira es gorda.	Yahaira está gorda.
(Yahaira is fat.)	(Yahaira has gained weight.)
Miguel es listo.	Miguel está listo.
(Miguel is clever.)	(Miguel is ready.)
María es bonita.	María está bonita.
(María is beautiful.)	(María looks good today.)

Although the words *loco* (crazy) and *borracho* (drunk) are slang, rather than clinical terms (and you'd never use them in connection with a patient), imagine the difference in meanings when *ser* and *estar* are used!

• Here's a reminder of the verb morphology of *ser* and *estar* in the present tense.

Sujeto	*Ser*	*Estar*
yo	soy	estoy
tú	eres	estás
él, ella, usted	es	está
nosotros/as	somos	estamos
ellos, ellas, ustedes	son	están

 2.13 Ejercicio

Read the following story. Choose between *ser* and *estar* and supply the correct form of the verb in the spaces provided.

Buenos días. Me llamo Hilda Rodríguez Portocarrero. _____

enfermera en el hospital Nuestra Señora de la Altagracia. El

hospital _____ grande y famoso. El hospital _____ en

Lima, Perú. Trabajo con la doctora Kathi Collins. La doctora

Collins _____ norteamericana. Ella _____ en el hospital

todos los días, pero yo no. Los sábados _____ en la clínica y

los domingos _____ en casa. Los domingos la clínica _____

cerrada. La doctora _____ alta y delgada. Yo _____ baja y

no muy delgada. La doctora y yo _____ muy contentas.

 ## 2.14 Actividad

Use *ser* or *estar* to ask questions that will elicit the following information from a partner. When you have finished, switch roles.

¿Quién?	Who?
¿Qué?	What?
¿Cómo?	How?
¿Dónde?	Where?
¿De dónde?	From where?
¿Cuál?	Which? What?

A. Where (*¿De dónde . . ?*) he or she is from (originally)
B. Where (*¿Dónde . . ?*) he or she is on a specific day of the week
C. What (*¿Cuál . . ?*) is his or her profession or specialty
D. What (*¿Cómo . . ?*) he or she is like
E. How (*¿Cómo . . ?*) he or she is feeling

 ## 2.15 Reciclaje

Play a *Jeopardy*-like guessing game with the class to recycle the personal descriptions from chapter 1. Use what you know about your classmates as well as what you can observe. One person tells something about a classmate, and the rest of the class tries to guess the person's identity by asking the question that would have elicited that information. For example,

Estudiante:	Es una estudiante alta y rubia.
Clase:	¿Cómo es Mary?
Estudiante:	Es de Nueva York.
Clase:	¿De dónde es Phyllis?
Estudiante:	Él es dentista.
Clase:	¿Quién es Vladimir?

UN CHISTE (A JOKE)

Estudiante:	¿Cuál es correcto: Buenos Aires *está* en Brasil, o Buenos Aires *es* en Brasil?
Profesor:	Buenos Aires *está* en Brasil.
Estudiante:	¡No, profesor. Buenos Aires *está* en Argentina!

2.16 Drama imprevisto

Act out the following situations in Spanish without previous preparation.

A. *Llego a las cuatro* (I arrive at four). You and a partner have never met. Have a telephone conversation in which you describe yourselves to each other so that you'll connect when your partner picks you up at the airport.

B. *Soy soltero* (I'm single). On the blackboard, write an ad for the personals section of a Spanish-language newspaper, either for yourself or for a famous person. In the case of a famous person, the class must then guess his or her identity.

C. *¡Vamos al cine!* (Let's go to the movies!) With your partner, spontaneously act out a conversation in which you negotiate a day to go to the movies together. Unfortunately you are never available at the same time. For example, one proposes a day of the week, and the other says where he or she is already scheduled to be. Cover all days of the week, and demonstrate your growing frustration.

Test a Patient's Orientation

Health care workers at times must assess whether a patient is oriented to person, place, and time. You can begin to do this in Spanish with three questions you have already learned.

¿Cómo se llama usted?	What is your name?
¿Qué día es hoy?	What day is today?
¿Dónde estamos?	Where are we?

You'll learn to ask the date and the time in chapter 4. The question *¿Dónde está usted?* does not always work well with patients who think concretely. Such patients tend to answer, *Estoy aquí* (I am here). Then you may prefer *¿Dónde estamos?* or find it helpful to give multiple choice. For example, *¿Estamos en una casa, una escuela o una clínica?*

Video Program: *La orientación*

Watch the *Demostración* segment of the video for chapter 2 and do the activity that follows.

Dr. Vargas:	Buenas tardes.
Sr. Flores:	Buenas tardes.

Dr. Vargas:	¿Cómo se llama usted?
Sr. Flores:	Me llamo Francisco Flores.
Dr. Vargas:	Señor Flores, ¿Sabe usted dónde estamos?
Sr. Flores:	Estamos en el consultorio.
Dr. Vargas:	Bueno, ¿En qué ciudad estamos?
Sr. Flores:	New Haven.
Dr. Vargas:	¿Cuál es el nombre de este lugar?
Sr. Flores:	No sé.
Dr. Vargas:	¿Estamos en una escuela, una clínica o una casa?
Sr. Flores:	Estamos en una clínica.
Dr. Vargas:	¿En qué año estamos?
Sr. Flores:	En el dos mil nueve.
Dr. Vargas:	Bien. ¿En qué mes estamos?
Sr. Flores:	Agosto.
Dr. Vargas:	Perfecto. ¿Qué día es?
Sr. Flores:	Hoy es lunes.
Dr. Vargas:	Muy bien. Gracias.

Dr. Vargas y Francisco Flores

¿Sabe usted?	Do you know?
ciudad	city
lugar	place
No sé.	I don't know.

 ## 2.17 Actividad

Determine whether people in the class are oriented to the three spheres of person, place, and day.

Vocabulario: Las especialidades (Specialties)

In chapter 1, we learned the names for various professions. Here, you'll notice a pattern in the formation of most of the names for specialties and the adjective forms that indicate *what kind* of evaluation, procedure, or operation. The instructor will help you with the pronunciation of accents. A guide to pronouncing accents follows this section.

Profesión	*Especialidad*	*Adjectivo*
el/la cardiólogo/a	la cardiología	cardiológico/a
el/la dermatólogo/a	la dermatología	dermatológico/a
el/la endocrinólogo/a	la endocrinología	endocrinológico/a
el/la ginecólogo	la ginecología	ginecológico/a

el/la neurólogo/a	la neurología	neurológico/a
el/la obstetra	la obstetricia	obstétrico/a
el/la odontólogo/a	la odontología	odontológico/a
el/la oftalmólogo/a	la oftalmología	oftalmológico/a
el/la oncólogo/a	la oncología	oncológico/a
el/la ortopeda	la ortopedia	ortopédico/a
el/la pediatra	la pediatría	pediátrico/a
el/la psicólogo/a	la psicología	psicológico/a
el/la psiquiatra	la psiquiatría	psiquiátrico/a
el/la radiólogo/a	la radiología	radiológico/a
el/la urólogo/a	la urología	urológico/a

The adjective forms are often used with the following nouns. Recall that adjectives must agree in gender and number with the nouns that they modify, for example, *el hospital psiquiátrico* and *la clínica psiquiátrica.* Words that end in *-ción* are feminine.

El hospital de otorrinolaringología

El centro oncológico

Masculino	Femenino
el hospital	la clínica
el examen	la examinación
el procedimiento	la operación
el tratamiento	la evaluación

 2.18 Reciclaje

Ask where various professionals are, and answer using the adjective form for the profession. You may choose between *clínica* and *hospital*.

Example: Student 1:   ¿Dónde está el oftalmólogo?
            Student 2:   El oftalmólogo está en la clínica
                          oftalmológica.

2.19 Reciclaje

Tell people what kind of evaluation they need, where, and with whom, as in the example. The place can be a hospital or a clinic. Use either the name for the specialty, as in *la clínica de psiquiatría,* or its adjective form, as in *la clínica psiquiátrica.*

> Example: Sr. Ramos, a psychiatric evaluation
>
> Student 1:   Sr. Ramos, usted necesita una evaluación psiquiátrica.
> Student 2:   ¿Dónde?
> Student 1:   En el hospital psiquiátrico.
> Student 2:   ¿Con quién?
> Student 1:   Con el psiquiatra.

¿Con quién?   With whom?

> A. Señora Camacho, a cardiac operation
> B. Doña Olga, a gynecologic exam
> C. Señor Durán, a neurologic examination
> D. Don Alfredo, a urologic procedure
> E. Señora Quiñones, an ophthalmic treatment
> F. Don Roberto, a psychological evaluation

 ## 2.20 Actividad

Make brief conversations based on the following ailments, whose names are close cognates with English. Tell people what kind of evaluation or procedure they need, and where to get it. After using the ailments below, propose your own to the class.

> Example: Student 1:   Sufro de prostatitis (I suffer from prostatitis).
>   Student 2:   Necesita consultar con un urólogo. Hay un buen urólogo en la clínica de urología.

> A. cáncer   D. dermatitis
> B. glaucoma   E. ataques epilépticos
> C. angina   F. esquizofrenia

La pronunciación del acento prosódico y el acento ortográfico (The Pronunciation of Stress and the Written Accent)

The oral stress point or prosody of a word is sometimes indicated by an acute accent. For example, the word *está* is stressed on the last syllable, and the word *clínica* is stressed on the first syllable. In the absence of a written accent mark, there are two rules.

- In words that end with a vowel, the letter *n*, or the letter *s*, the oral stress is on the next-to-last syllable. Examples are *plaza, mano, pulso, hablan, examen,* and *epidermis.* The instructor will help you with the pronunciation of these words.
- In words ending with consonants other than *n* or *s*, the oral stress or accent is on the last syllable, as in *hospital, general,* and *regular.*
- Written accent marks are used when a word will otherwise break these two rules, as in *pulmón* and *útil.* Written accent marks are also used when the spoken accent is before the penultimate syllable, as in *clínica* and *estómago.* (For these words, an easy rule to remember is to write the accent mark wherever there are two syllables left over after the syllable that receives the oral stress.) To know whether to use a written accent mark, you first must know how to pronounce the word properly. In other words, a written accent mark is required when a word ending in a vowel, *n,* or *s* is stressed on any syllable other than the penultimate, and when a word ending in any other consonant is stressed on any syllable but the last.

With help from the instructor, practice saying the following words.

amigo	farmacia	ambulancia
aspirina	natural	social
hablar	colon	gastritis
diurética	resucitación	antibiótico

Trabalengua

El otorrinolaringólogo está en el hospital de otorrinolaringología para una operación otorrinolaringológica.

Cultural Note: Attitudes and Ourselves

Exploring our attitudes toward groups that differ from our own is an essential step in learning a new language. There are two common outcomes when groups coexist in society. When *pluralism* prevails, groups retain and preserve their unique cultural characteristics, such as foods, language, and traditions. When there is *assimilation,* the norms, values, and practices of the majority culture are embraced. Although Latinos tend to assimilate by the third generation in the United States, many have rejected the melting pot image of the late nineteenth century. Some non-English-speaking Latinos go to their own neighborhood grocers and churches, watch television in Spanish, and fill out government forms in their own language. How do you feel about pluralism and assimilation?

Some U.S. citizens today remind us that their immigrant parents or ancestors learned English. Indeed, many European immigrants of the last century were able to escape ethnic discrimination by learning English and adopting customs of the host culture. A study by the Pew Hispanic Center revealed that Spanish-speakers learn English at a rate that is similar to that of immigrants who arrived a century ago. The first-generation immigrant retains native-speaker proficiency for their original language; bilingualism peaks in the second generation; and Spanish fades during the third generation.

Many consider it to be especially controversial to impose English on people of Puerto Rican heritage, who are not considered immigrants. They are born U.S. citizens, serve in the U.S. military, and speak Spanish as their native tongue. These are among the arguments advanced by some Latinos for bilingual government services.

It may take five years or more for an immigrant to become proficient in English as a second language. Individuals who do not have native language literacy may learn English less quickly than those who are literate in their primary language. Because of advances in communication and transportation, Spanish-speakers who immigrate to the United States today are more likely to maintain close ties to their native countries than the immigrants of a generation ago. This makes them more likely to keep speaking their native language.

There seems to be a basic human tendency to "fill in the blanks," by assuming that we can perceive more about a person than what is apparent by appearance alone. Thus, we are prone to make generalizations based on skin tone, ethnicity, accent and English proficiency, and socioeconomic status. The illogical aspects of such stereotypes are that they over-emphasize the similarities between members of a group and the differences between groups. Stereotypes and over-generalized beliefs, when combined with judgment about what is favorable, constitute prejudice. It can be argued that most of us hold some prejudicial views. Discrimination, on the other hand, is the unfair *treatment* of another person based on prejudice. When we become aware of our beliefs, we can strive to keep them from causing us to treat others unfairly.

We can observe ourselves for signs of unhealthy attitudes. Complete the following sentences. (Do not share your answers.)

1. My parents think that Spanish-speakers are . . .
2. I like Spanish-speakers who . . .
3. I am afraid of Spanish-speakers who . . .
4. Latino men are . . .
5. Latina women are . . .
6. Immigrants . . .
7. Undocumented aliens . . .
8. Government forms ought to be in English (or ought to be bilingual) because . . .

Do your answers betray either positive or negative generalizations, or both? Even positive stereotypes, for example that Latinos like to hug, respect doctors, and value family, tend to rob individuals of their individuality. How might your generalizations influence your treatment of others? Remember that in the United States there are Hispanic people who speak only Spanish, those who speak only English, and those who are bilingual or multilingual. Most are U.S. citizens, others are resident aliens, and some are without documents. There are those whose skin tones resemble those of their European ancestors, and those who have the physical characteristics of the West African people who were

Discrimination based on skin tone is common to many cultures.

enslaved and traded to the Spanish colonies. There are indigenous Indians from Latin America, some of whom do not speak fluent Spanish but have their own languages, and many shades and mixtures of all races. The Hispanic individual may face discrimination based on diverse prejudices involving race, ethnicity, language, customs, immigration, legal status, or socioeconomic situation.

Chapter 3
«¿Qué le pasa?»

Communication Goals

Discuss Colds and
Influenza
Ask Whether a Patient
Feels Comfortable
Discuss Pain
Diagnose Injuries

Vocabulary

What Is the Matter?
Colds and Flu Symptoms
Comfort
Parts of the Body
How Much Does It Hurt?
Injuries

Structure

The Verb *Tener*
The Verb *Doler*
The Past Participle
The Pronunciation of *G, C,
J,* and *H*

Video Program

Trama: «*¿Qué le pasa?*»
*Demostración: La
comodidad*

Cultural Note

Expressions for Every Day

By the end of this chapter you will be able to ask patients what symptoms and how much pain they are experiencing. You will know the complaints associated with the cold and flu season, and how to ask whether a patient feels hot, cold, hungry, or thirsty. You will be familiar with the Spanish names for parts of the body and for injuries like cuts, burns, broken bones, swelling, and infections.

Tengo gripe.

Discuss Colds and Influenza

Vocabulario: ¿Qué tiene?
(What Is the Matter?)

Preguntas útiles

¿Qué tiene?	What is the matter?
¿Qué tiene el niño?	What is the matter with the boy?
¿Qué le pasa?	What is happening (with you, him, or her)?
¿Qué síntomas tiene?	What symptoms do you have?
¿Qué problema tiene hoy?	What problem do you have today?

Expresiones útiles

Tengo gripe.	I have the flu.
Estoy resfriado/a.	I have a cold.
No tengo nada.	There's nothing wrong with me.

¿Qué tiene? means literally, "What do you have?" The question elicits a description of symptoms. Unlike English, the double negative is necessary in Spanish: that is why we say, *No tengo nada.* After reviewing the verb *tener,* we shall learn a group of the most common complaints: cold and flu symptoms.

Estructura: El verbo *tener* (To Have)

yo	*Tengo* gripe.	I have the flu.
tú	¿Qué síntomas *tienes?*	What symptoms do you have?
él, ella, usted	¿*Tiene* usted fiebre?	Do you have a fever?
nosotros/as	Juan y yo *tenemos* diarrea.	Juan and I have diarrhea.
ellos, ellas, ustedes	Los niños *tienen* fiebre.	The children have fever.

 ## 3.1 Actividad

Form meaningful sentences by choosing a subject pronoun from column A, supplying the correct form of the verb *tener* from column B, and an object or object phrase from column C, as in the example. The vocabulary follows this exercise.

> Example: Juan tiene gripe.

A	B	C
Juan		fatiga.
Ana		gripe.
Yo	tengo	diarrea.
Tú	tienes	escalofrío.
La niña	tiene	dolor de cabeza.
Nosotros	tenemos	una gripe terrible.
Los pacientes	tienen	catarro y dolor de garganta.
Mi madre		una fiebre de cuarenta grados.

Vocabulario: Los síntomas de la gripe (Colds and Flu Symptoms)

Note that these terms are often used with the verb *tener* and without the direct object pronoun. An exception is *Estoy resfriado/a* (I have a cold).

El resfriado / el resfrío (Common Cold)

la influenza	influenza
la gripe	flu, common cold
el resfriado, el resfrío	common cold
el catarro	mucus, common cold, congestion
la alergia	allergy
la monga	cold (colloquialism, Puerto Rico)
la gripa	cold (colloquialism, Colombia)

Los síntomas (Symptoms)

la congestión nasal	stuffy nose
la nariz tapada	stuffy (blocked) nose
el goteo post-nasal	post-nasal drip
la flema verdosa	greenish sputum
la fiebre	fever
la náusea	nausea
el vómito	vomit, vomiting
la tos	cough
el estornudo	sneeze
el mareo	dizziness
los escalofríos	chills
los sudores nocturnos	night sweats
la falta de aire	shortness of breath
la fatiga	fatigue, shortness of breath
la diarrea	diarrhea
el estreñimiento	constipation
el malestar general	malaise

Tengo dolor de cabeza.

El dolor (Pain)

el dolor de cabeza	headache
el dolor en el cuerpo	body ache
el dolor de garganta	sore throat

Preguntas útiles

¿Tiene mareo?	Are you dizzy (lightheaded, faint)?
¿Está usted mareado/a?	Are you dizzy (lightheaded, faint)?
¿Tose mucho?	Do you cough a lot?
¿Es una tos seca?	Is it a dry cough?

Gripe, resfrío, resfriado, and *catarro* are interchangeable. However, an old adage says, *Gripe les da a los ricos; catarro a los pobres* (the rich get the flu; the poor get a common cold). A similar refrain says, *Alergia les da a los ricos; raquiña a los pobres* (the rich get allergies; the poor get itching). Latinos may be prone to the belief that exposure to the cold, such as leaving a window open at night, may allow *frío* to enter the body, resulting in a cold or something worse.

Video Program: *«¿Qué le pasa?»*

Watch the *Trama* for chapter 3 and do the activity that follows.

Dr. Vargas y Marisol Flores

Dr. Vargas:	Buenas tardes. ¿Cómo está usted, señora Flores?
Sra. Flores:	No me siento bien. Estoy enferma.
Dr. Vargas:	Lo siento. ¿Qué tiene?
Sra. Flores:	Tengo gripe. Estoy resfriada.
Dr. Vargas:	¿Qué síntomas tiene?
Sra. Flores:	Me duele la cabeza. Tengo dolor de garganta. Me pican los ojos. Me pican los oídos. La nariz la tengo congestionada.
Dr. Vargas:	¿Tose mucho?
Sra. Flores:	Sí, tengo una tos seca. Cuando toso, me duele mucho la garganta.
Dr. Vargas:	¿Tiene fiebre?
Sra. Flores:	En la noche. Cuando me da fiebre, me da escalofríos.
Dr. Vargas:	¿Tiene náusea o vómitos?
Sra. Flores:	No, pero no tengo hambre y casi no como.
Dr. Vargas:	¿Tiene diarrea?
Sra. Flores:	No.
Dr. Vargas:	Vamos a mirarle los oídos, la nariz y la garganta. Abra la boca y diga a-a-h.
Sra. Flores:	A-a-h. ¿Necesito un antibiótico?
Dr. Vargas:	No. Usted tiene un resfrío. Es un virus. Los antibióticos curan las infecciones bacterianas. Los antibióticos no curan los resfriados. Los resfriados duran una o dos semanas. Debe tomar muchos líquidos como té con limón y sopa de pollo. Debe tomar dos aspirinas o dos

> *Me pican los ojos.*
> My eyes itch.

pastillas de ibuprofén cada cuatro o seis horas si necesita para la fiebre y el dolor. Debe llamarme si tiene
una fiebre persistente o dolor en el pecho.

Sra. Flores: Gracias, doctor Vargas.

Dr. Vargas: Va a estar bien pronto.

 ## 3.2 Actividad

Ask a partner the following comprehension questions about the video.

A. ¿Cómo está la señora Flores?
B. ¿Qué tiene ella?
C. ¿Le duelen los ojos?
D. ¿Qué pasa cuando la Sra. Flores tose?
E. ¿Tiene náusea o vómito?
F. ¿Necesita la Sra. Flores un antibiótico?
G. ¿Cuándo debe llamar al doctor Vargas?

 ## 3.3 Actividad

Take turns (tastefully!) acting out the symptoms of colds and flu, while
other students guess which you are miming. The interchange might go like
this:

Class: ¿Cómo estás, William?

Student: No muy bien.

Class: ¿Qué te pasa?

Student: (Mime a symptom.)

Class: ¡Tú tienes _____!

Student: ¡Sí! Tengo _____. (No, no tengo _____,

tengo _____.)

 ## 3.4 Drama imprevisto

Let's conduct some medical research. Find out what symptoms classmates
have when they have a cold. Using the questionnaire that follows, move
about the classroom asking, *Cuando estás resfriado/a, ¿qué síntomas tienes?* Report the results of your study to the class. *Los síntomas más comunes del resfriado son . . .* and, *William tiene dolor de garganta cuando
está resfriado.*

Cuestionario de síntomas	
Síntoma	Nombre de estudiante
Congestión nasal	
Catarro	
Goteo post-nasal	
Fiebre	
Malestar general	
Una tos seca	
Falta de aire	

Lectura: *El resfriado común* (The Common Cold)

Listen to the instructor read about the common cold. Then read the passage aloud yourself and answer the questions that follow. You will be able to guess the meaning of some of the new verbs. Less familiar verbs include *durar* (to last), *tomar* (to take), *fumar* (to smoke), *bajar* (to lower), *aliviar* (to relieve), and *descansar* (to rest).

Un virus causa el resfriado. Hay casi doscientos virus que causan el resfriado. Los síntomas incluyen catarro, dolor de garganta, tos, dolor de cabeza y malestares. El resfriado dura una o hasta dos semanas. Los niños normalmente tienen resfriado hasta seis veces al año. Los adultos usualmente tienen dos o tres resfriados cada año.

hasta	up to
remedios caseros	home remedies
debe	you should

Existen varios remedios caseros para el resfriado. Por ejemplo, debe tomar muchos líquidos como el agua o jugo (juice) para reducir la congestión de la nariz. La sopa de pollo o una infusión (un té) de limón y jengibre (ginger) son muy buenos para aliviar el frío del cuerpo. Debe usar un vaporizador en la casa. No debe fumar. La aspirina, el ibuprofén, y el acetaminofén bajan la fiebre y alivian los dolores. Los niños no deben tomar aspirina. Es muy importante descansar.

Los antibióticos no curan el resfriado, pero el resfriado a veces causa una infección bacteriana como la bronquitis, la sinusitis o la pulmonía. Los antibióticos son para curar las infecciones bacterianas. Debe llamar al médico o a la clínica si tiene síntomas

de una infección bacteriana como una fiebre
alta, fiebre con escalofrío, fiebre persistente,
dolor en el pecho cuando tose o esputo
amarillo verdoso o de un color oscuro.

amarillo verdoso oscuro	yellow-greenish dark

 ## 3.5 Actividad

Ask a partner the following reading comprehension questions.

    A. ¿Qué causa los resfriados?
    B. ¿Cuánto tiempo dura un resfriado?
    C. ¿Cuáles son los remedios caseros?
    D. ¿Curan el resfriado los antibióticos?
    E. ¿Cuáles son los síntomas de las infecciones bacterianas?
    F. ¿Cuáles son los remedios que bajan la fiebre y alivian los dolores?
    G. ¿Qué debo hacer si tengo una fiebre persistente?

 ## 3.6 Drama imprevisto

You are a doctor who is treating a patient who is suffering from a common
head cold. Your partner is your patient, who believes that he or she needs
an antibiotic. Educate your patient and negotiate the treatment, while your
partner insists that you are not doing your duty.

 ## 3.7 Drama imprevisto

Act in a *telenovela!* Elaborate an original dialogue using the following as a
plot or write your own. Choose volunteers for the roles of Amanda, Amador, and the doctor. Be creative with the script and over-express the emotions. Perhaps a narrator can read and then pause for players to embellish
their lines. As an option, film your improvisations and then review your
movies. Monitoring and correcting one's own speech is more effective than
instructor-originated correction.

Amanda y Amador son novios. Amanda
ama a Amador, y Amador ama a Amanda.
Amador tiene tos. Tose mucho. Tose día y
noche. Amanda cree que Amador tiene tuber-

novio/a	fiancé/fiancée
amar	to love
creer	to believe

culosis. Cree que va a morir. Un momento, por favor. La doctora
dice que Amador no tiene fiebre. No tiene sudores nocturnos. La
prueba del esputo es negativa. ¡Amador no va a morir! ¡Gracias a
Dios! ¡Va a vivir!

Ask Whether a Patient Feels Comfortable

Vocabulario: La comodidad (Comfort)

- *Tener* is also used to express hunger, thirst, sensations of heat and cold, and sleepiness. These expressions may be called "idiomatic," because they are translated for meaning, not word for word.
    ¿Tiene usted hambre?   Are you hungry?
- Because the drive states (hunger, thirst, and so on) are being used as nouns in Spanish, they do not change their spelling to agree with the gender of the person.
    Miguel tiene sueño.   María tiene sueño.
- Recall that the verb *estar* is used with the adjectives *contento* (happy) and *cansado* (tired). Here are some idiomatic expressions using *tener* to practice in the exercises that follow.

Tengo hambre.	I am hungry.
¿Tiene sed?	Are you thirsty?
No tengo calor.	I don't feel like it's hot.
Los niños tienen frío.	The children feel like it's cold.
¿Tiene sueño?	Are you sleepy?
¿Tiene prisa?	Are you in a hurry?
¿Tiene miedo el niño?	Is the child afraid?
Usted tiene razón.	You are right.

- *El niño está caliente* means the child has a fever (is hot to the touch). *El niño tiene calor* refers to the child's subjective experience of feeling that the day or the room is hot.

 ## 3.8 Ejercicio

To aid your memorization, associate the following cues with one or more of the *tener* idioms, as in the examples. *Buenísimo/a* means "exceptionally good."

Examples: el café   El café es buenísimo cuando tengo sueño.
            las frutas   Las frutas son buenísimas cuando tengo
                             hambre.

   A. una cama
   B. un carro deportivo (a sports car)
   C. una frazada
   D. un osito de peluche (a stuffed or "Teddy" bear)
   E. una hamburguesa

    F. un abanico / un ventilador (a fan)
    G. un vaso de agua (a glass of water)
    H. una discusión (an argument)

 ## 3.9 Actividad

Divide large areas of the blackboard into the categories *hambre, sed, frío, calor,* and so on. In the appropriate areas, draw and label the items or environs that you associate with these feelings, and create sentences from your drawings. These "semantic maps" help keep you thinking in Spanish and create memory cues.

 ## 3.10 Actividad

The instructor will hand out index cards, each with one of the *tener* idioms on it. Take turns miming the idiom on your card. Ask, *¿Qué tengo?* The rest of the class will report, *¡Tú tienes _____!* Perhaps the instructor will add a few trick cards, like *Tengo dolor de cabeza* or *Tengo catarro.*

 ## 3.11 Drama imprevisto

Circulate in the classroom with the following questionnaire and ask classmates whether they are hungry, thirsty, and so forth. After gathering your data, report your findings to the rest of the class. For example, *Susan tiene frío cuando está en el hospital y yo no.*

Circunstancia	Nombre de compañero
Tener razón siempre	
Tener frío cuando está en el hospital	
Tener miedo de las inyecciones	
Tener prisa por la mañana	
Tener sueño muy temprano	
Tener hambre en el trabajo	

Video Program: *La comodidad*

Watch the *Demostración* for chapter 3 and do the activity that follows.

Elsita:	Mami, soy enfermera.
Sra. Flores:	Eres enfermera. Qué linda. ¿Cómo te llamas?
Elsita:	Soy la enfermera Elsita.
Sra. Flores:	Mucho gusto enfermera Elsita.
Elsita:	¿Tienes sed?
Sra. Flores:	No, no tengo sed ahora. Tengo hambre. Tengo mucha hambre.
Elsita:	¿Tienes hambre? ¿Quieres un chocolate? Es delicioso.
Sra. Flores:	O, sí, muchas gracias. Me encanta el chocolate.
Elsita:	¿Tienes calor?
Sra. Flores:	No, tengo frío. Tengo mucho frío.
Elsita:	¿Tienes frío? ¿Quieres una sábana?
Sra. Flores:	O sí, muchas gracias. Eres una buena enfermera, Elsita. Ya no tengo frío, gracias.
Elsita:	¿Tienes miedo?
Sra. Flores:	Un poquito.
Elsita:	Acá está mi muñeca. No te preocupes. Todo va a estar bien.
Sra. Flores:	Qué linda. Ya no tengo miedo. Gracias.

Elsita Flores

 ## 3.12 Actividad

Ask a partner the following questions.

A. ¿Tiene sed la Sra. Flores?
B. ¿Tiene hambre la Sra. Flores?
C. ¿Tiene frío o calor la Sra. Flores?
D. ¿De qué tiene miedo la Sra. Flores?
E. Y tú, ¿tienes miedo a los doctores?
F. ¿Tienes miedo a las inyecciones?

Vocabulario: Las partes del cuerpo (Parts of the Body)

This section requires some memorization. Practice the following Spanish anatomical words during the next week while you are bathing, drying yourself, dressing, and so on. Name it as you dry it, so that kinesthesia cues memory as well. If you make index cards for studying, write the names in Spanish only. If needed, add a sketch of the body part represented. This will help you avoid forming memories that are dependent on English cues. Share with the class your techniques for memorization. Rote memory is a slow and tedious process. It is more helpful to elaborate on the new vocabulary, making drawings, sentences, and other associations.

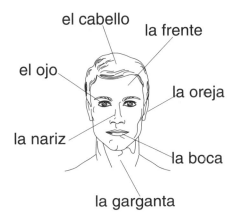

el cabello
la frente
el ojo
la oreja
la nariz
la boca
la garganta

La cabeza

La cabeza (Head)

el cráneo	cranium
el cabello, el pelo	hair

La cara (Face)

la frente	forehead
el ojo	eye
el pómulo, la mejilla	cheekbone, cheek
la nariz	nose
el seno frontal/paranasal	frontal/paranasal sinus
la oreja	ear (outer)
el oído	ear (inner)
la mandíbula	jaw
la barbilla	chin
la garganta	throat

La boca (Mouth)

el labio	lip
la lengua	tongue
el diente	tooth
la muela	molar
la encía	gum

 3.13 Actividad

Instructor: Bring a Mr. Potato Head to the class and distribute the face and head components to the students. Ask the class questions like *¿Quién tiene la oreja?* Students take turns naming the parts they picked as they put them on the model.

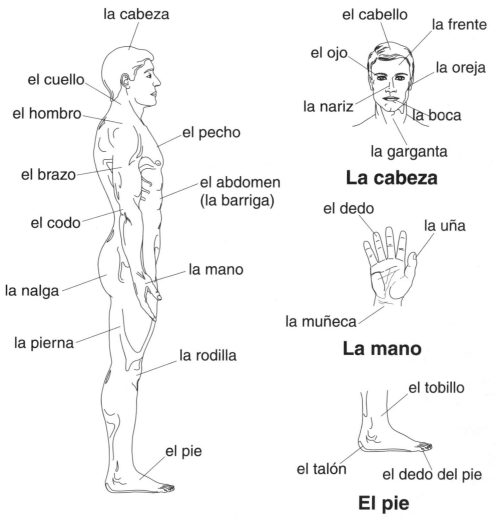

La cabeza

La mano

El pie

El cuerpo humano

3.14 Actividad

Students take turns as "police artist," drawing a face on the blackboard according to a description by other class members. Guidance may include, for example, *tiene la nariz grande; las orejas son pequeñas* (small); *y no tiene dientes.* Later, describe the various sketches while pointing to each aspect.

Las partes del cuerpo

el pecho, el tórax	chest
el pecho, el seno	breast, mammary gland
el brazo	arm
la mano	hand
el dedo	finger
la uña	fingernail
el abdomen, la barriga	abdomen
el ombligo	navel
el recto, el ano	rectum
el pene	penis
el escroto	scrotum
la vagina	vagina
el gluteo	buttock
la nalga, la pompis (*popular*)	buttock
la pierna	leg
el muslo	thigh
el pie	foot
el talón	heel
el dedo del pie	toe
la uña del dedo del pie	toenail

Las coyunturas (Joints)

la coyuntura, la articulación	joint
el cuello	neck
la espalda	back
la espina dorsal	spine
la vértebra	vertebra
el hombro	shoulder
el codo	elbow
la muñeca, el radio	wrist
el nudillo	knuckle
la cadera	hip
la rodilla	knee
el tobillo	ankle

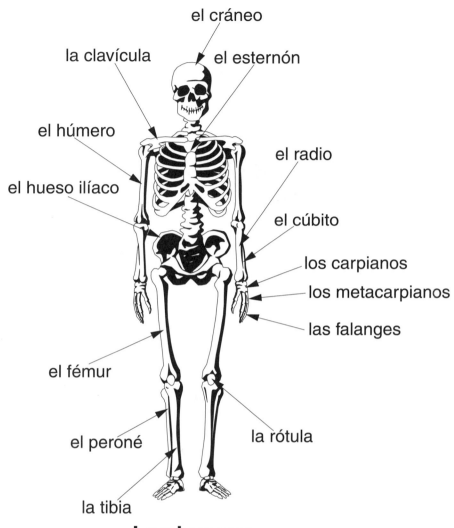

el cráneo

la clavícula   el esternón

el húmero

el radio

el hueso ilíaco

el cúbito

los carpianos

los metacarpianos

las falanges

el fémur

el peroné   la rótula

la tibia

Los huesos

Los huesos (Bones)

la clavícula	clavicle
el omóplato	scapula
el esternón	sternum
la costilla	rib
el húmero	humerus
el radio	radius
el cúbito	ulna
el carpo	carpus
el metacarpo	metacarpus
la falange	phalange

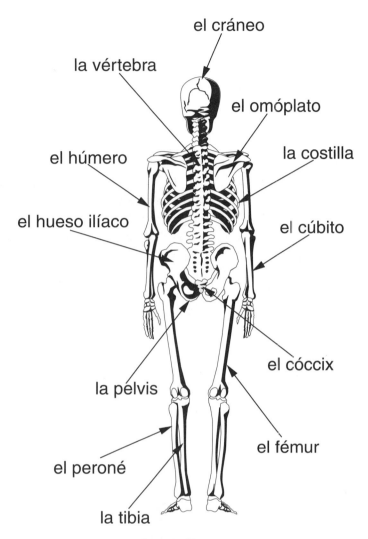

el cráneo

la vértebra

el omóplato

el húmero

la costilla

el hueso ilíaco

el cúbito

la pelvis

el cóccix

el peroné

el fémur

la tibia

Los huesos

el sacro	sacrum
el íleon	ilium
la pelvis	pelvis
el cóccix	coccyx
el fémur	femur
la patela, la rótula	kneecap
la tibia	tibia
el peroné	fibula

Note that although *nalga* (Caribbean) and *pompis* (Mexico, Central America) are not clinical terms, they are readily understood and their use is not likely to be offensive.

3.15 Ejercicio

A leader can drill the class by reading a list of body parts. Students must repeat the word and move or point to the part on their own bodies.

 ### 3.16 Actividad

Instructor: Obtain a Halloween skeleton and disassemble it. Distribute the body parts to students by asking them to pick the parts out of a bag; they must name the parts as they take them out. The instructor can lead in a drill by asking questions like, *¿Qué tiene Ana?* or *¿Quién tiene la cabeza?* Another idea is to make a variation of "pin-the-tail-on-the-donkey" by attaching a large cardboard person to the wall, or drawing one on the board. Distribute needed body parts drawn on paper or cardboard with double-stick tape (or drawn on sticky-note paper). Students take turns naming the part they were given and placing it on the model. Try it blindfolded anyone?

 ### 3.17 Actividad

Play *Simón dice* ("Simon Says"). Students stand while one class member chooses parts of the body and says, *Simón dice mueva la cabeza* or *No mueva las caderas.*

 ## Discuss Pain

 ### Estructura: El verbo *doler* (To Hurt, Ache)

- You learned that "pain" in Spanish is *el dolor.*

Tengo dolor de cabeza.	I have a headache.
¿Tiene dolor?	Do you have pain?
¿Dónde está el dolor?	Where is the pain?
Enséñame dónde duele.	Show me where it hurts.

- The verb *doler* means "to hurt." The third person (*duele* or *duelen*) is used because a part (or parts) of the body *does* the hurting. For example, *Me duele la cabeza* is literally "The head hurts me." "The head" is the subject of this sentence and (unfortunately) I am the object. Spanish-speakers use the indirect article *me* to indicate who feels the hurt. They avoid redundancy by saying *la cabeza.* English-speakers use the possessive article "my" to indicate who feels the hurt (if my head hurts, it must be hurting me).

- The indirect object pronouns—*me, te, le, nos,* or *les*—are placed before the verb. These represent the person who is the object of the pain. *Le* represents "you," "him," and "her."

Me duele el cuerpo.	My body hurts.
¿Te duele la garganta?	Does your throat hurt? (*familiar form*)
¿Qué le duele?	What hurts you (him, her)?
¿Qué le duele a Roberto?	What hurts Roberto?

- Remember that when the subject (what hurts) is plural, the verb must also be plural. "My left eye hurts" is *Me duele el ojo izquierdo.* "My eyes hurt" is *Me duelen los ojos.*

Me duelen los dientes.	My teeth hurt.
Me duelen las coyunturas.	My joints hurt.

 ## 3.18 Actividad

This is a guessing game. One student thinks of a body part and classmates guess, as in the example.

Example:	Student 1:	¿Le duele la cabeza?
	Student 2:	No, no me duele la cabeza.

Take turns guessing until the student says, *¡Sí, eso sí que es!* (Yes, that is it!). Pointing to the part of the body while saying the word may help you learn the vocabulary more quickly. (Does *eso sí que es* spell something in English?)

 ## 3.19 Actividad

Instructor: Make duplicate sets of index cards with the Spanish name (or a drawing) of a painful body part written on each and distribute them to the students. Students circulate in the classroom to find the partner with a card depicting the same ache or pain that they have by (quietly) asking,

¿Te duele el/la _____? Each student should answer in complete sentences:

No, no me duele el/la _____, or *Sí, me duele el/la _____.*

Vocabulario: ¿Le duele mucho? (How Much Does It Hurt?)

¿Cómo está el dolor?	How is the pain?
Me duele muchísimo.	It hurts a great deal.
. . . mucho	. . . a lot
. . . un poco	. . . a little
. . . un poquito	. . . a tiny bit

Está peor.	It's worse.
Está igual.	It's the same.
Está regular.	It's so-so.
Está mejor.	It's better.
¿Cuál es el brazo que le duele?	Which is the arm that hurts?
Es el brazo izquierdo.	It is the left arm.
Es el brazo derecho.	It is the right arm.
Señale con el dedo.	Point with your finger.

Right and *left* are adjectives and must agree in gender with the noun they modify. For example, *Me duele la pierna derecha y el brazo izquierdo.* Recall that Spanish-speakers use articles and not the possessive adjectives with parts of the body. *"My* arm hurts" is expressed *Me duele el brazo.*

 3.20 Reciclaje

Recall that in chapter 2 we learned to ask about pain. We asked, *¿Estás mejor, igual o peor?* Add this new information to what you know. Ask a partner about his or her pain. Begin with *¿Qué le duele?* and then work towards a more specific description, as in the example. You may also want to use the pain scale from chapter 2, which follows this exercise.

Example:	Student 1:	¿Qué le duele?
	Student 2:	Me duele la mano.
	Student 1:	¿Cuál es la mano que le duele?
	Student 2:	Me duele la mano izquierda.
	Student 1:	¿Cómo está el dolor? ¿Está peor, igual o mejor? Señale con el dedo cómo está el dolor.

¿Cómo está el dolor?
Señale el dibujo que corresponda.

0 1 2 3 4 5 6 7 8 9 10

No duele   Duele un poco   Tolerable   Duele mucho   Intolerable

Diagnose Injuries

Vocabulario: Las heridas (Injuries)

el golpe	bump
la laceración	laceration
la cortada, el tajo	cut
la cortadura	bad cut
la infección	infection
la hinchazón	swelling
la quemadura	burn
la fractura simple	simple fracture
la fractura compuesta	compound fracture
la fractura múltiple	multiple fracture

 ## Estructura: El participio pasado (The Past Participle)

- The preceding vocabulary words are nouns and are often used with *tener.*

   Tengo una cortada en el dedo.   I have a cut on my finger.
   Usted tiene una infección.   You have an infection.

- To report a diagnosis, you may use these or use the past participle of the related verb. The past participle may be used as an adjective. To form the past participle in Spanish, we add *-ado* to the stems of verbs that end in *-ar,* and *-ido* to the stems of verbs that end in *-er* or *-ir.* For example, the verb *quebrar* (to break) changes to *quebrado* (and *quebrada*) and *torcer* (to twist, sprain) changes to *torcido/a* (twisted, sprained).

cortar	to cut	→	cortado/a	cut
quemar	to burn	→	quemado/a	burned
hinchar	to swell	→	hinchado/a	swollen
torcer	to sprain	→	torcido/a	sprained
infectar	to infect	→	infectado/a	infected
inflamar	to inflame	→	inflamado/a	inflamed
quebrar	to break	→	quebrado/a	broken
fracturar	to fracture	→	fracturado/a	fractured
romper	to break	→	roto/a	broken

Note that *romper* is irregular in the past participle, and less clinical-sounding than *quebrar.* Here is a mnemonic device: if you can pinch an inch, it must be *hinchazón!*

- When the past participle is used as an adjective, it must follow the noun and agree with it in gender and number.

el brazo quebrado	the broken arm
la pierna quebrada	the broken leg
los ojos infectados	the infected eyes

- These can be used with the verb *estar* as well as with the verb *tener*.

  | El brazo está fracturado. | The arm is fractured. |
  | Joselito tiene el brazo fracturado. | Joselito has a fractured arm. |

 3.21 Ejercicio

With a partner, practice communicating the diagnosis of a broken bone to a patient, as in the example. Remember that gender and number must agree when you use a past participle as an adjective.

> Example: el brazo
>   Usted tiene el brazo quebrado.

A. el dedo   E. dos costillas
B. la pierna   F. tres dedos
C. el pie   G. el tobillo izquierdo
D. las rodillas   H. la muñeca derecha

Now repeat the exercise using the verb *estar*. For example, *El brazo está quebrado.*

 3.22 Ejercicio

Tell the patient that the body part is sprained but not broken, as in the example.

> Example: la muñeca
>   La muñeca no está quebrada, gracias a Dios; está torcida.

A. la rodilla   E. el dedo
B. los tobillos   F. la espalda
C. el cuello   G. el tobillo izquierdo
D. las muñecas   H. la muñeca derecha

3.23 Ejercicio

Give some more good news. Say that the indicated part of the body is swollen but not infected, as in the example.

Example: el dedo
El dedo está hinchado, pero no está infectado.

A. la encía
B. los labios
C. la rodilla
D. los tobillos
E. el dedo del pie
F. el codo
G. la lengua
H. el ojo derecho

 3.24 Actividad

Speak Spanish continuously—and test your memory—during this activity. The first student says, *Miguel tuvo* (had) *un accidente automovilístico, el pobrecito. Tiene el brazo quebrado.* The class repeats the report from the beginning. The next student adds yet another medical complaint, for example, *También tiene los tobillos hinchados.* The class repeats the entire report from the beginning before the next student adds to the list of injuries, and so on.

También	Also

 3.25 Drama imprevisto

When you have finished *actividad* 3.24, act out (or overact) a conversation with Miguel's parent or sibling in which you let him or her know what injuries Miguel sustained in the accident. The family member, repeating each portion of news, reacts with hyperbolic disbelief or anxiety, while you are a calming influence. Words of disbelief include *¡No puede ser!* (It can't be!). Words of assurance include *No se preocupe; todo va a estar bien* (Don't worry; everything is going to be alright).

 3.26 Actividad

Role-play a basic interview. Do not use English! Think of a set of cold symptoms or an ailing part of the body. Take turns in front of the class as *el/la paciente* while members of the class conduct an interview. The interview should elicit enough information to move from the patient's chief complaint to a finer definition of the problem and of the pain. As a frustrating but more challenging variation, try this exercise with a patient who answers only *Sí* or *No.*

The Pronunciation of *G, C, J,* and *H*

- The letter «g» is pronounced almost as the English "h" when it precedes the vowels «e» and «i». It is a fricative sound, which means that to produce it, air passes through a slightly constricted airway. Examples are *general, género,* and *ginecología.* It is pronounced as the English "g" in "go" before consonants and the vowels «a», «o», and «u». Examples are *gracias, gripe, garganta, gordo,* and *gusto.* To preserve this «g» sound before the vowels «e» and «i», the letter «u» is inserted in the written word, as in *guerra* (war), *guitarra,* and the family name *Rodríguez.*
- The letter «c» is pronounced like the English "c" in "cent" when it precedes the vowels «e» and «i». Examples are *cerebro* and *cirugía.* It is pronounced like the English "c" in "coin" before the vowels «a», «o», and «u», and before consonants. Examples are *cansado, catarro, cortar, codo, Cuba, clínica,* and *recto.*
- «J» is pronounced like the English "h," as in *ojo, oreja,* and *jueves.* The Spanish «h» is always silent, as in *herida, hambre,* and *hospital.* Note that the «g» is soft in the Spanish word for surgery, *cirugía,* because it is followed by an «i». To preserve the soft sound, the word for surgeon is written with a «j» (*cirujano*) as a spelling accommodation.

Cultural Note: Expressions for Every Day

You will become comfortable with the medical interview as a non-native speaker of Spanish. Listen carefully to Spanish conversations to become familiar with natural daily expressions. In faster-paced urban and industrial areas of the world some people have traded good manners for efficiency. Spanish-speakers in general strive to make social interactions warm, friendly, and courteous.

El tener respeto is a quality of the self in which one always expresses deference to the other person in an interpersonal exchange. It constitutes a cultural norm that accords value to the other person. Failure to do so is *una falta de respeto.* Many polite expressions are part of everyday life among Spanish-speaking people. For example, when you enter a room, it is customary to greet each person individually, which may involve standing for ladies and shaking hands with everyone. You might say, *Hola, ¿cómo está usted?* You'll notice that Latinos normally wait for a response after asking the question. Personal relationships are friendly. Kisses and hugs (*besos y abrazos*) are common. Sometimes Latino children do not make eye contact with an adult, having been taught that to do so would be disrespectful.

You may also notice that Latinos who have not fully assimilated into North American culture may have closer personal space tolerances. They may unconsciously judge the North American to be aloof for maintaining greater interpersonal distance. North Americans sometimes avoid eye contact when uncomfortable with physical closeness and unconsciously back off.

You'll recall the Spanish equivalents of some common courtesies:

por favor	please
muchas gracias	many thanks
de nada	you're welcome
un placer	a pleasure, you're welcome

After introducing oneself or being introduced to another person, it would be proper to say, *Encantado* (or *Encantada*), which means "enchanted" and expresses "Pleased to meet you." You can also say, *Mucho gusto,* to which the other person might respond, *El gusto es mío. Igual* or the adverb *Igualmente* is used for "Same here." In a professional context you might say, *A sus órdenes* (At your service) or *Para servirle* (In order to serve you).

When leaving a room, one customarily asks permission. *Con su permiso* means, "With your permission" and can be said simply, *permiso.* (The term *perdón* is reserved for asking forgiveness after bumping, interrupting, or otherwise offending, while *permiso* is used before the interruption.) "I am going to return soon" is *Voy a volver pronto,* or *Vuelvo ahora.*

«¡Mucho gusto!»

Chapter 4
El recepcionista

By the end of this chapter you will know the vocabulary that is used when receiving patients for admission at a medical office or hospital. You will be able to count to a thousand, give vital signs, and take telephone numbers. You will be able to negotiate with patients the dates and times of follow-up appointments. You'll be able to ask the patient's name, address, date of birth, insurance, and other information critical to the admissions process. Finally, you will learn why Latinos have two last names.

 Tell a Patient His or Her Vital Signs

Vocabulario: Los números del cero al diez
(Numbers from Zero to Ten)

Practice saying aloud the numbers from zero to ten. Build rhythm and fluency.

0	cero		
1	uno	6	seis
2	dos	7	siete
3	tres	8	ocho
4	cuatro	9	nueve
5	cinco	10	diez

 4.1 Actividad

Ask a fellow student the following questions. When you have finished, switch roles. Note that *¿cuántos?* or *¿cuántas?* means "how many?" and must agree in number and gender with the noun it precedes.

A. ¿Cuántas piernas tienes?
B. ¿Cuántos dedos tienes en la mano izquierda?
C. ¿Cuántos ombligos tienes?
D. ¿Cuántas orejas tienes?
E. ¿Cuántos dedos del pie tienes?
F. ¿Cuántos días hay en una semana?

hay	there is; there are

Los números del 11 al 1.000 (Numbers from 11 to 1,000)

11	once	21	veintiuno	31	treinta y uno
12	doce	22	veintidós	32	treinta y dos
13	trece	23	veintitrés	33	treinta y tres
14	catorce	24	veinticuatro	34	treinta y cuatro
15	quince	25	veinticinco	35	treinta y cinco
16	dieciséis	26	veintiséis	36	treinta y seis
17	diecisiete	27	veintisiete	37	treinta y siete
18	dieciocho	28	veintiocho	38	treinta y ocho
19	diecinueve	29	veintinueve	39	treinta y nueve
20	veinte	30	treinta	40	cuarenta

Notice the patterns. In Spanish, sixteen to twenty-nine are spelled as one word. After thirty, such numbers are spelled as three words. *Sesenta* has an *s* like *seis*. *Setenta* has a *t* like *siete*. (It helps to remember that *s* comes before *t* in the alphabet.) Whether one word or three, native pronunciation usually involves linking or blending the words together as if they were one. (Do you recall how fast you counted from one to ten when you played hide-and-seek as a child?) Pay extra attention to *once, doce, trece, catorce,* and *quince.* Heed the spelling of *quinientos, setecientos,* and *novecientos.*

50	cincuenta	190	ciento noventa
51	cincuenta y uno	199	ciento noventa y nueve
52	cincuenta y dos	200	doscientos
60	sesenta	225	doscientos veinticinco
70	setenta	300	trescientos
80	ochenta	351	trescientos cincuenta y uno

90	noventa	400	cuatrocientos
100	cien	500	quinientos
101	ciento uno	600	seiscientos
102	ciento dos	700	setecientos
130	ciento treinta	800	ochocientos
135	ciento treinta y cinco	900	novecientos
150	ciento cincuenta	1.000	mil

 4.2 Actividad

Tedious or not, you'll need to count from one to one hundred at least once in the classroom. Make it fun! Guess the number of candies in a jar and then count them to determine who will win a prize. Practice on your own this week counting people, cars, books, and so on, until you become fluent.

 4.3 Actividad

The instructor or a fellow student will practice asking how many of certain objects there are in the classroom. Arrive at the number as a group by counting aloud from the number *uno.* Recall that *cuánto/a/os/as* must agree with the noun in number and gender.

> Example: Leader: ¿Cuántos estudiantes hay en la clase?
> Class: Hay uno, dos, tres . . . estudiantes.

A. puertas (doors)
B. ventanas (windows)
C. enfermeros
D. escritorios (desks)
E. solteros (singles)
F. estudiantes
G. doctores
H. cabezas
I. diccionarios
J. ojos
K. vegetarianos (vegetarians)
L. bolígrafos (pens)

 4.4 Ejercicio

Ask your partner what your body temperature is, starting over and taking turns for each of the following readings. The decimal point is expressed *punto,* as in *noventa y ocho punto seis grados* (98.6 degrees). (This might frighten a patient who normally uses the metric system!)

> Example: 98.0 Student 1: ¿Cómo está mi temperatura?
> Student 2: Su temperatura está en noventa y ocho grados.

A. 98	E. 104.2
B. 100.8	F. 98.9
C. 97.4	G. 101.2
D. 103	H. 100.3

 ## 4.5 Ejercicio

Likewise, ask about blood pressure. The word "over" is *sobre,* as in *ciento veinte sobre ochenta* (120/80). *Presión arterial* may also be expressed *presión sanguinea.*

Example: (120/80)   Student 1:   ¿Cuál es mi presión arterial?
                     Student 2:   Ciento veinte sobre ochenta.

A. 110/68	E. 122/84
B. 166/110	F. 118/92
C. 134/80	G. 106/74
D. 128/70	H. 120/80

 ## 4.6 Actividad

Using the vital signs record that follows, answer the following questions in complete sentences. After identifying the person, tell the specific vital sign(s). For example, *el señor Duarte tiene la presión alta. Su presión es ciento sesenta sobre ciento diez.*

A. ¿Quién tiene la presión alta (la hipertensión)?
B. ¿Quién tiene taquicardia?
C. ¿Quién tiene la presión baja (la hipotensión)?
D. ¿Quién tiene fiebre?
E. ¿Quiénes no tienen fiebre?
F. ¿Quién tiene los signos normales?

Paciente	Presión arterial	Pulso	Temperatura
Sr. Bolívar	128/78	90	103.8
Sr. Duarte	160/110	160	98.9
Sr. Luperón	90/55	84	98.7
Sr. Vázquez	120/70	68	97.9

Take a Telephone Message

Los números telefónicos
(Telephone Numbers)

«¿Cuál es su número de teléfono?»

Telephone numbers are usually expressed orally by a single number followed by three groups of two-digit numbers. For example, 828-7932 is said 8-28-79-32, or *ocho, veintiocho, setenta y nueve, treinta y dos.* Zeros can change things. The number 679-7000 is *seis, setenta y nueve, siete mil,* and the number 679-7001 is *seis, setenta y nueve, setenta, cero uno.* When a double number such as 77 appears, you may hear *doble siete* or *par de siete* (pair of sevens). Write your office telephone number or other frequently used number here and practice saying it. *Mi número de teléfono es* _____. Take turns saying yours to the class to see how many can write it down correctly. Here is some additional vocabulary.

En este momento no está.	He or she is not here right now.
¿Quiere dejar un mensaje?	Would you like to leave a message?
¿Quién llama?	Who is calling?
¿Cuál es su número de teléfono?	What is your telephone number?
Mi número de teléfono es . . .	My telephone number is . . .

 ## 4.7 Actividad

The instructor will dictate several telephone numbers for you to practice. Next, take turns telling your work telephone or other important phone number in Spanish to the class. Students will write the numbers in Arabic numerals on paper, and the instructor will write them on the board for students to correct themselves.

 ## Video Program: *Los números de teléfono*

Watch the *Demostración* for chapter 4 and do the activity that follows. In the video, Rosmery the nurse takes several telephone messages, and you have the opportunity to take notes along with her and then check your accuracy.

4.8 Actividad

In pairs, practice role-playing telephone calls in which you leave and take telephone messages for a third party who is not there. Check each other's notes for accuracy.

La enfermera Rosmery es mexicana, de Guadalajara, y muy amable.

Estructura: Haciendo preguntas (Forming Questions)

- When questions are written, two question marks signal the event as intonation does when questions are spoken. Placing the subject after the verb may also indicate a question. For example, pitch is essential when asking aloud, *¿Su cita es a las cuatro?* Moving the subject after the verb, or even to the end of the sentence, makes the question more obvious. *¿Es su cita a las cuatro? ¿Es a las cuatro su cita?*
- You learned in chapter 2 that another way to ask a question is to make a statement followed by a marker such as *¿no?, ¿verdad?,* or *¿cierto?* For example, *Su cita es a las cuatro, ¿no?* The question mark is placed where the question portion of the statement begins.
- To solicit more than a yes-or-no answer, use an interrogative word. Two question marks and an accent on the interrogative word are necessary.

¿dónde?	where?	¿adónde?	to where?
¿de dónde?	from where?	¿cómo?	how?
¿cuándo?	when?	¿quién/quiénes?	who?
¿cuál/cuáles?	which?	¿qué?	what?
¿cuánto/a?	how much?	¿cuántos/as?	how many?
¿a qué hora?	at what time?		

- Here are some examples.

¿Dónde vive?	Where do you live?
¿De dónde es usted?	Where are you from?
¿Cómo está usted?	How are you?
¿Cuándo es su cita?	When is your appointment?
¿Quién es su doctor?	Who is your doctor?
¿Cuál es el tobillo hinchado?	Which is the swollen ankle?
¿Qué le duele?	What hurts you?
¿Cuántos años tiene?	How old are you?
¿A qué hora es su cita?	What time is your appointment?

- *¿Qué?* and *¿Cuál?* are not interchangeable. *¿Qué?* requests a definition or an explanation, and *¿cuál?* asks for a choice. For example,

¿Qué es la pulmonía?	What is pneumonia?
¿Qué le duele?	What hurts you?
¿Cuál es el hombro que le duele?	Which is the arm that hurts you?
¿Cuál es su número de teléfono?	What is your telephone number?

- To ask a name, you can say, *¿Cómo se llama usted?* or *¿Cuál es su nombre?* or even *¿Quién es usted?* The latter implies asking for a person's relationship to a situation, for example, job title or kinship to a patient. To ask an address, use *¿Cuál es su dirección?* Write your own information in the spaces below.

¿Cómo se llama usted?	Me llamo _____.
¿Cuál es su dirección?	Mi dirección es _____.
¿Quién es su doctor?	Mi doctor(a) es el/la _____.

- Note that with *¿Cómo se llama usted?* you do not need the verb *es* in the response. The question literally means, "How do you call yourself?"

Me llamo Rigoberto.	My name is Rigoberto.
Ella se llama Graciela.	Her name is Graciela.

 ## 4.9 Actividad

Speak with other students. Practice several ways to ask for students' and their doctors' names and addresses. (This is called circumlocution and helps to build flexibility.) In addition to *¿Quién es su doctor?*, we can say, *¿Cómo se llama su doctor?* and *¿Cuál es el nombre de su doctor?* Suppose you forget how to ask the question. How would you substitute or act it out? It is possible, although somewhat less polite, to ask the questions in this manner: *¿Nombre y apellido? ¿Dirección?*

 ## 4.10 Drama imprevisto

Play an "answer-and-question" game show. Someone circulates in the "audience" pretending to have a microphone and asking for *respuestas,* or "answers." When called upon, a student will make up and say the answer to an unstated *pregunta,* or question. The roving microphone will then call upon another student to state the question that would have elicited that answer. Here are some examples.

Respuesta	*Pregunta*
Me llamo Rafael.	¿Cómo te llamas?
Es un doctor para el corazón.	¿Qué es un cardiólogo?
Es una inflamación del pulmón.	¿Qué es la pulmonía?
Guadalajara está en México.	¿Dónde está Guadalajara?

Make and Negotiate Dates for Future Appointments

Vocabulario: El año, el mes y la fecha
(The Year, the Month, and the Date)

1900 mil novecientos	1997 mil novecientos noventa y siete
	1999 mil novecientos noventa y nueve
2000 dos mil	2009 dos mil nueve

Note that years are not expressed "nineteen ninety-six" as in English. This number is expressed "one thousand, nine hundred, ninety-six" in Spanish.

4.11 Actividad

Ask students the current year and what year they were born. *¿En qué año estamos?* can be answered, *Estamos en el año* _____. *¿En qué año nació usted?* can be answered, *Yo nací en el año* _____. *Nació* and *nací* are past tense forms of the verb *nacer,* to be born.

La edad (Age)

We use the verb *tener* to express age. "How old are you?" is *¿Cuántos años tiene?* (This is an idiomatic expression, because it literally means "How many years do you have?") "I am 30 years old" is *Tengo treinta años.* Never forget the importance of pronunciation. *Año* (pronounced "anyo") means "year," and *ano* you know from chapter 3!

4.12 Ejercicio

It may be more comfortable to talk about someone else's age! Refer to the chart below and ask a partner, for example, *¿Cuántos años tiene don Samuel?*

Nombre	*Fecha de nacimiento*
Don Samuel	el 3 de octubre del 1945
Sara	el 14 de marzo del 1993
Doña Olga	el 2 de mayo del 1931
Paquito	el 27 de enero del 2004
El Sr. Arroyo	el 30 de junio del 1968

 ## 4.13 Actividad

Take turns asking fellow students, *¿Cuántos años tiene usted?* The student will answer, *Tengo _____ años.* (It's all right to stretch—or shrink—the truth!) Continue until you find a student who is the same age as you.

Los meses del año (The Months of the Year)

enero	January	julio	July
febrero	February	agosto	August
marzo	March	septiembre	September
abril	April	octubre	October
mayo	May	noviembre	November
junio	June	diciembre	December

La fecha (The Date)

Note: When writing dates for patients, it is best to write the name of the month. Using numbers for the months and days can be confusing because of the order in which they are written. Spanish-speaking people normally write the day before the month. Hence, October 15, 2008, is written 15-10-08. In countries that write the number for the month in roman numerals, this date would be 15-X-08. In the United States, writing the date 6-8-2009 might be understood as either August 6, 2009, or June 8, 2009, depending on the degree to which the patient has acculturated to the host culture. In Spanish, write *el 6 de agosto del 2009.* (Note that in Spanish, months of the year are not written with an initial capital letter.)

¿Qué día es?	What day is it?
Hoy es jueves.	Today is Thursday.
¿Cuál es la fecha de hoy?	What is today's date?
Hoy es el cinco de febrero del dos mil nueve.	Today is February 5, 2009.
¿Cuál es su fecha de nacimiento?	What is your birth date?

Note that the first of the month has special treatment.

Hoy es el primero de mayo.	Today is May first.

Febrero del 2009						
lunes	martes	miércoles	jueves	viernes	sábado	domingo
						1
2	3	4	5	6	7	8
9	10	11	12	13	14	15
16	17	18	19	20	21	22
23	24	25	26	27	28	

 4.14 Actividad

Ask fellow students their date of birth. Move around the classroom and find someone born in the same month as you and someone born the same year as you.

 4.15 Reciclaje

In chapter 2 you learned how to determine whether a patient was oriented as to person, place, and time. You have expanded your repertoire of helpful questions with regard to the date. Work with a partner to role-play for the class an interview to elicit whether a patient knows his or her name, where he or she is, and the day, date, and year.

Vocabulario: La hora (Telling Time)

¿Qué hora es?	What time is it?
Es la una.	1:00
Son las dos.	2:00
Son las tres.	3:00
Son las tres y cinco.	3:05
Son las seis y media.	6:30
Son las siete y cuarto (y quince)	7:15
Son las diez menos cinco.	9:55
Son las diez de la mañana.	It is 10:00 in the morning.
a las cuatro de la tarde	at 4:00 in the afternoon
a las diez de la noche	at 10:00 at night

> *Es la una* is singular, while *Son las dos* is plural. *Cuarto* means "quarter."

Notice that *y* is used for the first thirty minutes after the hour, while *menos* is used for the twenty-nine minutes that precede the following hour. With the worldwide proliferation of digital watches, some Spanish-speakers now use digital time. For example, 10:45 in digital time is *Son las diez, cuarenta y cinco;* however, the traditional analog method is more common.

 4.16 Ejercicio

Look at the clock faces and say the times, first as analog, and then as digital.

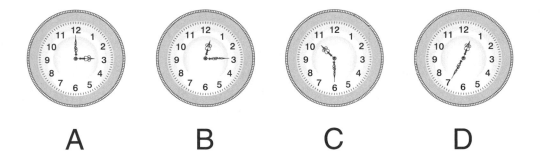

A   B   C   D

 4.17 Actividad

Play "Time Aerobics." The instructor stands with his or her back to the class, positions his or her hands like the hands of a clock, and chants the time represented. Students, who are standing as well, copy the instructor's position and repeat the time.

4.18 Ejercicio

Say the following times, translating from the English digital form to traditional analog Spanish. Afterwards, say them in Spanish digital time.

A. 10:45 AM	C. 8:30 PM	E. 3:56 PM
B. 6:15 AM	D. 11:55 PM	F. 6:05 PM

 4.19 Actividad

The instructor or a student should make a cardboard clock with movable hands (or secure a plastic "Will be back at . . ." sign from an office supplies store) to use as a prop in the classroom for practice in asking and telling the time.

 4.20 Ejercicio

To say, "You have an appointment with the doctor at 10:15," use *Usted tiene una cita con el doctor a las diez y cuarto.* Tell a partner about the following appointments in Spanish. When you have finished, switch roles.

A. You have an appointment with the dentist on Thursday, December 14 at 3:30 in the afternoon.
B. You have an appointment in the clinic on Tuesday, January 22 at 10:15 in the morning.
C. You have an appointment with Doctor Leicasch on Friday, February 28 at 6:45 in the evening.
D. You have an appointment with the neurologist, Dr. Solano, on Wednesday, May 30 at 1:00 in the afternoon.

 4.21 Actividad

Look at the doctor's appointment book. With your partner, role-play the part of the receptionist, calling the patients to remind them about their appointments. When you have finished, switch roles.

MARTA DURÁN LÓPEZ, MD

LUNES
3 DE OCTUBRE

1:00 _Sr. Acevedo_

1:15 _Sra. Martínez_

1:30 _Srta. Negrón_

1.45 _Sr. David García_

2:00 _Sr. Pedro Medina_

2:15 _Sra. Elsa Morel_

2:30 _Sra. López de Castro_

2.45 _Sr. Rentas_

3:00 _Sr. Julià-Vargas_

Conduct a Registration or Admissions Interview

Vocabulario: Los datos personales (Personal Information)

¿Cuál es su . . . ?	What is your . . .
nombre	name
apellido	last name
fecha de nacimiento	date of birth
número de Seguro Social	Social Security number
número de teléfono	telephone number
dirección	address

estado civil	marital status
soltero/a	single
casado/a	married
separado/a	separated
divorciado/a	divorced
viudo/a	widower/widow
¿Dónde vive usted?	Where do you live?
¿Qué . . . ?	What . . . ?
calle	street
número	number
ciudad	city
pueblo	town
¿Tiene usted plan médico?	Do you have health insurance?
¿Tiene seguro médico?	Do you have health insurance?
El Medicare	Medicare
El Medicaid	Medicaid
la asistencia pública	public assistance
¿Tiene la tarjeta?	Do you have the card?
¿Tiene usted la custodia legal?	Do you have legal custody?
¿Es usted el tutor / la tutora legal?	Are you the legal guardian?
¿A quién llamamos en caso de emergencia?	Whom do we call in case of emergency?
Favor de firmar el permiso para el tratamiento.	Please sign the consent to treatment form.

Another way to ask whether the patient is married is to ask, *¿Es usted casado/a?* "Do you have a partner?" or *¿Tiene pareja?* removes the marriage implication. Note that *¿Es usted señorita?* may imply a question about virginity.

El Medicare es un plan médico público en los Estados Unidos para las personas que tienen sesenta y cinco años o más o que son incapacitadas. El Medicaid es un plan médico público para las personas que son pobres y tienen hijos o que son incapacitadas.

Video Program: *La recepcionista*

Watch the *Trama* for chapter 4 and do the activity that follows.

Rosmery: Buenas tardes. Me llamo Rosmery. Soy enfermera y trabajo con el doctor Vargas.

La enfermera Rosmery y don Francisco

Sr. Flores: Mucho gusto. Soy Francisco Flores. Usted habla español. ¿De dónde es usted?

Rosmery: De México. De Guadalajara. Pero hace muchos años que vivo aquí en los Estados Unidos. Y usted, ¿De dónde es?

Sr. Flores: Soy de la República Dominicana, de Santo Domingo.

Rosmery: Dominicano. Excelente. La comida dominicana es deliciosa. ¿Usted tiene cita con el doctor hoy?

Sr. Flores: Sí, a las tres de la tarde. Para un examen físico.

Rosmery: Son las tres en punto. Es puntual. Muy bien. Gracias. Okay, nombre, Francisco Flores. ¿Es usted casado?

Sr. Flores: Sí, mi esposa se llama Marisol García de Flores.

Rosmery: ¿Cuál es su dirección?

Sr. Flores: Calle Main número quince, segundo piso.

Rosmery:: ¿En qué pueblo vive?

Sr. Flores: Aquí en New Haven.

Rosmery: ¿Cuál es su número de teléfono?

Sr. Flores: Cinco, cuarenta y ocho, treinta y seis, veinticuatro.

Rosmery: ¿Cuál es su fecha de nacimiento?

Sr. Flores: El cinco de mayo del mil novecientos setenta y nueve.

Rosmery: ¿Tiene plan médico?

Sr. Flores: Sí. Aquí está la tarjeta.

Rosmery: Gracias. ¿En caso de emergencia, a quién debemos llamar?

Sr. Flores: A mi esposa, Marisol Flores, al cinco, cuarenta y ocho, treinta y seis, veinticuatro.

Rosmery: Vamos a confirmar el número. Cinco, cuarenta y ocho, treinta y seis, veinticuatro. ¿Correcto?

Sr. Flores:	Sí, correcto. Ella tiene celular. Su número es nueve, setenta y siete, cuarenta y nueve, ochenta y siete.
Rosmery:	Vamos a confirmar el celular. Nueve, setenta y siete, cuarenta y nueve, ochenta y siete. ¿Verdad?
Sr. Flores:	Sí, preciso.
Rosmery:	Vamos a tomarle la temperatura. Su temperatura está en noventa y ocho punto ocho. Muy bien. No tiene fiebre.
Sr. Flores:	Me siento bien. Gracias a Dios.
Rosmery:	Tome asiento allí por favor. El doctor viene pronto.
Sr. Flores:	Gracias.

 4.22 Actividad

Work with a partner to fill out the form that appears below.

Clínica Abreu
Formulario de inscripción del paciente

Nombres: _____

Apellidos: _____

Idioma: _____

Dirección: _____

Teléfono: _____

Fecha de nacimiento: _____

Número de seguro social: _____

Estado civil: _____

Plan médico: _____

Contacto de emergencia: _____

The Pronunciation of *Ñ, R, RR, LL,* and *Y*

- The Spanish alphabet (*el alfabeto* or *el abecedario*) has twenty-seven letters (see appendix 1). The letter that appears in Spanish but not in English is the letter «ñ». Some grammars include «rr» in the alphabet.
- The letter «ñ» (called "enyay") is pronounced like the "ni" in "onion." Some examples are: *uña, señor, doña, año, sueño,* and *niño.*
- The letter «r» is pronounced by tapping the palate softly with the tip of the tongue, almost as in the English "tt" in "butter" or the "dd" in "ladder." When «rr» appears, it is trilled, meaning you must r-r-r-oll your tongue. Listen to good models and copy them. Practice saying *pero* (but) and *perro* (dog). Do not be discouraged. There are native Spanish-speakers who cannot trill the «rr», and regions where a dialect calls for a more throaty sound. Those who can, however, at times show off by rolling the letter «r» when it starts a word. Pronouncing the Spanish «r» like an English retroflex "r" can be irritating to a native Spanish-speaker. Some examples of the rolled «r» are: *diarrea, catarro, carrera, roto, regular,* and *rótula.*

    Perro raro, pero perro al fin (He's an odd dog, but a dog after all).

    Qué rápido corren los carros del ferrocarril (How fast the rail cars run).
- When the letters «ll» appear together, they are pronounced like "y." The letter «y» (*i griega,* or "Greek i") in Spanish is pronounced as it is in English (except when it stands alone in the word *y,* which is pronounced "ee"). Caribbean Americans often give an English "j" sound to both «y» and «ll». Some South Americans give them more of a "zsh" sound. Some examples are: *llamar, llegar, rodilla, yo, mayo,* and *yodo.*

 4.23 Drama imprevisto

Review the advertisement that follows. Take turns acting out telephone calls between a patient and the receptionist at the dental office of *La doctora Dolores D. Repente.* Choose the service that you need, and work to set up an appointment and another for six months later. Create—or randomly assign to other students—specific challenging scenarios. For example, you are experiencing a lot of pain, and the doctor's office is very busy; or the doctor's office does not seem to be very busy until you reveal that you do not have insurance.

 ## 4.24 Reciclaje

Integrate what you have learned in the first four chapters. Set up a small clinic in the front of the classroom. Students volunteer to play the part of patient, patient family member, receptionist, and practitioner. After the patient registers, demonstrate a courteous manner while the practitioner enters the room and each person is introduced. Diagnose the patient as having a swollen, broken, or sprained body part. Schedule a follow-up visit with an orthopedic surgeon.

Cultural Note: What's in a Name?

Spanish-speaking people (except in Argentina) use two *apellidos,* or last names. This can be complicated for persons who assist in filing for birth certificates or who read the medical records and try to figure out who is married to whom. It complicates the use of the computer for patient database searches. When only one last name is used, it is the last name of the father. When two are used, they are the last name of the father followed by the last (paternal maiden) name of the mother. Thus, Pedro Ortiz Pagán is the son of Señor Ortiz and Señora Pagán. You will see that it gets a bit more complicated than this, as we continue with the names of Pedro's family.

Pedro's parents' full names are Luis Ortiz Ruiz and María Pagán López. We already know that Pedro's full name is Pedro Ortiz Pagán, even if he chooses to go by the shorter name Pedro Ortiz. Now, suppose he marries Elsa Negrón García. Elsa can call herself Elsa Ortiz if she wishes, as an accommodation to North American culture. Or she can follow Spanish tradition and call herself Elsa Negrón de Ortiz, using her paternal last name followed by *de* and her husband's (paternal) last name.

If Pedro Ortiz Pagán and his wife, Elsa Negrón, have two children, Juan and Ana, the children's full names will be Juan Ortiz Negrón and Ana Ortiz Negrón. Now, if Juan Ortiz Negrón marries Marta Ortiz García, what will be the full name of their son, Juancito? Juan Ortiz Ortiz.

Chapter 5
La familia

By the end of this chapter you will be able to name the various members of a family and to ask about basic family medical history. In the process you will learn the present tense of regular verbs.

Ask About Family Constellation

Vocabulario: Los familiares (Family Members)

el padre (papá)	father	la madre (mamá)	mother
el esposo, el marido	husband	la esposa, mujer	wife
el hijo	son	la hija	daughter
el hermano	brother	la hermana	sister
el abuelo	grandfather	la abuela	grandmother
el nieto	grandson	la nieta	granddaughter
el tío	uncle	la tía	aunt
el sobrino	nephew	la sobrina	niece
el primo	male cousin	la prima	female cousin
el padrino	godfather	la madrina	godmother

Hijos means sons, but as a plural word it can refer to offspring in general (sons and daughters). *Hijas* refers only to daughters. To ask "Do you have children?" use *¿Tiene hijos?* The answer may be *Sí, tengo dos hijos: un hijo y una hija.* In the same way, *padres* refers to parents, but *padre* (in the singular) only to father; *hermanos* can refer to brothers and sisters or to brothers only.

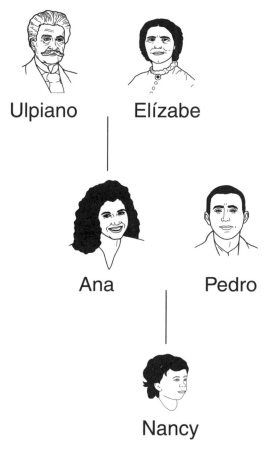

La familia de Ana. What questions or sentences
can you make about this family?

Hola. Soy Ana. Soy hija única de mi papá y mamá. No tengo
hermanos. Soy madre. Tengo una hija. Se llama Nancy y
tiene cinco años de edad. Mi esposo se llama Pedro. Aquí
está un diagrama de mi familia.

único/a	only

 ## 5.1 Actividad

The instructor and other members of the class show pictures of their families or of family members. Break into spontaneous conversation where
possible. Ask *¿Quién es?* (Who is that?) and ask for names and ages as well.

> Example: Student 1:   ¿Quién es? ¿Es su hija?
> Student 2:   Sí, es mi hija menor (youngest).
> Student 1:   ¿Cómo se llama y cuántos años tiene?
> Student 2:   Se llama Susan y tiene diez años.

Estructura: Adjetivos posesivos (Possessive Adjectives)

- We have learned that the word *de* is used to express possession. The possessive adjectives also express possession.

el hijo de Juan	Juan's son
su hijo	his son

- The possessive adjectives in Spanish are as follows:

mi	my
tu	your (*familiar*)
su	your (*formal*), his, her, its
nuestro	our (*modifies masculine noun*)
nuestra	our (*modifies feminine noun*)
su	your (*plural*), their

- Each of these adjectives may be made plural by adding *-s*. As adjectives, they must agree in number (and gender in the case of *nuestro/a*) with the noun they modify. Because the word *su* is used for *his, her, your, its,* and *their,* we may use the preposition *de* to be more specific. For example, when referring to Juan's son we say *su hijo* when we have already established that we are talking about Juan. Otherwise, we say *el hijo de Juan* to be more specific.

 ## 5.2 Ejercicio

Write the correct possessive adjectives in the spaces provided. The adjective must agree with the noun it modifies.

A. los padres de usted   _____sus_____ padres

B. la madre de usted   _____ madre

C. el abuelo de Pedro   _____ abuelo

D. los abuelos de Pedro   _____ abuelos

E. los hijos de nosotros   _____ hijos

F. las hermanas de nosotros   _____ hermanas

G. la familia de ustedes   _____ familia

Vocabulario: Más familiares (More Family Members)

el tío abuelo	great-uncle	la tía abuela	great-aunt
el/la bisabuelo/a	great-grandparent	el/la bisnieto/a	great-grandchild
el suegro	father-in-law	la suegra	mother-in-law
el yerno	son-in-law	la nuera	daughter-in-law
el cuñado	brother-in-law	la cuñada	sister-in-law
el padrastro	stepfather	la madrastra	stepmother
el hijastro	stepson	la hijastra	stepdaughter
el hermanastro	stepbrother	la hermanastra	stepsister
el hermano de padre	half-brother	la hermana de padre	half-sister
el hermano de madre	half-brother	la hermana de madre	half-sister
el ahijado	godson	la ahijada	goddaughter
hijo de crianza	foster child	como familia	just like family

To establish whether a caretaker who brings a child for medical care is the child's parent, asking *¿Es su hijo/a?* is more useful than asking *¿Es su niño?* A Spanish-speaker may say *Tengo dos hermanos* or *Somos tres hermanos.* The latter more explicitly includes the speaker in the siblingship.

Abuela paterna specifies the paternal grandmother, *abuela materna* the maternal grandmother, and so forth.

 5.3 Ejercicio

Quiz a classmate by asking for the following family relationships, as in the example. Make up some additional questions on your own.

> Example: el padre de mi abuela
> > Student 1:   ¿Quién es el padre de mi abuela?
> > Student 2:   El padre de su abuela es su bisabuelo.

A. la esposa de mi hermano   E. el hijo de mi tía
B. el hijo de mi hijo   F. la hermana de mi primo
C. el hijo de mi padrastro   G. la madre de mi esposa
D. la hermana de mi madre   H. el hijo de mi esposa y su ex esposo

5.4 Ejercicio

Fill in the following blanks with the relevant members of the family.

Hola. Me llamo Marta. Soy la primera _____ de mis padres.

Mi madre tiene una hermana. Ella es mi _____ y su nombre es

Linda. Yo soy _____ de mi tía Linda. Ella tiene un hijo. Él es

mi _____. Tengo otra tía. Ella es _____ de mi padre. Los

_____ de ella son mis primos también. El padre de mi padre

es mi _____. El hermano de mi abuelo es mi _____.

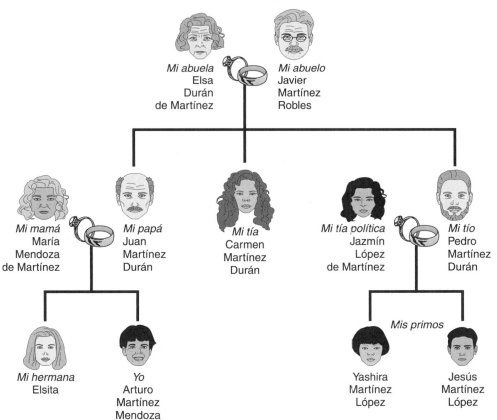

5.5 Actividad

Refer to the diagram *Mi familia, por Arturo Martínez Mendoza* and make as many questions and statements as you can about the family relationships. Ask classmates, for example, *¿Tiene hermanos Yashira?* or *¿Quién es doña Elsa?* Notice that Spanish-speaking people often use two last names, the father's followed by the mother's. A married woman may use her father's last name followed by *de* and her husband's (paternal) last name. This was explained in the Cultural Note at the end of chapter 4.

 5.6 Actividad

Circulate in the classroom and ask classmates whether they have children, siblings, nieces and nephews, godparents, and so on, and their names and ages. Take notes and report your findings to the class.

 5.7 Drama imprevisto

Play "Tangled Web." A group of five or six students goes to the front of the classroom and surrounds one member. A student declares his or her family relationship to the student in the middle, for example, *Soy tu madre.* The next student then states an accurate family relationship to each of the persons who went before. For example (to student in the middle), *Soy tu hermano* and (to second student) *Soy tu hijo.* Suppose someone in the group divorced (*Soy tu ex marido*) or married a person with children?

 Estructura: Los verbos regulares terminados en *-ar*
(Regular Verbs Ending in *-ar*)

- So far you have learned the three verbs *ser, estar,* and *tener.* Each changes its form according to the subject, or who is doing the action. These three verbs are considered "irregular" verbs because their forms are idiosyncratic.
- There are also "regular" verbs that change their endings more predictably than the irregular verbs. These may be divided into three groups: those whose infinitive forms end in *-ar,* in *-er,* and in *-ir.* Each group has a consistent set of forms, or endings.
- These are the endings for the regular verb *hablar* (to talk or to speak):

yo	hablo	Hablo inglés y un poquito de español.
tú	hablas	¿Hablas inglés?
él, ella, usted	habla	Mi mamá no habla inglés.
nosotros/as	hablamos	En casa, nosotros hablamos español.
ellos, ellas, ustedes	hablan	Mis hijos hablan inglés, pero soy bilingüe.

 ## 5.8 Actividad

The instructor may bring a "tin-can" telephone to class. (This can be more safely made with disposable cups, buttons, and yarn.) To actively and visually demonstrate how verbs change form depending on the subject or on who is doing the action, pass the ends of the phone around and create sentences that describe the action. For example,

> Yo hablo con Bill. Bill habla con Tom.
> Tom y yo hablamos. Tom y Bill hablan.

 ## Video Program: *¿Cuáles idiomas habla?*

Watch the *Demostración* for chapter 5 and do the activity that follows.

La enfermera Rosmery y Elsita.

Rosmery: Elsita, ¿hablas inglés?

Elsita: Sí. Hablo inglés y español. Mi padre habla inglés y español también, pero mi mamá sólo habla español. Ella no habla inglés.

Rosmery: Tú hablas dos idiomas. Es muy bueno hablar dos idiomas. Tienes mucha suerte.

Elsita: En casa siempre hablamos español, pero en la escuela hablo inglés porque mis profesoras y mis amigos no hablan español. Cuando estamos de vacaciones en Santo Domingo, hablo español con mis primos. Todos mis primos hablan español.

Rosmery: ¿Te gusta jugar con tus primos?

Elsita: Sí. Claro. Pero toditos viven en Santo Domingo, y mis padres y yo vivimos aquí en New Haven. A veces mi mamá está muy triste porque vivimos muy lejos de mi abuela, mis tíos y mis primos.

Rosmery:	Sí, es una pena cuando nuestros seres queridos viven lejos. Mi mamá vive en México y me hace mucha falta. Todos los meses le mando plata.
Elsita:	¿Plata?
Rosmery:	Plata es dinero en Centroamérica.
Elsita:	Mami dice que vivimos en los Estados Unidos porque papá tiene un buen trabajo y porque mi escuela es buena. Ella quiere vivir en Santo Domingo porque mi abuela está enferma. Mi abuela no tiene dinero. Cuando estamos en Santo Domingo mis padres le compran su medicina.
Rosmery:	Tus padres quieren mucho a tu abuela.
Elsita:	Sí. Y yo la quiero mucho también. Y quiero a mis primos. Quiero jugar con ellos hoy, pero tengo que esperar porque vamos de vacaciones en agosto.
Rosmery:	Qué bueno. Me alegro mucho.

 5.9 Actividad

Circulate in the classroom asking classmates what languages they speak. Ask about languages spoken by members of their family as well. Ask about any family member and any language. When you have finished, switch roles. Try to find someone who is bilingual and someone who is polyglot (multilingual). Report your findings. (In Spanish, names of languages are not capitalized.)

Example:	Student 1:	¿Qué idiomas (languages) habla tu familia en casa?
	Student 2:	Nosotros hablamos inglés.
	Student 1:	¿Qué idioma hablan tus abuelos?
	Student 2:	Mis abuelos hablan italiano.

Idiomas (Languages)

alemán	German
árabe	Arabic
chino	Chinese
español	Spanish
francés	French
inglés	English
italiano	Italian
japonés	Japanese
polaco	Polish
portugués	Portuguese

5.10 Actividad

The verb *tomar* means "to drink," among other meanings that you'll learn in chapter 6. It is a regular verb that ends in *-ar.* Treating *tomar* as you did *hablar,* ask whether classmates drink coffee in the morning, how many cups (*tazas*), and so on. Find ways to use each subject pronoun and verb form. For example, *Cheryl y Bill toman café,* and *Susan y yo no tomamos café por la mañana.* People who do not drink coffee may drink *té, leche, jugo* (juice), or *chocolate.*

 ## Estructura: Los verbos regulares terminados en *-er* e *-ir* (Regular Verbs Ending in *-er* and *-ir*)

- Regular verbs that end in *-er* have a consistent set of verb endings. These are the endings for the regular verb *comer* (to eat):

yo	como	En un restaurante como espaguetis.
tú	comes	¿Comes arroz con pollo?
él, ella, usted	come	Mi hijo come muy bien.
nosotros/as	comemos	Mi esposa y yo comemos a las seis.
ellos, ellas, ustedes	comen	Los empleados comen en la cafetería.

- Regular verbs that end in *-ir* also have a consistent set of verb endings. Notice that the verbs that end in *-ir* differ from those that end in *-er* only in the first person plural (*nosotros/as*). These are the endings for the regular verb *vivir* (to live):

yo	vivo	Vivo en un apartamento grande.
tú	vives	¿Dónde vives?
él, ella, usted	vive	Mi hija vive en una casa pequeña.
nosotros/as	vivimos	Vivimos cerca del (near the) hospital.
ellos, ellas, ustedes	viven	Mis hijos viven en Florida.

 5.11 Actividad

All students move around the room conducting the following survey (in Spanish!). Find someone who eats in the cafeteria *a veces* (occasionally), *a menudo* (frequently), and *siempre* (always). Find out the same about how often people eat at a restaurant, eat at home, eat broccoli, and eat pizza in the morning. Write names in the spaces provided, and try to fill in all of the spaces. Then share your results with the class.

Comer . . .	A veces	A menudo	Siempre
. . . en la cafetería			
. . . en casa			
. . . en restaurante			
. . . brócoli			
. . . pizza en la mañana			

 ## 5.12 Actividad

Circulate in the classroom asking where classmates live. Find someone who lives in the same town as you. Find out who lives in an apartment (*un apartamento*) and who lives in a private house (*una casa particular*). Ask classmates if they live alone (*solo/sola*) or with their parents (*con tus padres*), and so on.

Vocabulario: Algunos verbos regulares (Some Regular Verbs)

ayudar	to help	recetar	to prescribe
caminar	to walk	tomar	to take, drink
cocinar	to cook	trabajar	to work
comprar	to buy	usar	to use
cuidar	to care for	visitar	to visit
enseñar	to teach, show		
escuchar	to listen to	beber	to drink
estudiar	to study	comer	to eat
examinar	to examine	leer	to read
llamar	to call		
llegar	to arrive	abrir	to open
necesitar	to need	escribir	to write
preguntar	to ask	sufrir de	to suffer from

 ## 5.13 Reciclaje

Recycle the names of professions and the days of the week as you practice the verb *trabajar*. Ask classmates what they do for work, what days they work, and whether they work on Saturdays and Sundays, as in the example.

Example: Student 1:   ¿En qué trabajas?

Student 2:   Trabajo como enfermero.

Student 1:   ¿Qué días trabajas?

Student 2:   Trabajo de lunes a viernes.

Student 1:   ¿Trabajas los sábados y domingos?

Student 2:   Trabajo un fin de semana sí y un fin de semana no.

UN CHISTE (A JOKE)

Cirujano: El paciente necesita una operación inmediatamente.

Enfermero: ¿Qué tiene él?

Cirujano: Un buen plan médico.

Enfermero: ¡Caramba!

 ## 5.14 Actividad

Choose a partner and ask the following questions. When you have finished, switch roles.

A. trabajar   ¿Qué días de la semana trabajas?
B. llegar   ¿A qué hora llegas al trabajo?
C. beber   ¿Bebes bebidas alcohólicas todos los días?
D. tomar   ¿Tomas antiácidos por la noche?
E. caminar   ¿Caminas a la clase?
F. abrir   ¿Abre el hospital todos los días?
G. leer   ¿Lees el libro de español por la noche?
H. estudiar   ¿Cuántas horas estudias los fines de semana?
I. ayudar   ¿Quién ayuda a tus padres?

 ## 5.15 Actividad

Go to the blackboard in a large group and write "dehydrated sentences." These are sentences in which the verb has been replaced by a blank line. Next, the instructor will review all of the sentences and make any necessary corrections or clarification before all students return to the board and each completes a sentence other than his or her own. Finally, the group will edit and discuss the accuracy of all responses. An example is *Mi hermano _____ libros de medicina,* which becomes, *Mi hermano lee libros de medicina.*

Estructura: La *a* personal (The Personal *a*)

- When a specific person is the direct object of a verb (receives the action of the verb directly), a preposition called the personal *a* is placed before the object (person).

  Visito a mi mamá todos los días.

  Escucho a mi padre cuando él me habla.

- Note that the personal *a* is not needed when a person is not the direct object of the verb.

  Escucho música en el coche.

  Necesito aspirina para el dolor de cabeza.

- The personal *a* and the masculine definite article *el* form the contraction *al* (*a* + *el* = *al*).

  Visito al señor Vega.

  La madre llama al doctor cuando el niño está enfermo.

 5.16 Actividad

Practice active listening in Spanish by rephrasing your partner's statements, as in the example. Close your book as your partner reads the statements. When you have finished, switch roles. Note which sentences call for the personal *a* and which do not.

Example: Student 1:   Tengo dolor de estómago cuando como.
            Student 2:   Tú tienes dolor de estómago cuando
                          comes.

A. Aprendo español rápidamente.
B. Mi esposa y yo hablamos español en casa.
C. Visito a mi mamá todas las semanas.
D. Enseño inglés a mis padres.
E. Llamo a mi hermana por teléfono los domingos.
F. Mi hermano llega a la casa a las seis de la tarde los jueves.
G. Cuido a mis padres en la casa.
H. Mi tío bebe tres tazas de café por la mañana.

 5.17 Actividad

Make lucid sentences, choosing from the following lists of subjects, verbs, and objects. Remember to use the correct form of the verb according to the subject selected. Do not read straight across the lines in every case, as the verbs and objects may be scrambled.

Subject	Verb	Object
A. Yo	recetar	tres veces al día.
B. La doctora	cuidar	insulina para controlar la diabetes.
C. Mi hermano	comer	a su primo en agosto.
D. Los pacientes	visitar	a las ocho de la mañana.
E. Tú	estudiar	medicamento para mi tía abuela.
F. Tú y yo	llegar	a su hijo Freddy después de la escuela.
G. Mi abuelo	necesitar	español en la biblioteca por la mañana.

 ## 5.18 Drama imprevisto

The instructor will place items on a table in front of the room. These are common household objects associated with the list of verbs we are studying. These may include, for example, a CD or headphone (*escuchar música*), a snack (*comer*), a book (*leer*), a drink (*beber*), and a cellular phone (*hablar* and *llamar*). Two students stand behind the table and act out a story that the rest of the class tells. For example, *Susan escucha música y Bill lee el libro.*

 ## 5.19 Reciclaje

In chapter 1 you learned words that describe people (commonly used with *ser*). These appear below for review. Use these and your new verbs to describe family members. For example, *Mi tío William es rubio. Es alto y delgado. Trabaja como profesor y siempre llega tarde a la escuela.*

rubio	moreno	anciano	joven	grande
pequeño	alto	bajo	mediano	gordo
delgado	flaco	bonito	guapo	feo
bueno	inteligente	simpático	amable	agradable

 ## 5.20 Reciclaje

Recycle the names for injuries from chapter 3. You are an emergency room nurse, and your partner is a relative of an accident victim. Call the patient's home and speak to the family member. Establish the family relationship of the person with whom you are speaking and explain the extent of the injuries. Creatively find ways to use the family relationships vocabulary. For example, you want to speak to a parent, but a nosy cousin answers the phone. Answer—or don't answer—questions that may arise.

Take Family Medical History

Vocabulario: Las enfermedades hereditarias
(Hereditary Illnesses)

el alcoholismo	alcoholism
el asma	asthma
el cáncer	cancer
la depresión	depression
la diabetes	diabetes
la distrofia muscular	muscular dystrophy
la enfermedad de Alzheimer	Alzheimer's Disease
la enfermedad de Huntington	Huntington's Disease
la hemofilia	hemophilia
la hipertensión	hypertension
la presión alta	high blood pressure
los problemas cardíacos	cardiac problems
los problemas emocionales	emotional problems
el síndrome de Down	Down Syndrome

Expresiones útiles

Su padre tiene la presión alta.	Your father has high blood pressure.
Mi madre tuvo cáncer.	My mother had cancer.

Preguntas útiles

¿Están vivos sus padres?	Are your parents alive?
¿Qué enfermedades tenían?	What illnesses did they have?
¿De qué murió su madre?	From what did your mother die?
¿Qué enfermedades hay en su familia?	What illnesses are there in your family?
¿Hay asma en la familia?	Is there asthma in the family?

Asma, like *agua,* is a feminine word that often uses the masculine definite article *el* and a feminine adjective, for example, *el asma crónica.* Note that the definite article (*el, la*) is not used after the word *hay,* for example, *¿Hay asma en la familia?* To say that someone *had* an illness, use the past tense *tuvo,* which we'll learn in chapter 9.

 5.21 Actividad

Form small groups and ask each other whether various relatives are living, as in the example. Ask about the cause of death, which may prompt you to refer to the glossary that appears at the end of this text. (Recall that the adjectives must agree in gender and number.)

Example: Student 1:   ¿Está vivo su abuelo?

Student 2:   Sí, mi abuelo está vivo (or) No, mi abuelo murió.

Student 1:   (If grandfather died) ¿De qué murió?

Student 2:   Mi abuelo murió de un infarto cardíaco.

 5.22 Actividad

In the same small groups, ask about several aspects of medical history, using the preceding vocabulary.

Example: Student 1:   ¿Hay asma en su familia?

Student 2:   No, no hay asma (or) Sí, mi madre tiene asma.

 ## Estructura: Los complementos directos
(Direct Object Pronouns)

- The direct object pronoun represents the person or thing that directly receives the action of the verb. It can be used to replace the direct object noun. It sounds natural and reflects economy of language. It is used after the object noun is already mentioned.

  ¿Tomas café?   Sí, pero no *lo* tomo por la tarde.

  ¿Cuándo visitas a tu mamá?   *La* visito los domingos.

- These must agree in gender and number with the object noun. For example,

  ¿Usa usted insulina?   Sí, *la* uso dos veces al día.

  ¿Necesita el inhalador?   No, no *lo* necesito.

  ¿Tiene los supositorios?   No, no *los* tengo.

- The direct object pronouns are:

me	¿Me necesitas?	Do you need me?
te	Te necesito.	I need you.
lo/la	Lo/La visito.	I visit you/him/her/it.
nos	Ellos nos esperan.	They are waiting for us.
los/las	Los cuido.	I take care of them.

 5.23 Actividad

Notice the efficiency of the direct object pronoun. Take turns asking members of the class about what they drink. Use the direct object pronoun to answer the questions.

Example: Student 1:   ¿Tomas café?
             Student 2:   Sí, *lo* tomo por la mañana.
             Student 1:   ¿Tomas cerveza (beer)?
             Student 2:   Sí, pero *la* tomo solamente los sábados.

A. el té   D. las bebidas alcohólicas
B. el vino (wine)   E. el jugo de naranja (orange juice)
C. el agua (*feminine*)   F. el jugo de ciruela (prune juice)
D. la leche   G. el té de manzanilla (chamomile tea)

 5.24 Actividad

Here we shall vary the verbs. Ask a partner the following questions. Use the direct object pronoun when answering. The symbols (*m*) and (*f*) are provided to indicate whether the direct object noun is masculine or feminine. You'll know whether they are singular or plural.

Example: Student 1:   ¿Toma aspirina (*f*) todos los días?
             Student 2:   Sí, la tomo (or) No, no la tomo.

A. ¿Toma antibióticos (*m*) cuando tiene resfriado?
B. ¿Usa insulina (*f*) para la diabetes?
C. ¿Usa un inhalador (*m*) para el asma?
D. ¿Usa lentes (*m*) para leer?
E. ¿Visita a sus hermanos (*m*) en Puerto Rico?
F. ¿Necesita medicamento (*m*) para el dolor?
G. ¿Bebe bebidas alcohólicas (*f*)?

 ## Ask Who Helps an Infirm Family Member

 ### Estructura: Los complementos indirectos
(Indirect Object Pronouns)

- Unlike the direct object pronouns, which represent the person or thing that directly receives the action of the verb, the indirect object pronouns indicate to whom or for whom something is done. It is almost always necessary.
- The indirect object pronouns are:

me   Me duele el brazo.   My arm hurts (me).
te   Te cuido al niño.   I take care of the child for you.
le   Le escribo una receta.   I write you a prescription.

nos   El radiólogo nos lee la placa.   The radiologist reads the film
                                          for us.

les   Les compro la medicina.   I buy the medicine for them.

- Note that the indirect object pronouns *le* and *les* are both masculine and feminine, and are less specific than *me, te,* and *nos.* Therefore, they are often clarified by using *a* and the person to whom they refer.

  El doctor le examina a su padre.   The doctor examines your father.

  El doctor le examina a ella.   The doctor examines her.

- The speaker chooses between the direct and indirect object depending on the message. In the sentence *Su madre la cuida bien* (Her mother cares for her well), the direct object pronoun (*la*) represents the direct receiver of the action (her). In the sentence *La enfermera le pone una inyección a la niña* (The nurse gives an injection to the child), the indirect object pronoun (*le*) represents the person for whom the action is being done (the child). In chapter 6 we'll learn how to use these together in the same sentence. For now, here are some other examples of both direct and indirect object pronouns:

La enfermera le pone una
inyección a la niña. Su mamá
la cuida bien.

Le examino los oídos.   I examine your ears (for you).

Los examino ahora.   I examine them (the ears) now.

Le pongo una inyección a José.   I give José an injection.

La pongo ahora.   I give it (the injection) now.

 5.25 Ejercicio

Give the correct indirect object pronoun in the following sentences, as in the example.

Example: Receto un medicamento para su padre.
            Le receto un medicamento para su padre.

A. Receto un medicamento para sus hijos.
B. Escribo una carta a usted.
C. Llamo una ambulancia para la paciente.
D. Enseño español a los estudiantes.
E. Contesto el teléfono por la secretaria.
F. Leo el libro a usted.
G. La doctora contesta la pregunta para nosotros.

5.26 Actividad

Add the correct indirect object and the correct form of the verb to form sentences, as in the example. Note that with *le* or *les,* it may be necessary to further specify the object of the action.

Example: La enfermera _____ (tomar) la temperatura (a mí).
La enfermera *me toma* la temperatura.

A. El doctor _____ (recetar) un medicamento para Juan.

B. Tú _____ (preguntar) su historia médica a él.

C. Yo _____ (escribir) una carta al plan médico.

D. La anestesióloga _____ (explicar) el procedimiento (a mí).

E. El enfermero _____ (hablar) español a los pacientes.

F. Usted _____ (comprar) la medicina a sus padres.

G. La pediatra _____ (recetar) un antibiótico para mi bebé.

 5.27 Actividad

Your partner has an infirm grandmother who needs help. Ask who helps with the following. Your partner must name a different family member for each. Recall that the indirect object will be necessary.

Example: Cocinar   Student 1: ¿Quién le cocina a tu abuela?
Student 2: Mi madre le cocina todos los días.

A. ayudar con la casa
B. comprar la comida
C. recetar los medicamentos
D. enseñar a usar la insulina
E. examinar los pies para ver si hay úlceras
F. llamar al consultorio para hacer una cita con el doctor

Video Program: *La historia clínica familiar*

Watch the *Trama* for chapter 5 and do the activities that follow. In the video, Dr. Vargas takes Mr. Flores's medical history.

Dr. Vargas:	Buenas tardes, señor Flores.
Sr. Flores:	Buenas tardes, doctor.
Dr. Vargas:	Usted está aquí para un examen físico. ¿No?
Sr. Flores:	Sí, pero me siento bien, gracias a Dios.
Dr. Vargas:	Muy bien. Usted está casado y tiene una hija, ¿verdad?
Sr. Flores:	Sí, usted conoce a mi esposa Marisol y a nuestra hija Elsita.
Dr. Vargas:	Claro. ¿Cómo están ellas?
Sr. Flores:	Bien, bien gracias.
Dr. Vargas:	¿Cuántos años tiene Elsita ahora?
Sr. Flores:	Tiene diez años.
Dr. Vargas:	Diez años. Es una muchacha muy lista.
Sr. Flores:	Gracias.
Dr. Vargas:	Vamos a hablar de su historia médica familiar. ¿Están vivos sus padres?
Sr. Flores:	No. Están muertos. Mi padre murió el año pasado y mamá murió hace ya cinco años.
Dr. Vargas:	¿De qué murieron sus padres?
Sr. Flores:	Mi mamá murió de cáncer del seno, y metástasis en el cerebro. Cuando murió Mamá, mi papá tuvo una depresión muy grande.
Dr. Vargas:	¿Qué otros problemas médicos tenía su padre?
Sr. Flores:	Mi padre tenía hipertensión y diabetes. Al final murió de un ataque al corazón.
Dr. Vargas:	Lo siento. Es muy triste.
Sr. Flores:	Hay que seguir adelante.
Dr. Vargas:	Eso es verdad. ¿Tiene hermanos?
Sr. Flores:	Somos cuatro hermanos. Dos hermanos y dos hermanas. Tengo un hermano menor y dos hermanas mayores.

Dr. Vargas:	Son cuatro hermanos entonces. ¿Cómo están ellos de salud?
Sr. Flores:	Todos están bien, gracias a Dios. Pero mi hermano menor, Pablito, padece del asma y usa una pompa. Cuando está muy mal, usa la máquina para nebulizar el medicamento.
Dr. Vargas:	Y usted, ¿tiene algún problema médico?
Sr. Flores:	Tengo tres enfermedades. Diabetes, la presión alta y el colesterol alto.
Dr. Vargas:	¿Usa insulina?
Sr. Flores:	No. No la necesito. Tomo una pastilla dos veces al día.
Dr. Vargas:	¿En qué trabaja usted?
Sr. Flores:	Soy contable y trabajo para un banco internacional.
Dr. Vargas:	¿Toma café?
Sr. Flores:	Sí. Tomo una taza por la mañana y una a como las tres de la tarde.
Dr. Vargas:	¿Toma bebidas alcohólicas?
Sr. Flores:	Tomo cerveza.
Dr. Vargas:	¿Cuánto toma y con qué frecuencia?
Sr. Flores:	Nada los días laborales. Los fines de semana tomo como dos o tres botellas de cerveza al día.
Dr. Vargas:	¿Fuma?
Sr. Flores:	No, no fumo. Me disgusta el olor de los cigarrillos.
Dr. Vargas:	¿Fuma marihuana o usa alguna droga ilegal como la cocaína o la heroína?
Sr. Flores:	No, doctor. Nada de eso.
Dr. Vargas:	Muy bien.

 5.28 Actividad

Work with a partner to ask each other the following comprehension questions based on the video.

A. ¿Están vivos los padres del Sr. Flores?
B. ¿De qué murieron?
C. ¿Tiene hermanos el Sr. Flores?
D. ¿Sufre el Sr. Flores de algún problema médico?
E. ¿Necesita el Sr. Flores usar insulina?
F. ¿En qué trabaja él?
G. ¿Toma bebidas alcohólicas el Sr. Flores?
H. ¿Fuma el Sr. Flores?

5.29 Drama imprevisto

Play "Competitive Hypochondriac," a game show in which a small group of students stands in front of the class and each contestant tells of his or her aches, pains, and personal and family medical history. The object of the game is to amplify your own complaints while minimizing those of your opponent. Draw on vocabulary from the list of hereditary illnesses in this chapter, and the lists of flu symptoms, aches, pains, and injuries in chapter 3.

 5.30 Drama imprevisto

Improvise skits in which a practitioner interviews a patient to determine his or her family medical history, current conditions, and habits with regard to tobacco, alcohol, and illicit drugs. Assign unusual roles, for example, a "heart attack waiting to happen," or a person who may already be en route to canonization.

The Pronunciation of *B* and *V*

- The letters «b» and «v» are pronounced very similarly, both spoken a bit more softly than the English "b," and neither quite like the English "v."
- If there were a clear difference in the pronunciation, then Spanish-speaking people would not ask for clarification so often:

  ¿«V» de vaca, o «b» de burro?

vaca	cow

Practice the following words, and then try a pair of *trabalenguas*.

biopsia	fiebre	aborto
varicela	viruela	vivir

Veinte viudas con venas varicosas viven en una vivienda vieja.

¿Qué bebe el bebé? El bebé bebe leche buena de un biberón blanco.

Cultural Note: *La familia*

In North America an agrarian, extended family was typical prior to the industrialization that occurred between the world wars. As people in search of work moved farther from their parents, this multigenerational family shrank to a smaller, idealized nuclear family composed of father, mother, brothers, and sisters.

Often the Latino family is an extended family. Speaking of *mi familia,* one may have in mind aunts, uncles, and cousins as well as brothers, sisters, and in-laws. This is no surprise to health care workers who have had the responsibility of limiting the number of visitors at the bedside. In some countries, a family member must stay with a hospitalized patient for the purpose of delivering food, providing personal care, and making trips to a local pharmacy to purchase medications.

A *padrino* (godfather) or *madrina* (godmother) has almost equal standing with a parent, having promised to raise the child in the event the parents cannot. The child is expected to respect a godparent as a parent, although godparents count primarily as a support to the parents, or *compadres.* Although children are highly valued and well cared for, they are not always the center of attention at family gatherings. In times past, an old saying dictated that *los muchachos hablan cuando las gallinas orinan* ("children talk when chickens urinate," which means, "children should be seen and not heard").

Family boundaries are flexible. Even a neighbor can be considered part of the family. A close friend might be called *primo,* or cousin. People say of these relationships, *Somos como familia,* or "We're just like family." This may lead to misunderstanding. A hospital security guard outside the intensive care unit of a North American hospital once told a family member that visits were restricted to "immediate family only," to which the visitor replied, "I am his godfather."

The Latino family is a strong, primary support network for its members. Immigrants to the United States who are separated from family and homeland may suffer a profound sense of loss—greater than a clinician from a (now typical) North American nuclear family might expect. Many who emigrate leave their family unwillingly to work abroad and send money to support those who remain. They may leave behind children in the care of other relatives. This is often misunderstood by people whose culture defines the family more narrowly. Individuals separated from their family through unresolved conflict or family dysfunction may have a heightened sense of shame, loneliness, or abandonment.

Some immigrants have made the sacrifice of leaving children with relatives while they work abroad to better provide for their family.

Some Spanish-speakers say, *Tengo tres hermanos;* others say, *Somos cuatro hermanos.* The latter demonstrates a cultural view that includes oneself in the count, unlike the concept of sibling rivalry. This is an example of the relation between worldview and language.

When working with a Latino family, a helper must assess the degree to which the family has retained, for its members, its highly influential cultural value. Family boundaries may be vague. Policies regarding confidentiality of a patient vis-à-vis the family may be misunderstood. What the broad family system believes about the nature of the distress itself will be a powerful factor in the patient's view of the problem being treated. The worth of the family to the individual and of the individual to the family must never be underestimated.

Chapter 6
La farmacia

By the end of this chapter you will be able to write and explain basic instructions for taking medicines. You will be able to ask about drug allergies and educate patients about side effects and allergic reactions. You will know how to make polite and direct commands and to use these when educating patients about medication regimens, the management of asthma, and the use of pill organizers.

Give Medication Instructions

In some areas, the pharmacist is the most accessible health care provider. Many people will consult a pharmacist prior to going to see a doctor. The pharmacist may dispense a medication that would be controlled in the United States. Many countries are trying to end this practice because of the emergence of treatment-resistant infections.

The noun *receta,* which is used for "prescription," also means "recipe." What does that say about the history of pharmacotherapy? This is related to the verb *recetar,* which means "to prescribe."

Vocabulario: Formas de medicamentos (Forms of Medication)

el/la farmacéutico/a	pharmacist
recetar	to prescribe
la receta	prescription
el medicamento, la medicina	medication, medicine

Las tabletas

la tableta, la pastilla, la píldora   tablet, pill
media tableta   half of a tablet
la cápsula   capsule
la botella, el frasco   bottle

Las inyecciones e infusiones

la inyección   injection
la jeringuilla   syringe
el suero   IV

Los líquidos

el jarabe   syrup
el elíxir   elixir
la suspensión   suspension
la cucharadita   teaspoonful
media cucharadita   half a teaspoonful
la cucharada   tablespoonful

Los medicamentos tópicos

la crema   cream, ointment
el ungüento*   ointment, balm

Otras formas

el aerosol   aerosol
el gel   gel
la gota   drop
el inhalador, la pompa (slang)   inhaler
el nebulizador (la máquina)   nebulizer (machine)
el parche   patch
el supositorio   suppository

Preguntas útiles

¿Es usted alérgico/a a algún medicamento?   Are you allergic to any medication?
¿Tiene usted alergia a algún medicamento?   Do you have an allergy to any medication?
¿Toma algún medicamento todos los días?   Do you take medicine every day?
¿Necesita una receta nueva?   Do you need a new prescription?

Expresiones útiles

Hay que darle . . .   You must give him/her . . .

---

*The «ü» in *ungüento* is pronounced like English "w."

Estructura: El verbo *tomar* (To Take)

- The verb *tomar* is a regular *-ar* verb, and it means "to take." It can be used for taking classes, taking a bus, and drinking a liquid.

    Tomo español y biología este semestre.

    Mis hijos toman el autobús por la mañana.

    ¿Por qué no tomamos un café?

- Here we are interested in how *tomar* is used to talk about taking medicine.

    ¿Toma usted algún medicamento todos los días?

    Tomo una pastilla para controlar la diabetes.

    Mis padres toman una vitamina y una aspirina por la mañana.

La farmacia está cerrada.

La farmacia está abierta.

 ## 6.1 Ejercicio

Ask your partner if the indicated persons take the following medications, as in the example. Remember that the subject of the sentence determines the form of the verb.

    Example: Usted, vitaminas todos los días
                Student 1:   ¿Toma usted vitaminas todos los días?
                Student 2:   Sí, tomo vitaminas todos los días. (or)
                              No, no tomo vitaminas.

A. Usted, antiácidos por la noche

B. Doña Violeta, una aspirina todos los días

C. Tú, medicamento para los ataques epilépticos

D. El señor Altamirano, un diurético para quitar el agua

E. Los padres de Juan, medicamento para la hipertensión

F. Los pacientes, antibióticos para curar las infecciones bacterianas

6.2 Actividad

Conduct a survey. All students circulate in the room asking fellow students whether they or members of their family take an aspirin, a vitamin, or an antacid every day. Ask what time the medicine is taken (*¿A qué hora . . .*). Ask classmates what medicine they take for a headache (*¿Qué tomas cuando tienes dolor de cabeza?*). Students may, of course, choose what information they wish to disclose or not to disclose. The following survey may help you to report your findings afterwards.

Nombre de estudiante	Aspirina, sí o no y la hora	Vitamina, sí o no y la hora	Antiácido, sí o no y la hora	Preferencia de analgésico

 Estructura: Los imperativos con *favor de, hay que y tener que* (Commands with *Favor de, Hay que,* and *Tener que*)

- There is a gentle way to make a request. Use *favor de* and a verb infinitive.
    Favor de sentarse.   Please sit down.
    Favor de llamar a la clínica.   Please call the clinic.
    Favor de tomar la pastilla.   Please take the pill.
- Note that the word *hay* means "there is" and "there are." (Spanish «h» is silent, and *hay* rhymes with the English word "buy.") The next time you are looking for pineapples in a Latin American open-air market, ask, *¿Hay piña?* The attendant will respond, *Sí, hay,* or *No, no hay.*
    Hay un paciente nuevo.   There is a new patient.
    Hay efectos secundarios.   There are side effects.

- Another option is to form an impersonal request using *hay que* and the infinitive. This tells something that one must do. *Hay que tomar la medicina* is "One must take the medicine." It functions as a soft command, "Take the medicine."

    Hay que tomar mucha agua con el medicamento.

    Hay que tomar el medicamento a la misma hora cada día.

- When a stronger or more direct command form is indicated, tell the patient that he or she "has to" do something. The formula *tener que* + infinitive means "to have to _____." The verb *tener* is conjugated and the second verb is not.

Tengo que ir a la clínica.	I have to go to the clinic.
Tienes que tomar la tableta.	You have to take the pill.
Usted tiene que ir al laboratorio.	You have to go to the laboratory.

- When you ask whether the patient understands the instruction, he or she may say, "Yes." It is more helpful to ask more direct questions, such as, *¿A qué hora toma el ibuprofén?* or *¿Cuántas pastillas toma a las nueve?*

Doctor Carlos Guzmán González
Avenida del Sol, número 1025
Pueblo del Rey

Rx   Por 60 CC
                                                          Frasco # 2

Amoxicilina Suspensión
    250 mg / 5 ML
USO: Tome 5 cc vía oral.
    cada 8 horas por 5 días

[signature]

Licencia número 65413

6.3 Ejercicio

Give your Spanish-speaking patient the following instructions using *favor de*. Practice writing the instructions as well.

A. Please call the doctor tomorrow.

_____

B. Please wait (*esperar por*) five minutes.

_____

C. Please go to (*ir a*) the pharmacy today.

_____

D. Please take the medicine every day.

_____

E. Please take 2 *acetaminofén* when your head hurts.

_____

F. Please use the *nitroglicerina* when you have chest pain.

_____

G. Please make (*hacer*) an appointment in the clinic.

_____

 6.4 Actividad

You are the nurse and your partner is the resistant patient. Tell the patient that he or she must take the following doses at the indicated times. Use *hay que* or *tiene que* as in the example. The patient may protest, *No quiero* (I don't want to) or *No me gusta* (I don't like it).

Example: Una cucharadita por la mañana
            Student 1:   No me gusta la medicina.
            Student 2:   Hay que (Tiene que) tomar una
                          cucharadita por la mañana.

A. media tableta por la mañana y 1 tableta por la noche
B. 2 cucharaditas 3 veces al día
C. 1 cucharada a las nueve de la noche
D. media cucharadita cada 4 horas
E. 2 pastillas 4 veces al día
F. 3 píldoras a las ocho de la mañana
G. una cápsula todos los días por la mañana

Vocabulario: Instrucciones para la dosificación y vías de administración (Dosing Instructions and Routes of Administration)

La dosis

pastilla(s) o tabletas	pill(s)
cucharadita(s)	teaspoonful(s)
cucharada(s)	tablespoonful(s)
miligramo(s)	milligram(s)
mililitro(s)	milliliters(s)

La vía de administración

tomar, poner, inyectar, aplicar	to take, to put, to inject, to apply
por vía intravenosa, por suero	intravenously
por vía oral, por la boca	by mouth
por vía intramuscular	intramuscularly
por vía subcutánea	subcutaneously
por inhalación	by inhalation
debajo de la lengua	under the tongue
en el ojo derecho/izquierdo	in the right/left eye
en el oído	in the ear
por la nariz	in the nose
por el recto	in the rectum
por la vagina	in the vagina
en el área afectada	to the affected area

La frecuencia (Frequency)

una vez al día, diario	once per day, daily
( ) veces al día	( ) times a day

cada ( ) horas	every ( ) hours
a las 9 de la mañana/noche	at 9 AM/PM
por la mañana/noche	in the morning/at night
al acostarse	at bedtime
un día sí, un día no	every other day
todos los días	every day
por ( ) días	for ( ) days
media hora antes de comer	a half hour before eating
una hora después de comer	an hour after eating
con las comidas	with meals
con leche	with milk
con mucha agua	with plenty of water
cuando es necesario	as needed
sin falta	without fail

Propósito (Purpose)

para el dolor	for pain
para dormir	for sleep
para quitar la picazón	to take away the itching
para bajar el colesterol	to lower cholesterol
para aliviar la ansiedad	to relieve anxiety
para eliminar el agua	to eliminate the water
para evitar el embarazo	to avoid pregnancy

 6.5 Ejercicio

Now say the following medication instructions in Spanish. Use *hay que* or *tiene que* as in the example.

Example: You must take 2 pills twice a day.
            Hay que tomar dos pastillas dos veces al día.

A. You must take 1 pill every 4 hours.
B. You must take 1 teaspoonful in the morning and 2 at bedtime.
C. You must take the medicine with milk.
D. You must take 1 pill 4 times a day for 10 days.
E. You must drink plenty of water with the medicine.
F. You must take 1 teaspoonful in the morning.
G. You must take 2 pills every 4 hours as needed for pain.
H. You must put (*poner*) 2 drops in each (*cada*) eye twice a day.
I. You must apply (*aplicarse*) the cream in the morning and at night.

6.6 Ejercicio

Practice writing medication instructions for your patient in the space provided. Express numbers in Arabic numerals to avoid misunderstandings based on spelling errors.

A. Acetaminophen, take 2 tablets every 4 to 6 hours as needed for pain.

_____

_____

B. Mylanta®, take 2 tablespoonfuls at bedtime.

_____

C. Omeprazole, take 1 capsule at 8:00 AM.

_____

D. Isoniazid, take 1 tablet every day in the morning.

_____

E. Fluoxetine 20 mg, take 1 capsule in the morning.

_____

F. Phenytoin 100 mg, take 1 capsule 3 times a day.

_____

G. Loperamide, take 1 capsule every 2 to 3 hours as needed for diarrhea.

_____

_____

Video Program: *¿Qué medicamentos toma?*

Watch the *Trama* for chapter 6
and do the activities that follow.
In the video, Dr. Vargas talks to
Mr. Flores about medication allergies and his current medications.

Dr. Vargas:	Señor Flores, ¿es usted alérgico a algún medicamento?
Sr. Flores:	No tengo ninguna alergia.
Dr. Vargas:	No tiene alergia a nada.
Sr. Flores:	Perdón. Creo que soy alérgico a la penicilina.
Dr. Vargas:	¿Qué pasa cuando toma la penicilina?
Sr. Flores:	La penicilina me da problemas con la piel. Cuando la tomo me pican los brazos.
Dr. Vargas:	Cuando toma la penicilina, ¿se le hincha la cara o los labios o tiene dificultad para tragar?
Sr. Flores:	No.
Dr. Vargas:	Cuando toma la penicilina, ¿tiene dificultad para respirar?
Sr. Flores:	No, gracias a Dios.
Dr. Vargas:	¿Toma algún medicamento todos los días?
Sr. Flores:	Sí, aquí está la lista de mis medicamentos.
Dr. Vargas:	A ver. El lisinopril. Es para la presión arterial. ¿Cuánto toma?
Sr. Flores:	Del lisinopril tomo una pastilla de cinco miligramos dos veces al día. Una por la mañana con el desayuno y la otra en la noche antes de acostarme.
Dr. Vargas:	¿Tiene efectos secundarios, como hinchazón de la cara o la garganta?
Sr. Flores:	No.
Dr. Vargas:	La hidroclorotiazida. Es también para la hipertensión, como el lisinopril. Es un diurético, para eliminar el líquido del cuerpo. ¿Cuánta hidroclorotiazida toma?
Sr. Flores:	Tomo cincuenta miligramos al día. Las pastillas son de veinticinco miligramos, y tomo dos pastillas por la mañana.

Dr. Vargas:	El lisinopril y la hidroclorotiazida pueden provocar problemas con el estómago. Tiene que tomarlos con comida o leche. Otra vez a la lista . . . La metformina es para la diabetes tipo dos. ¿Cuánta toma?
Sr. Flores:	Tomo quinientos miligramos dos veces al día.
Dr. Vargas:	¿Tiene algunos efectos secundarios como náusea o vómitos?
Sr. Flores:	No.
Dr. Vargas:	¿Diarrea?
Sr. Flores:	No.
Dr. Vargas:	Bien. Finalmente, el salbutamol. ¿Usted usa la tableta, el líquido o el aerosol?
Sr. Flores:	Es una pompa.
Dr. Vargas:	El inhalador, entonces. ¿Con qué frecuencia lo usa?
Sr. Flores:	Como dos veces al día, pero sólo cuando tengo fatiga.
Dr. Vargas:	Bien. Lisinopril, hidroclorotiazida, metformina y salbutamol. Usted toma cuatro medicamentos. Toma tres medicamentos todos los días y sólo usa el inhalador cuando tiene dificultad para respirar. ¿Siempre toma los medicamentos todos los días?
Sr. Flores:	Sí. Mi esposa Marisol insiste.
Dr. Vargas:	Me alegro. Es muy importante tomar todos los medicamentos de la manera indicada. Llámame si tiene un problema con los medicamentos.
Sr. Flores:	Está bien. De acuerdo.

insistir	to insist
de acuerdo	agreed

 ## 6.7 Actividad

Ask a partner the following comprehension questions.

- A. ¿Es el señor Flores alérgico a algún medicamento? ¿Qué le pasa?
- B. ¿Cuáles medicamentos toma el Sr. Flores todos los días?
- C. ¿De cuáles enfermedades crónicas sufre el Sr. Flores?
- D. ¿Tiene el Sr. Flores efectos secundarios de la metformina?
- E. ¿Usa el Sr. Flores un medicamento de alivio rápido para el asma?
- F. ¿Con qué frecuencia usa el inhalador?

 ## 6.8 Reciclaje

In the spaces below, write prescriptions to renew Mr. Flores's medications for a month.

A. <u>Lisinopril,</u><u>   </u>.

B. <u>Hidroclorotiazida,</u><u>   </u>.

C. <u>Metformina,</u><u>   </u>.

D. <u>Salbutamol,</u><u>   </u>.

Vocabulario: Algunas clases de medicamentos
(Some Classes of Medications)

el analgésico, el calmante	analgesic
el antiácido	antacid
el antialérgico, el antihistamínico	antihistamine
el antibiótico	antibiotic
el anticoagulante	anticoagulant
el anticolinérgico	anticholinergic
el anticonvulsivo	anticonvulsive
el antidepresivo	antidepressant
el antidiarreico	antidiarrheal
el antiespasmódico	antispasmodic
el antigripal	cold reliever
el antihipertensivo	antihypertensive

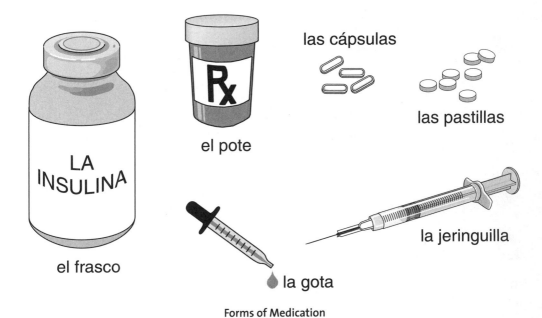

las cápsulas

las pastillas

el pote

LA INSULINA

el frasco

la gota

la jeringuilla

Forms of Medication

el antiinflamatorio no esteroide drug	nonsteroidal anti-inflammatory (NSAID)
el antitusígeno	cough suppressant
el barbitúrico	barbiturate
el broncodilatador	bronchodilator
el descongestionante	decongestant
el diurético	diuretic
el esteroide	steroid
el expectorante	expectorant
el laxante	laxative
la pastilla anticonceptiva	birth-control pill
la pastilla para bajar de peso	diet pill
la pastilla para dormir	sleeping pill
el sedante, el calmante	sedative
el tranquilizante	tranquilizer
la vitamina	vitamin

Note: The NSAIDs can be called *calmante, analgésico,* or *antipirético,* depending on the use. Some of the newest immigrants may not be familiar with the brand names for certain medicines. They may be more familiar with generic names like *acetaminofén* or *ibuprofén* because pharmaceutical companies in their country of origin may have their own brand names or may import generic medications.

6.9 Ejercicio

Say the type of medication corresponding to each of the following products. As always, you must use complete sentences.

     Example: Maalox®   Maalox® es un antiácido.

A. Advil®   F. Ex-Lax®
B. Proventil®   G. Benadryl®
C. Bactrim®   H. Prozac®
D. Coumadin®   I. One-a-Day®
  E. Lasix®   J. Sudafed®

6.10 Actividad

The instructor will hand out two index cards to each student. On card one, write either the name of a medication, such as *la amoxicilina,* or the class of a medication, such as *antibiótico.* On card two, write a symptom or illness that might respond to that medication: *una infección en los oídos.* Next, the instructor should collect card one from everyone, shuffle the cards, and redistribute them at random. Students will then circulate in the room simultaneously, speaking only Spanish and seeking the appropriate treatment for their condition. For example, *Tengo una infección en los oídos. ¿Qué medicamento tienes?*

 ## Estructura: El imperativo (Formal [*Usted*] Commands)

- You learned several ways to give commands in the context of the pharmacy. These were versatile and uncomplicated because the verb representing the action remained in its infinitive form. You learned,

  Favor de + infinitivo   Favor de llamar al doctor si tiene alguna
                              pregunta.
  Hay que + infinitivo   Hay que tomar la tableta con mucha agua.
  Tener que + infinitivo   Tiene que tomar la medicina con comida.

- Spanish-speakers also use direct commands, which are especially useful when a concise imperative is appropriate. When stitching a laceration, you might say, "Don't move!" During a physical exam you might say, "Breathe deeply!" and during an x-ray you might say, "Don't breathe." Here is how to make a formal (*usted*) command.

- Remove the *-o* from the first person singular form of the present tense and then add *-e* for verbs that end in *-ar* and *-a* for verbs that end in *-er* or *-ir.*

  tomar   ¡Tome la medicina!   Take the medicine!
  comer   ¡No coma nada!   Don't eat anything!

- If a verb is irregular in the *yo* (first person singular) form, the command is also irregular. To say "Put the nitroglycerine under your tongue," think in three steps. Think *poner* (the verb infinitive); *pongo* (the first person singular); and *ponga* (the formal command). Then say, *Ponga la nitroglicerina debajo de la lengua.* (Because *poner* is an *-er* verb, we used *a*.)

- Of course native and fluent speakers do not have to think first about construction. For novices, however, starting with the first person singular form eliminates memorizing many of these morphologies individually as "irregular" verb forms. For now this shortcut may help. "Think *yo* and use the wrong letter." In chapter 11 we'll address commands using reflexive verbs, which are often used in activities of daily living, and in chapter 12 you'll learn informal commands.

> Native speakers may include the reflexive pronoun *se*, as in *Tómese una aspirina,* or *Hay que tomarse dos pastillas.*

6.11 Ejercicio

Use the formal command form to write and say the following medication instructions in Spanish, as in the example.

> Example: Ibuprofén 600 mg, take 1 tablet by mouth 3 times a day.
> *Ibuprofén 600 mg, tome 1 tableta 3 veces al día.*

A. Take the medicine every day without fail.

_____

B. Amoxicilina (250 mg/5 ml), take 1 teaspoonful 3 times a day for 5 days.

_____

_____

C. Guaifenesina, take 1 tablespoonful 4 times a day for congestion.

_____

D. Salbutamol, take 1 puff (inhalación) every 4 to 6 hours as needed for shortness of breath.

_____

_____

E. Donepezilo, take 10 mg by mouth once a day in the morning.

_____

F. Ginkgo, take 160 mg by mouth at 8:00 AM and 8:00 PM.

_____

 ## Video Program: *Cómo usar el inhalador*

Review the *Demostración* for chapter 6, in which Dr. Vargas explains how to use an inhaler.

6.12 Ejercicio

In the spaces below, supply the correct formal commands using the following verbs. You'll then have a transcript of the video portion that you have just seen.

agitar	to shake
quitar	to remove
exhalar	to exhale
mantener*	to maintain
abrir	to open
poner	to put
inhalar	to inhale
oprimir	to press
contener*	to hold, contain
retirar	to retire, take away
enjuagar†	to rinse

Quiero enseñarles cómo usar el inhalador para recibir el máximo beneficio del medicamento. Primero, _____ (agitar) bien el inhalador. Así. _____ (quitar) la tapa protectora. _____ (exhalar) completamente a través de su nariz y _____ (mantener) la boca cerrada. _____ (abrir) la boca completamente y _____ (poner) la boquilla a una o dos pulgadas de su boca. Así. _____ (inhalar) lentamente y profundamente y, al mismo tiempo, _____ (oprimir) la parte de abajo del envase para rociar el medicamento en la boca. Así. _____ (contener) el aliento durante cinco a diez segundos, _____ (retirar) el inhalador y _____ (exhalar) lentamente a través de la nariz o boca. Así. _____ (poner) la tapa protectora en el inhalador. Después de cada tratamiento, _____ (enjuagar) su boca con agua o enjuague bucal.

Mantener and *contener* are treated like *tener* (the *yo* form ends in -*go*).
†*Enjuagar* requires an added *u* to maintain its «g» sound. ¡*Enjuague* usted!

Estructura: Los adjetivos demostrativos y los adjetivos afirmativos y negativos
(Demonstrative Adjectives and Affirmative and Negative Adjectives)

- The demonstrative adjectives specify a particular person or thing. These are the demonstrative adjectives.

	Singular	*Plural*	*Inglés*
Masculino	este	estos	this, these
Femenino	esta	estas	this, these

- The demonstrative adjective must agree in gender and number with the noun that it modifies. For example,

  Este medicamento es para el dolor.

  Estos supositorios son para la náusea.

  Esta inyección es para quitar las voces.

  Estas pastillas son para la diarrea.

- These are the affirmative and negative adjectives in Spanish.

	Singular	*Plural*	*Inglés*
Masculino	alguno, algún	algunos	some, any
	ninguno, ningún*		not any
Femenino	alguna	algunas	some, any
	ninguna*		not any

- *Alguno* and *ninguno* drop the -*o* before a masculine singular noun, but *alguna* and *ninguna* keep the final -*a*.

  ¿Es usted alérgico a algún medicamento?

  No soy alérgico a ningún medicamento.

  ¿Sufre usted de alguna enfermedad?

- The double negative is necessary in Spanish. Think in terms of agreement. In an affirmative sentence, use the affirmative adjective. In a negative sentence, use the negative adjective.

  ¿Toma algún medicamento todos los días?

  No, no tomo ningún medicamento.

 ## 6.13 Ejercicio

Explain to your Spanish-speaking patient Don Ignacio the anticipated benefits of the following medicines. (Act as if the items were laid out on the desk in front of you.) Insert the correct form of the demonstrative adjective (*este, estos, esta, estas*) in the spaces provided. Recall that adjectives and their nouns must agree.

*The adjectives *ningún, ninguno,* and *ninguna* are almost always used in the singular form.

Don Ignacio, es muy importante usar _____ medicamentos

en la manera indicada. _____ crema es para aliviar el dolor de

la quemadura. En caso de fiebre, _____ pastillas son para

quitar la fiebre. Si tiene mucho dolor, _____ pastillas son para

el dolor. _____ jarabe es para la tos. Si está peor mañana, favor

de llamar a _____ número de teléfono. Finalmente, _____

recetas son para comprar más medicamentos.

ACETAMINOFÉN 60 ml. **Pediátrico** ANALGÉSICO Y ANTIPIRÉTICO QUITA EL DOLOR Y LA FIEBRE COMPOSICIÓN: Cada cucharadita (5ml) contiene: Acetaminofén..................125 mg. Sorbitol.............................0.2 ml. Excipiente C.S.P...................5 ml.	**MANTÉNGASE FUERA DEL ALCANCE DE LOS NIÑOS** INDICACIONES: Acetaminofén jarabe está indicado en estados febriles, resfriados comunes, reacciones febriles pos vacuna y en enfermedades que producen dolor y fiebre. DOSIFICACIÓN: Niños de 1 a 3 años: Según receta médica. Niños mayores de 3 años: 1-2 cucharaditas 3 ó 4 veces al día.

PARA EL CATARRO
TOME

GRIPELINA™

EL JARABE ANTIGRIPAL

●DESCONGESTIONANTE
●EXPECTORANTE
●SEGURO Y EFECTIVO
PARA TODA LA FAMILIA

dist. en Perú por los Laboratorios Martínez, s.a.

 6.14 Ejercicio

Explain to your Spanish-speaking patient the anticipated benefits of the following medicines. You will need three verbs for this exercise; *quitar* (to take away), *bajar* (to lower), and *eliminar* (to eliminate). All are regular *-ar* verbs. For example, *Estas pastillas son para eliminar el agua.*

A. This ointment is to take away the itching.
B. This medicine is to lower your cholesterol.
C. This syrup is to take away the diarrhea.
D. This IV is to take away the infection.
E. This pill is to lower your blood pressure.
F. This injection is to take away the pain.
G. This medicine is to take away the swelling.
H. These pills are to eliminate the water.

6.15 Reciclaje

Review the symptoms of colds and flu in chapter 3 and state the common uses for the following over-the-counter medicines.

> Example: Tylenol®
> El Tylenol® es para quitar el dolor y bajar la fiebre.

A. El Pepto Bismol®   F. El Robitussin DM®
B. La leche de magnesia   G. La aspirina
C. El Sudafed®   H. El Imodium®
D. Las mentas Hall's®   I. El Benadryl®
E. Las gotas antialérgicas   J. El ibuprofeno

 6.16 Drama imprevisto

Working in small groups, make a radio or television commercial for one of the medicines from *Reciclaje* 6.15. As an alternative, use the following packaging for *acetaminofén pediátrico* as a basis for an unscripted role play in which you are a pediatrician and your partner is the mother of an ill child.

 Ask About Medication Allergies and Educate Patients About Allergic Reactions

Vocabulario: Las reacciones alérgicas
(Allergic Reactions)

las alérgias	allergies
la anafilaxis	anaphylactic shock
la eczema	eczema
la epenefrina (adrenalina)	epinephrine (adrenaline)
la erupción (manchas rojas)	rash (red marks)
la falta de aire	shortness of breath
la hinchazón	swelling
el jadeo	gasping
la picazón, la comezón	itch, itching
la raquiña (slang)	itching
el sarpullido, las ronchas	hives, rash
el silbido	wheeze

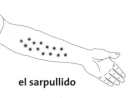

el sarpullido

Lectura: Los efectos secundarios

Los doctores recetan los medicamentos para los beneficios de curar enfermedades o aliviar síntomas. Muchos medicamentos también tienen efectos secundarios. A veces los efectos secundarios son molestos pero desaparecen con el tiempo o con bajar la dosis. Los efectos secundarios incluyen la náusea, el mareo, la indigestión, el vómito, el estreñimiento, la diarrea, la sequedad en la boca, el dolor de cabeza, el insomnio, la irritabilidad y el sueño.

> *molesto* bothersome

Muchas veces los efectos secundarios son benignos, pero algunas personas tienen una reacción alérgica. La reacción alérgica ocurre cuando el sistema inmunológico responde al medicamento. Los síntomas de una reacción alérgica incluyen hinchazón, picazón, manchas rojas, inflamación en la garganta, asma, ritmo cardíaco irregular y/o dificultad para respirar. Hay que llamar al doctor o al hospital inmediatamente si tiene una reacción alérgica después de tomar un medicamento. La reacción alérgica más severa es la anafilaxis. La dificultad para respirar siempre es una emergencia médica. Si hay dificultad para respirar o anafilaxis, necesita llamar al 911 o llevar al paciente a la sala de urgencia.

Educate a Patient About Asthma

Lectura: El asma (Asthma)

El asma es una enfermedad crónica que causa una inflamación en los pulmones y las vías respiratorias. El asma no es una enfermedad contagiosa. Durante un ataque (un episodio agudo) del asma, el paciente sufre de dificultad para respirar. Otros síntomas incluyen:

la comezón en la barbilla o garganta	itching in the chin or throat
la dificultad para hablar	difficulty speaking
la falta de aire	shortness of breath
los jadeos	gasping, panting
el pecho apretado	tight chest
la respiración silbante	wheezing
los silbidos	wheezing
la tos	cough

El asma no tiene cura pero es posible controlar los síntomas con medicamentos que un doctor receta. Todas las personas que sufren de asma necesitan un medicamento de alivio rápido para usar durante un ataque. Muchas personas necesitan también usar todos los días un medicamento preventivo. Los medicamentos son en forma líquida, en forma de tableta o cápsula y en aerosol (para inhalar).

También hay que evitar las cosas que provocan los ataques. Algunas de las cosas que provocan los ataques son:

los ácaros del polvo	dust mites
las alérgias	allergies
las alfombras	carpets
la caspa de animal	animal dander
la contaminación del aire	air pollution
las cucarachas	cockroaches
el frío	cold weather
el humo	smoke
el moho	mold
los perfumes	perfumes
el polen y el polvo	pollen and dust

Algunos episodios o ataques de asma son severos y son una emergencia médica de vida o muerte. Es necesario llamar al doctor o a la clínica si el efecto del medicamento de alivio rápido dura menos de cuatro horas (o si no quita la tos o la respiración silbante). Es importante tener un plan para ir al hospital cuando el medicamento no alivia los síntomas y la respiración está rápida y difícil.

 ## 6.17 Actividad

Work with a partner to check each other's comprehension of the two preceding readings.

    A. ¿Son todos los efectos secundarios una emergencia médica?

    B. ¿Cuál es la reacción alérgica más severa?

    C. ¿Cuáles son los síntomas de la anafilaxis?

    D. ¿Qué tienen en común un ataque de asma y una reacción alérgica?

    E. ¿Es una enfermedad contagiosa el asma?

    F. ¿Cuáles son algunas de las cosas que provocan los ataques de asma?

    G. ¿Qué es un medicamento de alivio rápido y cuándo es necesario usarlo?

    H. ¿Cuándo es necesario llamar al doctor o a la clínica?

    I. ¿Cuándo es necesario ir rápidamente al hospital?

6.18 Drama imprevisto

Work with a partner to make a skit in which a practitioner educates the parent of a child with asthma about the disease and ways to control it. Discuss an emergency plan for when rescue medication, *un medicamento de alivio rápido,* does not resolve an acute episode. Instead of acting out your skit with your partner, switch partners in order to demonstrate a less-scripted and more spontaneous version for the class. Parents of the child may choose to play the role of an exceptionally nervous parent or a parent who minimizes the possible dangers.

 ## Estructura: El verbo *dar* y los complementos directos e indirectos
(The Verb *Dar* and Direct and Indirect Objects)

- *Dar* takes an irregular form in the first person singular (*yo*) form.

yo	doy	Le doy agua de arroz al bebé.
tú	das	¿Le das comida sólida al bebé?
él, ella, usted	da	¿Le da al bebé leche del pecho?
nosotros/nosotras	damos	Le damos un medicamento a Juan.
ellos, ellas, ustedes	dan	Las pastillas me dan salpullido.

- The verb *dar* may require the use of the indirect object. Recall that the indirect object represents the person to/for whom the action of the verb is done.

  | Le doy a usted la receta. | I give you the prescription. |
  | Mi madre me da la inyección. | My mother gives me the injection. |

- With the instruction "*hay que* + infinitive" attach the indirect object (as a suffix) to the infinitive. Where increased clarity is needed, add *a* and identify the person to whom the action is to be done.

  Hay que darle al niño el jarabe cada cuatro horas sin falta.

  Hay que darle a su madre la insulina después de comer.

- Direct and indirect objects may be used together. The indirect object always goes first. The objects may be placed before a conjugated verb or as a suffix to a verb infinitive. It makes no difference which way you do this.

  La enfermera tiene que inyectarme la insulina.

  La enfermera tiene que inyectármela.

  La enfermera me la tiene que inyectar.

- Never use two objects beginning with *l* together. When the indirect object *le* or *les* would appear before *lo, la, los,* or *las,* change the indirect object to *se.* For example, to say "You have to give it to him every six hours," use either of the following expressions.

  Se lo tiene que dar cada seis horas.

  Tiene que dárselo cada seis horas.

6.19 Actividad

Look at Juancito's medication regimen and assume that medication times are at nine, one, five, and nine. Ask his caretaker whether he or she is giving the prescribed treatments. For example, *¿Le da a Juancito la amoxicilina tres veces al día?* The answer may use the direct and indirect objects together: *Sí, se la doy a las nueve de la mañana, la una de la tarde y las nueve de la noche.* How many different questions can you make?

| | Hora de administración | | | |
Medicamento	9	1	5	9
Amoxicilina, 1 cucharadita	X	X		X
Acetaminofén, 2 cucharaditas	X			X
Robitussin®, 1 cucharada	X	X	X	X
El inhalador albuterol	X			X

 6.20 Actividad

Work with a partner to create a Spanish dialogue to present to the class. Here are a few ideas to get you started.

A. Ask if he/she takes medicine every day and about any allergies to medications.
B. Discover that he/she has an allergy to a specific drug, such as penicillin, and what happens.
C. Give instructions for a medication or over-the-counter preparation, and answer questions about its use. Provide information about possible side effects.
D. Discuss the problems associated with drinking alcoholic beverages (*las bebidas alcohólicas*) when using a particular medication.
E. Teach about the flu vaccine (*la vacuna para la gripe*) and ask about allergy to eggs (*los huevos*).

 6.21 Drama imprevisto

The instructor will supply a bag of M&M's® or Skittles®. Consider each color to be a medication, and assign a type or purpose to each. Invent and demonstrate a television commercial to promote the drug or a didactic session to educate a patient about its use. Include the diagnosis; purpose of the medication; dosing, frequency, and route of administration; side effects; and instructions about what to do if any problems or further questions arise. You'll need to know the colors.

los rojos	the red ones	los anaranjados	the orange ones
los amarillos	the yellow ones	los verdes	the green ones
los azules	the blue ones	los morados	the purple ones
los marrones	the brown ones	-claros/-oscuros	light-/dark-

Explain How to Use a Pill Organizer

Lectura: El recordatorio de pastillas (The Pill Organizer)

The following new verbs appear in this description of how to use a pill organizer:

olvidar	to forget	vender	to sell
usar	to use	preparar	to prepare
poner	to put	corresponder	to correspond

El recordatorio de pastillas (también se llama el organizador de pastillas) es una caja que tiene siete compartimientos, uno para cada día de la semana. El recordatorio es para no olvidar tomar el medica-

caja box

mento. Las farmacias los venden. Use el organizador todos los días. Prepárelo el primer día de la semana, y ponga las pastillas de cada día en el compartimiento que corresponde al día. Por ejemplo, ponga las pastillas que usted toma los lunes en el compartimiento que corresponde al lunes. Siempre tome el medicamento en la forma indicada.

El recordatorio
de pastillas

6.22 Actividad

The instructor will bring a pill organizer for demonstration, or students may use the illustration to educate another student about its use. Students prepare a medication regimen on a sheet of paper and role-play to explain the regimen in relation to the use of the pill organizer. Include and discuss a medication that is taken every other day.

Cultural Note: *La confianza*

Now you can give medication instructions in Spanish. This may improve treatment adherence. However, when in doubt about the accuracy of your instructions or the patient's understanding, seek a qualified interpreter. Despite the accuracy of your instructions, you may miss cues about comprehension and about the patient's cognitive competence even when the directions seem intuitive, with potentially serious consequences.

You may also improve treatment adherence by making a conscious effort to help the patient to address issues of trust. Some people believe—with good reason—that if you do not cross the language boundary, you will never earn the *confianza* of the patient. *Confianza* is facilitated by one's being genuine and empathetic, which may include having an authentic interest in Spanish language and the patient's culture or origin. *Confianza* is more than the literal translation, "confidence," implies. It combines trust and respect. When a health care provider earns the *confianza* of the patient, the patient will express feelings, listen more carefully, and be more likely to follow advice. Direct eye contact from the patient may be a sign of *confianza*. The health professional who earns *confianza* has communicated a genuine interest in the patient, beyond the requirements of his or her job.

In many cultures, it is common to expect relationships to feel as if they were personal rather than business. Latinos call this *el personalismo.* In Latin America, one may build brand loyalty as much by making customer relationships feel personal as by advertising one's expertise and modern equipment. In the United States, when the doctor doesn't take a moment to greet each person in the room individually, a North American might assume the doctor is busy or has a lot of important things to do. A Latino in the same situation may feel that something is out-of-the-ordinary and attribute this to a lack of courtesy or respect. Practitioners should consider the possible effects of maintaining strict boundaries on their relationships with patients from other cultures. Perhaps there is some personal information one might disclose—in the interest of making a relationship feel more natural to the patient—while not violating a necessary parameter of self-disclosure.

Many new Latino immigrants find it difficult to adjust to the time pressures of the managed care system in the United States. Returning home from the doctor's office, one new arrival began to list the questions she had wanted to ask the doctor. "It is not like my country," she said. "Here they do not sit down and talk to you; they hurry out." Courtesy and "small talk" are more conventional in Latino culture than in the managed care system, where time and efficiency may be measured in patients per hour. It may take time to warm up. One often asks about the patient's family. The Spanish-speaking patient may not mention his or her most urgent health concern first. He or she may wait until after discussing a subordinate concern and sensing the *confianza* needed before talking of more important or more intimate problems. It must be established that the practitioner has time to listen.

Communication styles may affect *confianza.* For example, Latinos tend to be "high-context" communicators. That is, they tend to focus as much on the nonverbal cues and context of a conversation as on the content. Saying coolly, "If you do not take the medication, you will get sick," without appropriate affect may dilute the message. The patient may think unconsciously, "He told me I'd get sick, but he did not appear very worried, so it may not be so important." A precept of successful cross-cultural communication is to learn the way that a particular patient population—or individual—may wish to be treated, and to strive to treat people that way.

Many Latinos who are proficient in English will prefer Spanish for talking about intimate and personal feelings or topics like sexuality. This is in part due to speaking Spanish at home or having spoken Spanish as a child. They may speak Spanish in times of distress. Coping mechanisms like "self talk" may be inseparable from one's native language. Some patients have denied that they speak English at all in the hopes of being assisted by a Spanish-speaking helper in whom they may sense more *confianza.* When English is a second language and the patient becomes psychotic, proficiency in English may diminish or disappear because of the psychotic disorganization. (Conversely, the concentration used in speaking a second language may temporarily repress the psychosis.) As the patient improves, the use of English also improves and can be a cognitive sign of recovery. Brain damage, as from a stroke, has been known to disable a second language while leaving the first language intact.

Chapter 7

La nutrición y las dietas

By the end of this chapter you will know the names of common foods in Spanish and be able to ask patients about their dietary habits and preferences. You will be able to give basic instructions for weight-reducing, low-fat, and clear-liquids diets.

Ask Patients About Food Preferences

Vocabulario: La pirámide (The USDA Food Pyramid)

Granos: «Consuma la mitad en granos integrales»

el arroz (el arroz integral)	rice (whole-grain rice)
el cereal cocido	cooked cereal
el cereal seco	dry cereal
el maíz	corn
el pan	bread
la pasta	pasta
la tortilla*	tortilla

Verduras: «Varíe sus verduras»

la calabaza	squash
los guisantes	peas
la lechuga	lettuce
el plátano de cocinar	plantain
el repollo	cabbage
el tomate, el jitomate	tomato
los vegetales, las verduras	vegetables, green vegetables
la zanahoria	carrot

*In Mexico a *tortilla* is a flat cake usually made from corn, but in the Caribbean region it is an omelet.

Frutas: «Enfoque en las frutas»

banana, guineo, plátano	banana
la ciruela	prune
la manzana	apple
el melón	melon
la naranja (la china)	orange
la piña	pineapple
la toronja	grapefruit
la uva	grape

Leche: «Coma alimentos ricos en calcio»

el helado	ice cream
la leche baja en grasa	low-fat milk
la leche descremada	fat-free (no-fat) milk
el queso bajo en grasa	low-fat cheese
el yogur bajo en grasa	low-fat yogurt

Proteínas, carne y frijoles: «Escoja proteínas bajas en grasa»

la carne de res	beef
el cerdo	pork
los frijoles, las habichuelas	beans, pea beans
el huevo	egg
la manteca de cacahuate	peanut butter
el pescado	fish
el pollo	chicken

Aceites: «Los aceites son parte de una buena dieta»

el aceite de maíz	corn oil
el aceite de oliva	olive oil
las grasas	fats
la manteca	lard
la mantequilla	butter
la margarina	margarine
la mayonesa	mayonnaise

Espresiones útiles

Debe comer más vegetales.	You should eat more vegetables.
Debe comer menos grasa.	You should eat less fat.
No debe usar mucha sal.	You should not use a lot of salt.
En vez de comer dulce,	Instead of eating candy,
coma frutas.	eat fruit.

 ## Estructura: Verbos como *gustar* (Verbs Like *Gustar*)

- One meaning of the verb *disgustar* is "to disgust." Like the verb *doler*, which you know from chapter 3, it is most frequently used in the third person (singular and plural), and it is used with indirect objects (*me, te, le, nos, les*). For example,

Me disgustan las arañas.	Spiders disgust me.
A Luisa le disgustan las anchovas.	Anchovies disgust Luisa.

- The verb *gustar* is the opposite of *disgustar* and means "to please." It may be confusing because the meaning-based translation of *Me gusta el café* is "I like coffee." The literal translation, "Coffee pleases me" explains why we use the form *gusta*. That which pleases is the subject of the verb *gustar*.

Me gusta el café.	I like coffee.
¿Te gusta el café?	Do you like coffee?
A Luisa le gusta la leche.	Luisa likes milk.
No nos gusta la cerveza.	We don't like beer.
A mi papá le gusta la cerveza.	My dad likes beer.

- If the subject (that which pleases) is plural, use the third person plural form of the verb.

Me gustan las comidas.	I like the meals.
¿Le gustan las uvas?	Do you like grapes?

- We can also express our fondness for an activity by following the verb *gustar* with a verb infinitive.

No me gusta cocinar.	I do not like to cook.
¿Qué le gusta comer?	What do you like to eat?

- Other verbs that are used like *gustar* include *interesar* (to interest), *importar* (to matter), *aburrir* (to bore), and *fascinar* (to fascinate). For example,

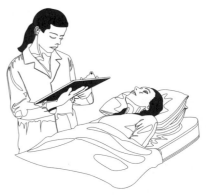

Me interesa la medicina.	Medicine interests me.
¿Le importa comer bien?	Does eating well matter to you?
Me aburre la televisión.	Television bores me.
A Juan le fascina comer.	Eating fascinates Juan.

¿Qué le gusta comer?

 ## 7.1 Actividad

On the board, a volunteer writes the headings *Me gusta, No me gusta, Me disgusta,* and *Me fascina.* Students draw representations of what they like or dislike in the appropriate areas of the board and then write full-sentence captions. Recall that these verbs may be followed by infinitive verbs as well. For example, under the heading *Me fascina* could be a drawing of two people talking and the caption *Me fascina hablar español.* Edit the finished work as a class.

Vocabulario: Más alimentos y bebidas
(More Foods and Beverages)

El desayuno (Breakfast)

la avena	oatmeal
el cereal	cereal
la ciruela	prune
la fruta	fruit
el huevo	egg
el pan tostado, la tostada	toast
el panqueque	pancake
la salchicha	sausage
el tocino	bacon
la toronja	grapefruit

El almuerzo (Lunch)

la ensalada	salad
el jamón	ham

las papas fritas	french fries
el queso	cheese
el sándwich	sandwich
la sopa	soup

La cena (Supper, Dinner)

el arroz	rice
la carne	meat
la carne de res	beef
el cerdo	pork
los frijoles, las habichuelas	beans, pea beans
el pan	bread
la papa	potato
la pasta	pasta
el pescado	fish
el pollo	chicken
el vegetal	vegetable
la verdura	vegetable

Las bebidas (Beverages)

el agua*	water
el café	coffee
la cerveza	beer
el chocolate	hot cocoa
el jugo de ciruela	prune juice
el jugo de manzana	apple juice
el jugo de naranja[†]	orange juice
el jugo de tomate	tomato juice
la leche	milk
el refresco	soft drink
el té	tea
el vino	wine

Preguntas útiles

¿Toma usted bebidas alcohólicas?	Do you drink alcoholic beverages?
¿Toma café descafeinado?	Do you drink decaffeinated coffee?

Agua and *azúcar,* like *asma* and *área,* are feminine nouns that are used with the masculine definite article (*el*). Adjectives take their feminine form, however (*El agua está fría. Mi azúcar está alta.*).

[†]In the Caribbean, orange juice is *el jugo de china.*

el cereal

la leche

la mantequilla

el jugo de naranja

el pan tostado

el café

el tocino

el huevo

la salchicha

 7.2 Ejercicio

Make a diagram that organizes according to food groups some of the foods commonly associated with breakfast, lunch, and dinner.

	Desayuno	*Almuerzo*	*Cena*
Granos	_____	_____	_____
	_____	_____	_____
Verduras	_____	_____	_____
	_____	_____	_____
Frutas	_____	_____	_____
	_____	_____	_____
Leche	_____	_____	_____
	_____	_____	_____
Carnes y frijoles	_____	_____	_____
	_____	_____	_____

 7.3 Actividad

Interview a fellow student. Take turns asking each other about likes and dislikes, as in the example. Use the familiar, or *tú,* form.

la calabaza

la toronja

la zanahoria

la manzana

los guisantes

Varíe sus verduras y enfóquese en las frutas.

Example: tomar café por la mañana

Estudiante 1: ¿Te gusta tomar café por la mañana?

Estudiante 2: Sí, me gusta tomar café por la mañana (*or*) No, no me gusta el café. No lo tomo por la mañana.

A. tomar cerveza con el desayuno
B. tomar jugo de naranja por la mañana
C. comer una banana con el desayuno
D. comer un sándwich para el almuerzo
E. tomar jugo de ciruela con la cena
F. tomar bebidas alcohólicas todos los días
G. tomar un refresco por la mañana

 ## Estructura: Los verbos *querer* y *preferir* para expresar gustos y preferencias
(The Verbs *Querer* and *Preferir* to Express Likes and Preferences)

- "I like coffee" is *Me gusta el café.* "I want coffee" is *Quiero café. Querer* is an irregular -*er* verb. The stem changes from *e* to *ie* except in the first person plural (*nosotros*).

yo	quiero	Quiero una ensalada.
tú	quieres	¿Quieres un vaso de leche?
él, ella, usted	quiere	¿Quiere usted una taza de café?
nosotros/as	queremos	Queremos comer una dieta balanceada.
ellos, ellas, ustedes	quieren	Mis padres quieren bajar de peso.

- Like *gustar,* the verb *querer* can precede a noun or another verb. The second verb is not conjugated.

Quiero tomar un vaso de agua.	I want to drink a glass of water.
¿Quiere cenar en la cafetería?	Do you want to eat dinner in the cafeteria?

- The phrase *si Dios quiere* means "God willing." Some Spanish-speakers may use this phrase instead of a more direct "yes" or "no" when answering a question or telling plans.
- *Preferir* is an irregular *-ir* verb. Like *querer,* the stem changes from *e* to *ie* except in the first person plural (*nosotros*). Also like *querer* it can precede a verb.

yo	prefiero	Prefiero el arroz a las papas.
tú	prefieres	¿Prefieres el arroz o las papas?
él, ella, usted	prefiere	Sandra prefiere el refresco a la leche.
nosotros/as	preferimos	Sergio y yo preferimos beber leche.
ellos, ellas, ustedes	prefieren	Mis padres prefieren tomar té.

 7.4 Actividad

Practice the vocabulary you have learned this far. Make suggestions for meals to your partner, following the example. Your partner will decide whether or not to play the role of a picky eater. Agree on something for breakfast, lunch, and dinner.

> Example: desayuno, huevos
> > Estudiante 1: Para el desayuno, ¿quiere huevos?
> > Estudiante 2: Sí, quiero huevos (Sí, los quiero).
> > > (*or*) No me gustan los huevos. Quiero pan tostado y café.

 7.5 Actividad

Put all three of your new verbs together. Ask a partner about his or her preferences. Your partner follows the example but indicates his or her own preferences.

> Example: Café o té
> > Student 1: ¿Quiere usted café o té?
> > Student 2: Bueno, me gusta el café, pero prefiero el té.

A. la leche o el chocolate
B. la carne de res o el pollo
C. las papas, la pasta o el arroz
D. el tocino o la salchicha

E. la ensalada o la sopa
F. la cerveza o el vino
G. los vegetales o las frutas
H. el pescado o el cerdo

Video Program: *Para una buena hambre no hay pan duro*

Watch the *Demostración* portion of the video for chapter 7. Do the activity that follows. In the video, Rosmery shares her lunch with Sra. Flores.

Rosmery:	Hablando de dietas me da mucha hambre. ¿Tienes hambre?
Sra. Flores:	Ay, sí. Tengo mucha hambre.
Rosmery:	Tengo mi almuerzo aquí. Vamos a ver qué podemos compartir.
Sra. Flores:	Eres muy amable Rosmery.
Rosmery:	Gracias, pero antes de llamarme amable, vamos a ver qué tenemos para comer.
Sra. Flores:	Para una buena hambre no hay pan duro.
Rosmery:	Del grupo de las frutas, presento una banana y unas uvas. ¿Te gustan las bananas?
Sra. Flores:	Sí, me gustan las bananas, pero prefiero las uvas.
Rosmery:	Quieres las uvas entonces. Te las doy. Del grupo de los granos, tenemos pan.
Sra. Flores:	Sí, el pan me gusta. Cuando hace frío, me encanta comer pan con mantequilla y tomar una taza de chocolate caliente. Pero a Francisco no le doy ni mantequilla ni chocolate. Tú sabes, la dieta.
Rosmery:	Hablando de chocolate. ¿Sabes qué?
Sra. Flores:	No, dime.
Rosmery:	Mi esposo está un poco gordito, así que para ayudarle con su dieta, cuando compramos chocolate, yo me lo como primero. Así él sigue con su dieta y evita el chocolate.
Sra. Flores:	Eres simpática y generosa, Rosmery.

7.6 Drama imprevisto

After two minutes or less of planning, act an unscripted skit for the class. The last line of the skit should fit the plot perfectly and must be *Para una buena hambre no hay pan duro.* This means, "For a good hunger there's no stale bread," which is similar to the English, "Don't look a gift horse in the mouth!"

 ## Educate Patients About Special Diets

Vocabulario: Las comidas y las dietas (Meals and Diets)

la nutrición	nutrition	la dieta	diet
comer	to eat	ayunar	to fast

Las comidas (Meals)

el desayuno	breakfast	desayunar	to eat breakfast
el almuerzo	lunch	almorzar	to eat lunch
la cena	supper	cenar	to eat supper
la comida	dinner, meal	la merienda	snack
la bebida	beverage	el alimento	food

Las dietas (Diets)

seguir	to follow	dieta balanceada	balanced diet
la sal	salt	el sodio	sodium
la grasa	fat	el colesterol	cholesterol
el azúcar	sugar	la fibra	fiber
la proteína	protein	el almidón	starch
el carbohidrato	carbohydrate	el calcio	calcium
la libra	pound	la onza	ounce
la caloría	calorie	el gramo	gram

Preguntas útiles

¿Come bien el niño?	Does the child eat well?
¿Cuánto pesa usted?	How much do you weigh?
¿Ha bajado de peso recientemente?	Have you lost weight recently?
¿Ha subido de peso recientemente?	Have you gained weight recently?

Estructura: El verbo *deber* (Should, Ought To)

- The verb *deber* is a regular *-er* verb. It is useful for discussing diets because it expresses what one should or should not do.

yo	debo	Debo comer porciones más pequeñas.
tú	debes	No debes comer mucha grasa.
él, ella, usted	debe	Usted no debe comer comida rápida.
nosotros/as	debemos	Debemos comer una dieta balanceada.
ellos, ellas, ustedes	deben	Los pacientes no deben comer mucha sal.

Lectura: Un plan para bajar de peso (A Weight-Reducing Diet)

Para tener una dieta saludable y balanceada, debe comer cada día comidas de cada grupo de alimentos. También es importante tener un equilibrio entre lo que come y su actividad física. Una dieta balanceada tiene de siete a ocho porciones del grupo de los granos, de cuatro a cinco porciones del grupo de las verduras, de cuatro a cinco porciones del grupo de las frutas, de dos a tres del grupo de la leche, dos o menos porciones del grupo de la carne y no mucha grasa. Cada día se debe comer por lo menos cinco porciones de frutas y vegetales. Para bajar de peso, es importante comer una dieta balanceada, hacer ejercicio regularmente, comer menos calorías y no comer mucha grasa ni azúcar. Para comer menos calorías, debe comer menos porciones, o comer porciones más pequeñas.

Datos nutricionales	
Tamaño por porción 1 taza (236 ml) Porciones por envase 1	
Cantidad por porción	
Calorías 120 Calorías de grasa 45	
	% Valor diario*
Grasa total 5g	8%
Grasa saturada 3g	15%
Ácido grasoso *Trans* 0g	
Colesterol 20mg	7%
Sodio 120 mg	5%
Carbohidrato total 11mg	4%
Fibra dietética 0g	
Azúcares 11g	
Proteínas 9g	17%
Vitamina A 10% • Vitamina C 4%	
Calcio 30% • Hierro 0% • Vitamina D 25%	
*Los porcentajes de valores diarios están basados en una dieta de 2,000 calorías.	

Las frutas y los vegetales tienen mucha fibra.

7.7 Ejercicio

Write a balanced diet here.

El desayuno   El almuerzo

_____   _____

_____   _____

_____   _____

_____   _____

La cena   La merienda (Snack)

_____   _____

_____   _____

_____   _____

_____   _____

Lectura: La dieta baja en grasa y colesterol
(Low-Fat, Low-Cholesterol Diet)

Una persona con el colesterol alto no debe comer mucha grasa. La carne y la grasa de animal tienen colesterol. Las personas con el colesterol alto deben tomar leche descremada o baja en grasa. No deben comer más de tres huevos a la semana. Los alimentos que son permitidos incluyen los panes y cereales, las tortillas de maíz, el arroz, los frijoles y todas las frutas, vegetales y verduras. El coco tiene mucha grasa. No coma la carne de res más de tres veces a la semana. Coma porciones pequeñas y quite la grasa antes de cocinarla. También quite la piel del pollo antes de cocinarlo. Debe comer pescado grasoso, como el atún y el salmón. Las grasas permitidas son el aceite de maíz, el aceite de oliva y el aceite de soja (soy). El aceite de maíz puede bajar el colesterol.

 7.8 Ejercicio

El señor López tiene el colesterol muy alto. Él tiene varias preguntas. Favor de contestarle las siguientes preguntas.

A. ¿Debo cocinar con manteca?   No, no debe _____.

B. ¿Debo comer pollo y pescado?   Sí, debe _____.

C. ¿Debo comer mucho coco (coconut)? _____.

D. ¿Debo tomar leche baja en grasa? _____.

E. ¿Debo comer queso bajo en grasa? _____.

F. ¿Debo comer papas fritas?   _____.

G. ¿Debo usar aceite de maíz?   _____.

H. En vez de la carne de res, ¿qué debo comer?   _____.

Lectura: La dieta baja en azúcares concentradas
(Diet Low in Concentrated Sugars)

Las personas que tienen un nivel alto de triglicéridos en la sangre y las personas que sufren de la diabetes deben seguir una dieta baja en azúcares concentradas. La diabetes es una enfermedad que afecta la forma en que el cuerpo usa la comida. El comer azúcar no causa la diabetes, pero las personas que tienen diabetes tienen demasiada (too much) azúcar en la sangre. No hay cura para la diabetes, pero es posible controlarla. Para controlar la diabetes hay que hacer ejercicio regularmente, comer una dieta balanceada, controlar el peso y evitar las azúcares concentradas. También, si el doctor o enfermero receta una medicina, hay que tomarla en la manera indicada. Con respecto a la dieta, no debe dejar de comer ninguna de las comidas (Don't skip meals). Coma las comidas a la misma hora y la misma porción todos los días (especialmente si usa medicamento). Coma alimentos ricos en fibra como granos, verduras y frutas. Debe usar menos sal, grasa, azúcar y alcohol. Los siguientes alimentos tienen mucha azúcar. Evítelos (Avoid them).

el azúcar de caña	cane sugar
el dulce	candy
la miel de abeja	honey
el almíbar, el sirope	syrup
la torta	cake
la leche condensada	condensed milk
el refresco	pop, soda, soft drink

 7.9 Ejercicio

El señor Vega tiene diabetes. También él tiene muchas preguntas. Favor de contestarle las siguientes preguntas.

A. ¿Debo usar mucha azúcar
   cuando cocino?   No, no debe _____.

B. ¿Debo comer ensalada?   Sí, debe _____.

C. ¿Debo beber vino?   _____.

D. ¿Debo comer muchos dulces?   _____.

E. ¿Debo comer frijoles?   _____.

F. ¿Debo usar leche condensada?   _____.

G. ¿Debo tomar refrescos dietéticos? _____.

H. ¿Debo usar azúcar artificial?   _____.

◯ Teach Patients How to Prepare for a Colonoscopy

Vocabulario: La colonoscopia y la dieta de líquidos claros
(Colonoscopy and the Clear-Liquids Diet)

el agua	water
los refrescos claros (no rojos)	clear soda (not red)
el café o té sin leche	coffee or tea without milk
el jugo de manzana	apple juice
el caldo	broth
la gelatina	gelatine
los laxantes	laxatives
el citrato de magnesio	magnesium citrate
el bisacodilo	bisacodyl
evitar	to avoid
la aspirina	aspirin
los anticoagulantes	anticoagulants

A soft diet may be indicated as an intermediate step between a clear-liquids diet and a regular diet or for persons who require choking precautions. Here is some vocabulary that may help.

la dieta blanda	soft diet
la dieta corriente	regular diet
la dieta de puré	soft diet (puree)
los frijoles majados	mashed beans
el puré de papa, arroz, manzana	puree of potato, rice, apple

 7.10 Reciclaje

Write colonoscopy-preparation instructions in Spanish. Integrate what you learned about writing prescriptions in chapter 6, what you learned about special diets in this chapter, and the new vocabulary that appears above. Here is a sketch in English. You should provide examples of what to drink and what to avoid when following a clear-liquids diet. When you have finished, read your work to the class.

> Your colonoscopy is (day, date, and time). Do not take aspirin after (day, date one week prior). The day before (*el día antes*), take bisacodyl 5 mg, 4 tablets by mouth at 8:00 AM and follow a clear-liquids diet. Do not eat food or drink milk products. At 6:00 PM, drink 10 ounces of magnesium citrate. At 9:00 PM drink another

10 ounces of magnesium citrate. Follow a clear-liquids diet all night. Do not drink anything two hours before your colonoscopy.

_____

_____

_____

_____

_____

 ## 7.11 Actividad

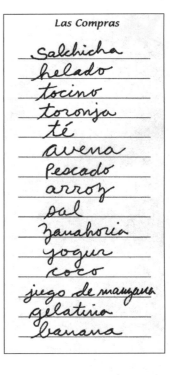

Las Compras

- Salchicha
- helado
- tocino
- toronja
- té
- avena
- pescado
- arroz
- sal
- zanahoria
- yogur
- coco
- jugo de manzana
- gelatina
- banana

Consult the shopping list in the illustration and advise the following patients about what they should or should not buy.

> Example: la señora Acevedo, la dieta baja en sal
> *Señora Acevedo, usted debe comprar las zanahorias. No compre las salchichas.*

A. Señora Blanco Peña, la dieta baja en grasa y colesterol.
B. Pedrito Jiménez, la dieta de líquidos claros.
C. Señora Medina Ortiz, la dieta para bajar de peso.

 ## 7.12 Actividad

Look at the diet slip in the illustration. Your partner is Señor/a Cintrón, speaks only Spanish, and would like your help in choosing what to order for breakfast. Role-play a conversation for the class.

 ## 7.13 Actividad

Students or the instructor may bring to class a snack, such as *flan* or *arroz con leche* and some *café con leche.* (For a simpler—and less tasty—exercise, bring only a few empty plates and cups.) Offer refreshment to fellow

---

Sunday Breakfast
Regular Diet

Name:_____ Room:_____

Your hostess will collect your menu at 10:00 a.m.

Please circle your selections

Cereals: *Fruits and Juices:*
Oatmeal   Orange Juice
Corn Flakes   Apple Juice
      Banana

Breakfast Entrees:
Cheese Omelet
Egg on Toast
Yogurt

Breads: *Beverages:*
Plain Bagel   Decaffeinated Coffee
Toast   Tea with Lemon
Margarine, Jelly   Lowfat Milk
      Non-Dairy Creamer

---

students using the verb *querer*. Ask about likes, dislikes, and preferences using the verbs *gustar* and *preferir*. If you like the food, trill the *r* when you say *¡Qué rico!*

Video Program: *Cómo bajar de peso*

Watch the *Trama* portion of the video for chapter 7. Do the activity that follows. In the video, Rosmery educates Sra. Flores about a weight-reducing diet for type 2 diabetes.

Rosmery: ¿Cómo está usted Sra. Flores?

Sra. Flores: Marisol. Llámame Marisol.

Rosmery: Marisol es un nombre bonito. Mi mamá se llama Marisol. ¿Cómo estás?

Sra. Flores: Bien. Bueno, un poco preocupada por Francisco. Tiene diabetes, el colesterol alto y la presión alta.

Rosmery: Bueno, son problemas crónicos, es verdad, pero hay tratamiento, y podemos ayudar a tu esposo.

Sra. Flores: ¿Qué podemos hacer? Dicen que si no controla el azúcar, la presión arterial y el colesterol, le puede dar un ataque al corazón, un derrame cerebral o quedarse ciego.

Rosmery: Ay, pobrecita, estás asustada porque lo quieres mucho. Pero no debes preocuparte tanto. Vamos a hablar de cómo lo podemos ayudar. Primero, ¿tienen un plan de alimentación para controlar la diabetes?

Sra. Flores: ¿Un plan de alimentación?

Rosmery: Sí, un plan de alimentación es decir una dieta especial para la diabetes.

Sra. Flores: Bueno, tratamos de evitar el azúcar. Compramos refresco dietético, pero Francisco no puede tomarse un café sin echarle tres cucharaditas de azúcar.

Rosmery: Bueno, es importante evitar el azúcar, pero más importante es controlar el peso. Don Francisco tiene diabetes tipo dos. Ese tipo de diabetes muchas veces mejora cuando bajamos de peso.

Sra. Flores: Es difícil bajar de peso.

Rosmery: Difícil, sí; pero imposible, no. Hablando en general, hay que comer porciones pequeñas y comer alimentos saludables que no tienen mucha grasa o azúcar. Frutas y verduras, pescado, las carnes que no tienen mucha grasa, frijoles, y la leche baja en grasa son buenos. Si come poco, y come alimentos saludables, puede controlar el peso. Y si baja de peso, se puede controlar mucho mejor el colesterol, la presión arterial y la diabetes.

Sra. Flores: Francisco no come mucho. Le hago arroz, habichuelas y carne casi todos los días, pero uso la pechuga de pollo porque dicen que la pechuga tiene menos grasa.

Rosmery: Excelente.

Sra. Flores: Bueno, sí, pero a Francisco le gusta comer su pollo frito y su salami. Sí, tienen mucha grasa, pero quiero hacerle la comida que a él le gusta.

Rosmery: Eres una buena esposa, Marisol. Explíquele a don Francisco que le estás preparando comida saludable para que estén más años juntos.

Sra. Flores: Me gusta la idea de estar más años juntos.

Rosmery:	Muy bien. Y ¿es físicamente activo don Francisco?
Sra. Flores:	Allí está el otro problema. Francisco trabaja en una oficina, donde tiene mucho estrés y hace poco ejercicio.
Rosmery:	Para bajar de peso, hay que tener un equilibrio entre lo que comemos y la actividad física. Es bueno hacer ejercicio. Debe hacer media hora a una hora de actividad física casi cada día. ¿Qué le gusta hacer?
Sra. Flores:	A él le gusta caminar, pero siempre dice que no tiene tiempo.
Rosmery:	¿Por qué no caminan en la tarde, después de la cena? Sería un buen momento para hablar. Incluso hasta sería romántico.
Sra. Flores:	Ahora estamos hablando el mismo idioma.

 ## 7.14 Drama imprevisto

It is dinner time at the Floreses' house later that night. Play the parts of Francisco, Marisol, and Elsita discussing what is for dinner. You may choose to play a more cooperative—or a less cooperative—Francisco. For example, *Pero mi amor, me gustan los dulces.*

 ## 7.15 Drama imprevisto

Play the game *afortunadamente, desafortunadamente.* Take turns adding to a string of statements. Start with *Tengo hambre* or *Tengo sed.* The next statement begins with *afortunadamente,* the statement after that begins with *desafortunadamente,* and so on.

Example:	Student 1:	Tengo sed.
	Student 2:	Afortunadamente, tenemos cerveza.
	Student 3:	Desafortunadamente, no me gusta la cerveza.
	Student 4:	Afortunadamente, hay café.
	Student 5:	Desafortunadamente, el café está frío.

 ## 7.16 Drama imprevisto

An old adage says *Por la boca muere el pez* (The fish dies by his mouth). With a partner, improvise a conversation about food and diets in which this gem of folk wisdom is the logical last line.

7.17 Reciclaje

Food and drink can be comforting, which can make dieting little more than wishful shrinking. Recycle the comfort idioms that use the verb *tener*. Find out what a partner likes or prefers to eat or drink when he or she feels hungry, thirsty, hot, cold, afraid, or in a hurry. *¿Qué prefieres tomar cuando tienes miedo?*

Cultural Note: Balancing Diet and Exercise

Hispanic cuisine has many starchy foods. In some areas, this may be due to their availability as compared to other foods. Although some are like vegetables in their vitamin content, their carbohydrate content is more similar to bread than to vegetables. These include rice, lima beans (*habas*), corn, and winter squash (*calabaza*). *Yuca* and *plátano* are two starchy vegetables that you may not know. *Yuca* is a root that must be cooked; it may be boiled (and topped with sautéed onions!) or grated, pressed, mixed with spices, and fried. It is one of the oldest foods in America. Before Columbus arrived in the "New World," the native people made a cake called *casave* by grating and pressing the *yuca,* adding salt, and cooking it on a hot rock. (To make *casave* at home, grate the *yuca,* press out the juice with cheesecloth, add salt, and cook it well on a dry cast-iron pan. A few drops of cold water will help you roll the dough. The raw juice is toxic.) The colonists took *casave* back to Spain because it did not

La yuca

spoil on the long voyages. *Plátano* is a vegetable that looks like a large, fat banana but has a flavor of its own (although when very ripe it tastes like a sweet potato). Fried, crushed, and re-fried it makes *tostones,* a real favorite in the Caribbean, but not good for low-fat diets. Other roots and tubers like *batata, yautía, malanga coco,* and *ñame* are carbohydrates that are boiled alone or in sauces and stews. People on a strict diabetic diet who use a system of exchanges or *intercambios* might be instructed to be consistent with carbohydrates and to use certain of these foods in place of bread.

Epidemiologically, Latinos born outside of the United States have a lower incidence of obesity and obesity-exacerbated illnesses such as hy-

El ñame

pertension and type two diabetes mellitus. After five years in the United States, however, they begin to close the gap with Latinos born in the United States and with a sample of all native-born North Americans. A recent study found that Latinos in the United States less than five years had a 16 percent rate of obesity, and after five years this had increased to 22 percent. Latinos born in the United States and U.S. citizens in general had a 30 percent rate of obesity. There were similar progressions for hypertension and type two diabetes.

For some natives of the United States, it is a challenge to find the right balance between calories taken in and calories burned, or between eating and exercise. One Latina proposed this explanation, "Before I moved to the United States, I ate a big breakfast and a heavy lunch to get enough calories for a long day at work. When I bought food from a street vendor, it was either fruit or corn on the cob. Sweet, fatty snacks were not as common as they are here, where anything placed on the table at the office disappears by lunchtime. I got substantial exercise walking to and from the bus stop. Here there is a surplus of food, and I drive everywhere because either there is no public transportation or it's too cold to walk. Since I do not burn as many calories, I have to eat much smaller portions and be especially careful not to eat too many of my favorite carbohydrates, like rice and yucca."

La banana («el guineo» en la región del Caribe)

Chapter 8
El examen físico

By the end of this chapter you will know the Spanish terms necessary to conduct the physical exam portion of a history and physical. You will be able to ask how long various symptoms have been present, to ask what makes things better or worse, to describe bowel habits, and to explain and schedule referrals for common tests. If this class can be held in an exam room, this may help you form kinesthetic memory cues and to think of the questions and expressions that you most frequently use in this setting.

⌕ Clarify the Chief Complaint

Vocabulario: El tiempo (Time)

¿Con qué frecuencia?	How often?
nunca, jamás	never
casi nunca	almost never
de vez en cuando	once in a while
a veces	at times
una o dos veces al día	once or twice a day
a menudo	often
frecuentemente	frequently
siempre; Es continuo.	always; It's continuous.
Va y viene.	It comes and goes.
¿Desde cuándo?	Since when?
desde esta mañana	since this morning
desde anoche	since last night
desde ayer	since yesterday
desde el lunes	since Monday
desde hace tres días	since three days ago
desde la semana pasada	since last week

¿Cuánto tiempo hace?   How long has it been?
    Hace una hora.   It's been an hour.
    Hace dos días.   It's been two days.

¿Cuánto tiempo dura el dolor?   How long does the pain last?
    Dura de una a dos horas.   It lasts for one or two hours.
    Dura varios días.   It lasts for several days.

 ## Estructura: ¿Cuánto tiempo hace?
(How Long Has It Been?)

- The verb *hacer* means "to do" and "to make." *Hacer* is irregular only in the first person singular (*yo*).

yo	hago	Hago la cena a las ocho de la noche.
tú	haces	¿Haces ejercicio todos los días?
él, ella, usted	hace	Mi mamá hace una torta deliciosa.
nosotros/as	hacemos	¿Qué hacemos hoy?
ellos, ellas, ustedes	hacen	Mis amigos no hacen nada hoy.

- The verb *hacer* is used in expressions of time. In such expressions, it is used in the third person singular.

¿Cuánto tiempo hace?	How long has it been?
Hace dos días.	It has been two days.
¿Hace mucho?	Has it been a long time?
Hace poco.	It has been a short time.

- To ask how long a symptom or condition has been happening, use the formula *¿Cuánto tiempo hace que* + verb phrase.

  ¿Cuánto tiempo hace que usted usa insulina?

  ¿Cuánto tiempo hace que le duele el brazo?

- In response, or to say how long the symptom or condition has been happening, use the formula *hace* + period of time + *que* + verb phrase.

  Hace dos años que uso insulina.

  Hace una semana que me duele el brazo.

- Word order is not critical. You may also hear the following.

  ¿Hace cuánto tiempo que tiene diabetes?

  ¿Qué tiempo hace que sufre de asma?

  Sufro de asma hace dos años.

- As another alternative you can ask *¿Desde cuándo?* which means "Since when?"

¿Desde cuándo le duele el ojo?	Since when does your eye hurt?
Me duele desde esta mañana.	It hurts since this morning.

 8.1 Actividad

When your partner makes the following statements, ask him or her how long it has been happening, as in the example. Your partner may answer ad lib. Switch roles when you are halfway through.

> Example: Student 1:   Me duele la espalda.
>
> Student 2:   ¿Cuánto tiempo hace que le duele la espalda?
>
> Student 1:   Hace tres días que me duele la espalda.

A. Tengo fiebre.	F. Toso mucho.
B. Estoy enfermo.	G. Estoy casado/a.
C. Tengo hipertensión.	H. Mi hijo tiene gripe.
D. Me duele la garganta.	I. Tengo dolor de cabeza.
E. Tengo rigidez en el cuello.	J. Mi suegra vive con nosotros.

8.2 Actividad

That was a little tedious; this is more challenging. After time-limited preparation, present to the class a less-scripted dialogue in which you and your partner are patient and practitioner. Exchange greetings and introductions, identify the chief complaint, and elicit answers to "how long," "since when," "how often," and "how long does it last." Here is an example, followed by sample chief complaints (*motivos de la consulta*) and their translations. As an alternative, feel free to offer your own.

> Example: Student 1:   ¿Qué le pasa?
> Student 2:   Me duele la mandíbula.
> Student 1:   ¿Cuánto tiempo hace que le duele la mandíbula?
> Student 2:   Hace una semana que me duele mucho.
> Student 1:   Cuando le duele, ¿cuánto tiempo dura el dolor?
> Student 2:   Dura una hora o hasta dos horas.

A. Tengo ardor en el estómago.   My stomach burns.
B. Tengo sudores por la noche.   I have night sweats.
C. Se me hinchan los tobillos.   My ankles get swollen.
D. Me da jaquecas.   I get migraines.
E. Cuando orino me arde mucho.   When I urinate it burns a lot.

 8.3 Actividad

Active listening, or reviewing the message with the speaker, is a way to seek confirmation of whether we understood correctly. First, ask questions as needed to fill in the required information. The patient should provide information ad lib. After you have written the information, repeat or summarize the patient's message until the patient confirms that you have correctly understood. For example, *Hace una semana que le duele la espalda todos los días, y el dolor dura de dos hasta tres horas. ¿Verdad?*

1. Motivo de la consulta: _____.

2. Desde cuando: _____.

3. Frecuencia: _____.

4. Duración: _____.

Here are more sample chief complaints.

A.	Me duele el pecho.	My chest hurts.
B.	Se me hinchan las manos.	My hands get swollen.
C.	Me duele la cabeza.	My head aches.
D.	Tengo dolor en el abdomen.	My belly hurts.
E.	Sangro por la nariz.	My nose bleeds.

UN CHISTE

Doctor:	¿Qué le pasa?
Paciente:	Tengo amnesia total.
Doctor:	¿Desde cuándo tiene amnesia?
Paciente:	Desde el sábado ocho de mayo del 2008 a las dos en punto de la tarde.
Doctor:	¡Caramba!

Vocabulario: ¿Qué le mejora? (What Makes You Better?)

mejorar	to improve
empeorar	to worsen

Preguntas útiles

¿Qué le ayuda?	What helps you?
¿Qué le mejora?	What makes you better?
¿Qué le empeora?	What makes you worse?
¿Qué le hace sentir mejor?	What makes you feel better?
¿Qué le hace sentir peor?	What makes you feel worse?
¿Hay algo que le mejora?	Is there something that makes you better?

Vocabulario: Las materias fecales (Bowel Movements)

heces, materias fecales	feces
defecar, evacuar, ensuciar hacer pupú	to move one's bowels, to "go poop" (juvenile)
¿Tiene diarrea o estreñimiento?	Do you have diarrhea or constipation?
¿Con qué frecuencia evacua?	How often do you move your bowels?
¿De qué color es la materia fecal?	What color is the stool?
¿Hay sangre?	Is there blood?

¿Cómo son las heces (materias fecales)?   How are the stools?
   ¿Son . . .   Are they . . .
    . . . blancas?   . . . white?
    . . . verdosas?   . . . greenish?
    . . . como la brea?   . . . like tar?
    . . . flotantes?   . . . floating?
    . . . blandas?   . . . soft?
    . . . líquidas?   . . . liquid?
    . . . mocosas?   . . . with mucus?
    . . . duras y secas?   . . . hard and dry?

 ## 8.4 Actividad

You are a gastroenterologist. Your partner suffers from a bowel problem. Find out what the problem is, and whether anything helps or makes it worse. Give advice as indicated. Recycle important vocabulary from chapter 7 and give advice about drinking water, exercising regularly, and eating fiber (papaya is a recognized home remedy for constipation).

Recall that in chapter 2 we asked, *¿Cómo está el dolor?* and answered, *No duele; duele un poco,* and so forth. In chapter 3 we asked, *¿Dónde está el dolor?* and reported changes in the pain (*Está peor; Está igual;* and *Está mejor*). Use the verb *ser* to describe the character of the pain. *¿Cómo es el dolor?* asks what kind of pain it is. Here is some new vocabulary that will be useful when refining the chief complaint.

   ¿Es un dolor sordo?   Is it a dull ache?
   ¿Es un dolor agudo/punzante? Is it a sharp pain?
   ¿Es un dolor quemante/ardiente? Is it a burning pain?
   ¿Es un dolor pesado?   Is it a crushing pain?
   ¿Es un dolor que corre? Is it a radiating pain?

 ## Video Program: *La pulmonía*

Watch the *Demostración* for chapter 8, in which Dr. Vargas asks questions to help clarify Mr. Vargas's complaint of malaise. Do the comprehension exercise that follows.

  Sr. Flores: Doctor, no me siento bien. Estoy enfermo.
  Dr. Vargas: ¿Qué le pasa?

Sr. Flores:	Toso mucho.
Dr. Vargas:	¿Tiene dolor?
Sr. Flores:	Me duele el pecho cuando toso y cuando respiro profundamente.
Dr. Vargas:	¿Cuánto tiempo hace que tiene la tos?
Sr. Flores:	Hace tres o cuatro días.
Dr. Vargas:	¿Desde cuándo le duele el pecho cuando tose?
Sr. Flores:	Hoy es viernes. Desde el martes entonces.
Dr. Vargas:	Cuando tose, ¿hay flema?
Sr. Flores:	Sí, una flema verdosa.
Dr. Vargas:	¿Hay sangre cuando tose?
Sr. Flores:	No.
Dr. Vargas:	¿Tiene fiebre?
Sr. Flores:	Ayer tuve una fiebre de treinta y nueve grados.
Dr. Vargas:	¿Hay algo que mejora el dolor y la fiebre?
Sr. Flores:	No me gusta tomar los calmantes, pero ayer tomé un calmante.
Dr. Vargas:	¿Qué tomó?
Sr. Flores:	Dos ibuprofén.
Dr. Vargas:	Le quitó la fiebre el ibuprofén?
Sr. Flores:	Sí, me mejoró bastante pero en cuatro horas la fiebre y el dolor volvieron.
Dr. Vargas:	Usted tiene una tos con dolor y fiebre alta de hace tres días. El ibuprofén ayuda pero los síntomas vuelven. Tiene esputo verdoso. Puede ser una pulmonía. Voy a escucharle los pulmones ahora. Respire profundamente. Respire por favor. Respire. Otra vez. Otra vez. Y una vez más. Señor Flores, usted tiene pulmonía. Es una infección bacteriana del pulmón izquierdo. Voy a recetarle un antibiótico. Levofloxacino, quinientos miligramos, por la boca, una vez al día por diez días, número diez. Lleve esta receta a la farmacia. Es para un antibiótico. Tome una pastilla todos los días por diez días. Es importante tomar todo el medicamento. Va a sentirse mejor pronto. Tenemos que hacer una radiografía del pecho hoy. Rosmery le va a hacer la cita.

8.5 Ejercicio

Test your comprehension by reading the following paragraph aloud, choosing the correct words or phrases from the options in parentheses.

> El señor Flores está (bien, enfermo). El problema es que hace tres o cuatro días que le duele (el pecho, la cabeza) cuando (evacua, tose). Cuando tose hay (flema, sangre) y el pobre don Francisco tiene (fiebre, calor). El doctor Vargas dice que el señor Flores tiene (un virus, pulmonía) y que necesita (antibióticos y una radiografía del pecho, una radiografía del pecho y un calmante). Tiene que tomar los antibióticos (por suero intravenoso, por vía oral). Pronto el señor Flores va a estar (peor, mejor).

 ## Conduct a Physical Examination

 ### Estructura: El verbo *ir* para hablar del futuro
(The Verb *Ir* to Talk About the Future)

- The verb *ir* is an irregular verb and means "to go." These are the forms of the verb in the present tense.

yo	voy	Voy a la clínica todos los viernes.
tú	vas	¿Vas al dentista cada seis meses?
él, ella, usted	va	¿Va usted a la farmacia hoy?
nosotros/as	vamos	Vamos a la cafetería para comer.
ellos, ellas, ustedes	van	Mis hijos van a la casa de su abuela.

- The verb *ir* can also be used to talk about something that "is going to" happen in the future. Use the verb *ir* (conjugated in the present tense), the preposition *a,* and a verb infinitive. Note that the *a* does not translate literally.

Vas a estar bien.	You are going to be fine.
Voy a consultar con un cirujano.	I am going to consult with a surgeon.

- When the direct or indirect objects are used, they can be placed either before the conjugated verb or as a suffix to the verb infinitive. It makes no difference which.

La doctora le va a recetar algo.	La doctora va a recetarle algo.
El enfermero lo va a examinar.	El enfermero va a examinarlo.

- *Vamos* also means "Let's." Its use highlights collaboration (without implying "talking down to" as it might in English).

Vamos a ver.	Let's see.
Vamos a esperar.	Let's wait; let's hope.
Vamos a tomarle la temperatura.	Let's take your temperature.

Estructura: Las contracciones *al* y *del*
(The Contractions *al* and *del*)

- The preposition *a* means "to." When followed by the definite article *el,* the two are contracted to form the word *al.* There is no contraction with *la, las,* or *los.*

Voy a la clínica.	I go (I'm going) to the clinic.
Voy *al* hospital.	I go (I'm going) to the hospital.

- The "personal *a*" also contracts with the definite article *el.*

Examino al señor Ulloa ahora.	I'll examine Señor Ulloa now.

- The preposition *de* means "of" or "from" and is used to express possession as well. When *de* is followed by the definite article *el,* the two are contracted to form the word *del.* There is no contraction with *de la, de las,* or *de los.*

Le llamo de la clínica.	I'm calling (you, him, her) from the clinic.
Le llamo *del* hospital.	I'm calling (you, him, her) from the hospital.
¿Cuál es el teléfono del Sr. Vega?	What is Sr. Vega's telephone number?

8.6 Reciclaje

Recall the food vocabulary from chapter 7 while practicing expressions with *ir + a +* infinitive to talk about what you plan to do at the big party. When it is your turn, you must first recite the plans of each student that went before you, as in the example. Be creative!

Example:	Bill:	Voy a la fiesta y voy a comer arroz. ¿Vas a la fiesta, Bob?
	Bob:	Sí. Voy a la fiesta. Vas a comer arroz, pero no me gusta el arroz. Voy a comer torta y tomar leche. ¿Vas a la fiesta, Ann?
	Ann:	Sí. Voy a la fiesta. Bill va a comer arroz. Tú vas a comer torta y tomar leche. Pero no voy a comer nada. Voy a bailar.

8.7 Actividad

This is a matching exercise. Your partner announces that he or she is off to one of the destinations listed below. Ask why, and your partner will select an appropriate response, as in the example. (Don't read straight across.) Remember to contract *a* and *el*.

Example: Student 1:   Voy al consultorio.
            Student 2:   ¿Para qué vas al consultorio?
            Student 1:   Voy para chequearme la presión.

Lugares	*Propósitos (Purposes)*
La clínica	para una cirugía
El consultorio	para un análisis de sangre
El hospital	para un examen físico
El laboratorio	para comprar una receta
La farmacia	para una radiografía del pecho

 8.8 Actividad

Play the jealous roommate. Your partner announces that he or she is going out, *¡Me voy!* Ask where he or she is going, and let it degenerate from there. A few groups may wish to demonstrate their transaction for the class. Here are some sample questions.

¿Por qué te vas?	Why (for what reason) are you going?
¿Para qué vas?	Why (for what purpose) are you going?
¿Con quién vas?	With whom are you going?
¿Qué vas a hacer?	What are you going to do?
¿A qué hora vienes?	What time are you coming back?

Vocabulario: El examen físico (The Physical Exam)

mirar	to look, to look at
escuchar, auscultar	to listen, to listen to, to auscultate
tocar, presionar, palpar	to touch, to press, to palpate
dar golpecitos, percutir	to tap, to percuss
mirar la garganta	to look at the throat
el estetoscopio	stethoscope
escuchar los pulmones	to listen to the lungs
escuchar el corazón	to listen to the heart
pesar al niño (a la niña)	to weigh the child

Escuchar (auscultar)

Tocar (palpar)

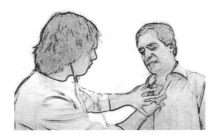

Dar golpecitos (percutir)

medir* al bebé (a la bebé)	to measure the baby
medir el nivel de oxígeno en la sangre	measure the blood oxygen level
tomar la temperatura	to take the temperature
tomar la presión arterial	to take the blood pressure
poner un suero	to put in an IV
poner una inyección	to give an injection
poner una curita	to put on a band-aid
poner puntos	to suture
sacar puntos	to remove stitches

*Medir is a stem-changing verb (*mido, mides, mide, medimos, miden*).

sacar sangre para un análisis	to draw blood for a test
hacer un electrocardiograma	to take an electrocardiogram
hacer un examen digital de la próstata	to do a digital exam of the prostate

When treating a minor injury, a mother may say, *Sana, sana, culito de rana; si no te sanas hoy, te sanas mañana* (Heal, heal, toad's little tail; if you don't heal today, you'll heal tomorrow).

 ## 8.9 Actividad

Two students playing the roles of practitioner and patient will mime (most of) the activities listed above, in random order. The rest of the class will say what is happening, for example, *Le pone un suero intravenoso.* This may be particularly beneficial to visual and kinesthetic learners. Which type of learner are you?

Voy a mirarle los oídos.

 ## 8.10 Drama imprevisto

Combine the physical exam vocabulary with the formula *ir a* + infinitive. Each student should choose one of the following patient chief complaints, although the instructor may choose to assign them by letter. Students then circulate in the classroom. Tell someone your chief complaint, and he or she will say what will happen next in the physical exam. That person then tells you his or her chief complaint, and it is your turn to say what you plan to do next. When finished, find another partner.

> Example: Sufro del corazón. Tengo taquicardia.
> Voy a escucharle el corazón.

A. Tengo fiebre.
B. Tengo una cortadura.
C. Me duele la garganta.
D. Sufro de asma y tengo la respiración corta.
E. Hace diez días que tengo puntos en la pierna.
F. Necesito la vacuna antitetánica (tetanus vaccine).
G. Mi bebé no come mucho y está demasiado chiquito.
H. Estoy aquí para chequearme la glucosa en la sangre.
I. Tengo pulmonía y necesito antibióticos por suero.
J. Sufro de la presión alta. Me duele la cabeza y estoy mareado.

8.11 Actividad

Associations and practice help with memorization. A volunteer will write *mirar, auscultar, palpar,* and *percutir* at the top of sentence-wide columns on the board. Students will brainstorm questions and statements associated with each column header. For example, under *auscultar* you may include, *Voy a auscultarle la arteria carótida para ver si hay un soplo. ¿Toma medicamento para bajar el colesterol? ¿Sigue una dieta baja en grasa?* If the activity goes well, try it with *poner* and *medir* as well.

 Video Program: *El examen físico*

Watch the *Trama* for chapter 8, in which Dr. Vargas completes the physical exam portion of a history and physical exam on Sr. Flores. Then do the exercise that follows.

Dr. Vargas:	Su temperatura y presión arterial son excelentes. Vamos a hacerle un examen físico ahora. ¿Está listo?
Sr. Flores:	Sí.
Dr. Vargas:	Muy bien. Primero voy a mirarle los ojos. Mire el punto de luz. Bien. ¿Tiene problemas con la vista?
Sr. Flores:	No tengo problemas con la vista. No uso lentes.
Dr. Vargas:	Muy bien. Ahora, voy a mirarle los oídos. ¿Le duelen los oídos?
Sr. Flores:	No.
Dr. Vargas:	Ahora, voy a mirarle la nariz y la garganta. Abra la boca, saque la lengua y diga «a-a-a-h-h-h». Muy bien. Ahora voy a tocarle el cuello. Bien. Ahora, voy a escucharle los pulmones y el corazón. Respire profundamente por la boca. De nuevo. Muy bien. Acuéstese por favor. Respire profundamente. Otra vez. Otra vez. Y una vez más. Ahora voy a darle golpecitos en el pecho. Ahora, voy a tocarle el abdomen. Dígame si le duele. Respire profundamente. Otra vez. Muy bien. Ahora, por favor, levante las piernas y trate de resistir cuando yo empujo. Muy bien. La otra pierna. Perfecto. Ahora voy a hacerle un examen de la próstata a través del ano. Por favor, póngase la bata.

la bata	robe

8.12 Actividad

Identify statements or questions that would likely go along with each of the following announcements during a typical physical examination, as in the example.

Example: Voy a mirarle los ojos.
                      Accompaniment: ¿Usa lentes? ¿Tiene problemas con
                                                         la vista?

A. Voy a mirarle los oídos.
B. Voy a mirarle la nariz y la garganta.
C. Voy a tocarle el cuello.
D. Voy a escucharle los pulmones y el corazón.
E. Voy a darle golpecitos en el pecho.
F. Voy a presionarle el abdomen.
G. Voy a hacerle un examen de la próstata a través del recto.

 ## 8.13 Actividad

Practice reading this sample exam while acting it out with your partner, who can answer questions ad lib.

MOTIVO DE LA CONSULTA

Favor de quitarse la ropa y ponerse la bata del hospital. Vuelvo pronto. ¿Qué le pasa? ¿Cuánto tiempo hace que usted tiene este problema (estos síntomas)? ¿Desde cuándo? ¿Con qué frecuencia? ¿Qué tiempo dura/n (la fiebre, los síntomas . . .)? ¿Toma usted algún medicamento todos los días? ¿Es usted alérgico a algún medicamento o a alguna comida? ¿Qué mejora el problema? ¿Qué lo empeora? ¿Fuma usted? ¿Toma usted bebidas alcohólicas? ¿Usa drogas, como la cocaína, la heroína o la marihuana?

bata	gown

EL EXAMEN FÍSICO

Voy a mirarle los ojos. Voy a mirarle los oídos. ¿Le duelen los oídos? Voy a mirarle la nariz y la garganta. Abra la boca, saque la lengua y diga «a-a-a-h-h-h». Míreme la nariz. Mire a ese punto de luz. ¿Tiene problema de la vista? ¿Usa lentes?

Voy a escucharle los pulmones y el corazón. Respire profundamente por la boca. Otra vez. Tosa. Tosa otra vez. ¿Hay flema cuando tose? ¿De qué color es la flema? ¿Es de un color claro, amarillo o verdoso? Cuando tose, ¿hay sangre? ¿Le duele cuando tose? ¿Tiene dolor de pecho? ¿Es un dolor fuerte (punzante, quemante, pesado, continuo)? ¿Tiene a veces los tobillos hinchados?

Favor de acostarse (lie down). ¿Tiene dolor en el estómago? ¿Le duele la barriga? ¿Le duele cuando presiono aquí? ¿Tiene diarrea? ¿Tiene estreñimiento? Cuando usted orina, ¿hay sangre? ¿Hay sensación de ardor? ¿Hay picazón? ¿Hay una secreción blanca? ¿Tiene relaciones sexuales? Tengo que examinarle la próstata a través del ano con el dedo, usando un guante. Levántese y ponga los codos en la camilla. Tengo que introducir un dedo para tocar la próstata. Es un poco incómodo, pero terminamos rápido.

A Word That Says a Lot: *Así*

Using only one Spanish word, you can teach a child how to tie shoelaces or to button a shirt. What word is that useful and versatile? When you are not sure how to verbalize an instruction, simply demonstrate the action you want the patient to perform and say the word *así,* which in this context means "in this way" or "like this."

Schedule Follow-up Tests

Vocabulario: Algunos análisis y procedimientos
(Some Tests and Procedures)

El laboratorio (The Laboratory)

la biopsia	biopsy
el cultivo	culture
el análisis de orina	urine test
el análisis de sangre	blood test
el análisis de glucosa en la sangre	blood glucose test
la concentración de alcohol en la sangre	blood alcohol level

Formas de radiografía (Forms of X-Ray)

la radiografía, los rayos equis	x-ray
la placa	film, x-ray
la tomografía computarizada	CT scan
el mamograma	mammogram
el angiograma	angiogram
las imágenes por resonancia magnética	MRI

Pruebas de los órganos (Tests of the Organs)

la broncoscopia	bronchoscopy
la espirometría	spirometry
el electrocardiograma	EKG
la prueba de estrés	stress test
la supervisión Holter	Holter monitor
el electroencefalograma	EEG
la colonoscopia	colonoscopy
la endoscopia	endoscopy

 8.14 Ejercicio

Play a *Jeopardy*-like game. Take turns reading the following simplified descriptions of tests. After each reading, students guess by asking *¿Qué es un (una) _____ ?*

A. Es una radiografía de una vena o arteria. Antes de hacerla, se introduce un catéter en una vena o arteria. Se inyecta una solución, o medio de contraste. La prueba es para descubrir si hay depósitos de colesterol u otra enfermedad.

B. Es una grabadora portátil para grabar información del ritmo cardíaco durante un tiempo, como un electrocardiograma.

> *grabadora portátil*
> a portable recorder

C. Son para hacer unas imágenes muy específicas de una parte del cuerpo sin usar rayos equis.

D. Es un procedimiento en que se introduce un tubo o un catéter por la nariz o por la boca para examinar los bronquios o los pulmones.

E. Es una prueba en la cual un patólogo examina una muestra de tejido con un microscopio para descubrir si hay cáncer u otra enfermedad.

F. Es un examen de rayos equis de los senos para descubrir si hay tumores o quistes.

> *muestra de tejido* tissue sample
> *O* changes to *u* before words that begin with *o* or *ho*.
> *quiste* cyst

G. Es una prueba en la cual el paciente exhala en un instrumento que mide cuánto aire entra y sale de los pulmones para medir la capacidad respiratoria de los pulmones.

H. Es una exploración del interior del intestino grueso con un colonoscopio.

8.15 Drama imprevisto

Look at the photo of the girl who underwent a CT scan. You are the x-ray technician and your partner is the patient, who suffers from persistent headaches. Demonstrate an interview in which you introduce yourself to the girl and explain the procedure. Remember to use the familiar (*tú*) form of the verbs. The class may play the role of the girl's family.

La tomografía computarizada

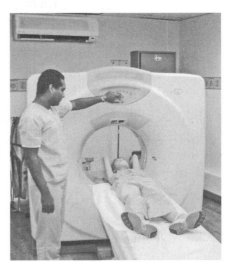

Soy técnico de radiografía.

Vocabulario: Haciendo citas
(Scheduling Appointments)

de/por* la mañana	in the morning
de/por la tarde	in the afternoon/evening
de/por la noche	in the nighttime
de una vez	at once
mañana	tomorrow
pasado mañana	the day after tomorrow
la semana que viene	next week
dentro de dos semanas	within two weeks
el mes que viene	next month

*Note that *de* is used when a specific time is mentioned, as in *Tomo el medicamento a las cinco de la mañana.* *Por* is used when a specific hour is not mentioned, as in *Tomo el medicamento por la mañana.*

el año que viene	next year

Preguntas útiles

¿Puede venir el lunes a las cinco?	Can you come on Monday at five?

8.16 Actividad

Recommend to your partner that he or she have one of the tests or procedures. Describe something about the test and answer any questions that arise.

> Example: análisis de glucosa en la sangre

> Usted necesita un análisis de glucosa en la sangre. Tenemos que sacarle una gota de sangre del dedo para determinar cuánta glucosa, o azúcar, hay en la sangre.

8.17 Actividad

Role-play a receptionist and patient making an appointment for one of the following tests or procedures. Make the appointment for a time that is not only convenient to both the clinic and the patient but within the indicated time guidelines as well.

A. sacar los puntos	(dentro de dos semanas)
B. hacer un análisis de sangre	(dentro de una semana)
C. una endoscopía	(dentro de un mes)
D. un electroencefalograma	(mañana)
E. un angiograma	(la semana que viene)
F. un análisis de orina	(dentro de una semana)
G. un electrocardiograma	(dentro de dos semanas)

8.18 Drama imprevisto

Look at the photograph of Dr. Willie Contreras examining a patient. What is he saying? Using the blank *Historia clínica,* reenact the examination with a partner. Note that the abbreviations on the form are for *presión arterial* (PA), *frecuencia cardíaca* (FC), and *frecuencia respiratoria* (FR). Several dyads should demonstrate their interviews for the class.

El doctor Contreras Medina

Historia clínica

Fecha: _____

Apellidos: _____ Nombre: _____

Fecha de nacimiento: _____

Sexo: _____ Nacionalidad: _____ Teléfono: _____

Motivo de consulta: _____

Historia familiar: _____

Antecedentes médicos: _____

Medicamentos: _____

Alergias: _____

Tabaco, alcohol, drogas: _____

PA _____ FC _____ FR _____ Altura _____ Peso _____

Cuello _____ Tórax _____ Pulmones _____

Abdomen _____ Extremidades _____

Impresión diagnóstica _____

_____

Tratamiento _____

_____

_____

Firma

Cultural Note: A Dynamic Process

Culture is dynamic, and frontiers are disappearing. Culture is imported and exported. Countries and cultures are interdependent, and no group is isolated. Groups are penetrated by outside cultures, for example via products and media, such as Internet, television, and advertisements. People export culture as they migrate. Then they acculturate gradually, generally in three generations, although children are fast. The host culture, or receiving culture, is changed also. Thus, an individual's culture of origin and the receiving mainstream culture are not always vastly different. As the world shrinks, flattens, and globalizes, cultures encounter situations that are easily assimilated and others that are not, forcing them to adapt.

Immigrants and others who have cross-cultural experiences may decide that there are aspects of both cultures that they like and dislike. They may either consciously or unconsciously cling to—or reject—specific aspects of their culture of origin while embracing aspects of the host culture. In the chapter 7 video, Sra. Flores says, "*A Francisco le gusta comer su pollo frito y su salami. Sí, tienen mucha grasa, pero quiero hacerle la comida que a él le gusta.*" She may have been experiencing conflict between a traditional gender role and the new information that she was learning about diets. In chapter 9, Rosmery compares Halloween and *El día de los muertos* and laments, "*Mis hijos están muy americanizados* (My children are very Americanized)."

Language competency is an essential component of acculturation. Families may resist acculturation by recognizing that the way to preserve cultural views and traditions is to speak Spanish at home. Children, on the other hand, may resist speaking Spanish, as a way to avoid appearing different among peers. This may create intergenerational communication gaps. The same children may one day regret not speaking Spanish, and decide to take classes in order to rediscover their heritage or connect with elderly family members.

Children may be pressured to choose between cultures rather than to skillfully navigate both worlds. Families eventually choose what parts of culture to preserve and what to leave behind in order to comfortably assimilate. With some experience, families and individuals may function very successfully in both cultures. For example, a wedding planned by a Latin

American family may not begin at the time printed on the invitation. This is because it must begin when everyone is ready, and all guests have arrived. The same family, when scheduling a business appointment, may insist, *Empezamos a la una, hora americana* (We'll start at one o'clock, American time), to encourage punctuality.

During the process of acculturation individuals may feel lonely, frustrated, and incompetent to function in the new society. Parents may struggle with communicating with their children's teachers or pediatrician. They may not understand why their children would rather play with friends than go to Tío Alfredo's birthday party, and wonder why neighbors do not collaborate in rearing each other's children. Relief is available in enclaves, or neighborhoods that keep the cultural identity of their members while coexisting with the surrounding dominant culture. These enclaves also provide great opportunities for dominant culture members to have cross-cultural experiences.

Models for comparing health across ethnic groups have focused on genetics and racial differences, on cultural lifestyles (diet and exercise, for example), on socioeconomic status, and on proximity to pathogens (living in cities, for example). Although each view has merit, controlling socioeconomic factors in health care access (literacy, insurance, transportation, and the linguistic competency of the patient and provider) can erase some of the health differences between groups.

Chapter 9
«¿Qué pasó?»

In this chapter you will learn to talk about things that occurred in the past. You will learn to ask, "What happened?" and "Did you take your medicine?" You will be able to ask, "When was the last time that you . . . ?" You'll also be able to talk about habitual actions in the past and to ask, "What was going on when this happened?" Contextual themes will incorporate pre-surgical interviews, cardiac rehabilitation, and the work of visiting nurses and paramedics.

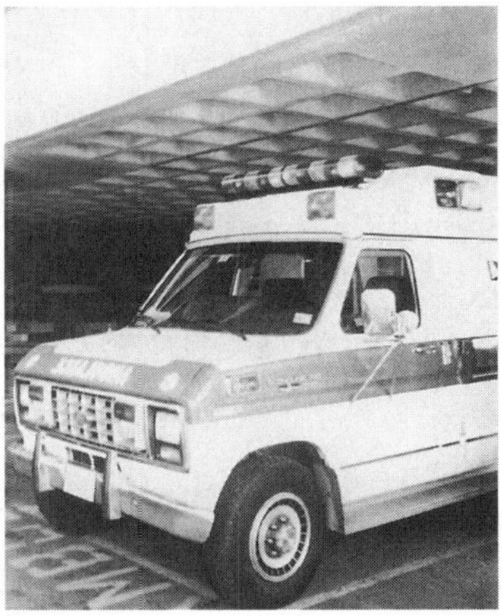

Ask What Happened

Vocabulario: Tiempos pasados (Times in the Past)

esta mañana	this morning
hoy	today
anoche	last night
ayer	yesterday
anteayer	the day before yesterday
el jueves pasado	last Thursday
la semana pasada	last week
el mes pasado	last month
el año pasado	last year

lunes	martes	miércoles	jueves	viernes
anteayer	ayer	hoy	mañana	pasado mañana

9.1 Actividad

Share with the class experiences you have had speaking Spanish with your patients and their families. How did they react? How did you feel? What other grammar or vocabulary do you need? In which circumstances will it be helpful to be able to talk about things that happened in the past?

 9.2 Actividad

Over the next two weeks, prepare a project to present to the class. Work with partners if you wish. This may be a skit in which you examine or educate a patient, or it may be a graphic presentation, such as a patient satisfaction questionnaire or a poster or educational pamphlet related to your specific area of work. The instructor may ask for a draft for editing and coaching before you finalize your project.

 ### Estructura: El pretérito de los verbos regulares
(The Preterit of Regular Verbs)

- There are two simple past tenses in Spanish, the preterit and the imperfect. We shall learn both. Let's start with the preterit tense, which is used to describe actions that were completed in the past. The preterit tense is formed (as is the present tense) by changing the form of the verb according to the subject (who or what is doing the action). Notice that the first and third persons have written accents that guide you to stress that syllable when speaking. The other forms are stressed on the next-to-last syllable. Here are the forms of the verb *tomar* in the preterit. All regular *-ar* verbs follow this pattern.

yo	tomé	I took, I did take
tú	tomaste	you took, you did take
él, ella, usted	tomó	he, she, you took, did take
nosotros/as	tomamos	we took, did take
ellos, ellas, ustedes	tomaron	they, you took, did take

- The preterit of regular verbs ending in *-er* and *-ir* is formed similarly by changing the form of the verb according to the subject. Here are the forms of the verb *comer* in the preterit. All regular *-er* and *-ir* verbs follow the same pattern.

yo	comí	Comí arroz anoche.
tú	comiste	¿Comiste bien?
él, ella, usted	comió	Juan no comió nada.
nosotros/as	comimos	Ada y yo comimos en la cafetería.
ellos, ellas, ustedes	comieron	Los niños comieron en la escuela.

- The first person plural, or *nosotros,* form is the same in both the present and the preterit tenses. They are differentiated by the context.

  Nosotros siempre tomamos café por la mañana (*present tense*).
  Ayer tomamos una taza de té antes de salir para el hospital
  (*past tense*).

 9.3 Actividad

Ask about treatment adherence. Ask your partner whether the following people took their medicine or otherwise followed the plan for today. Switch halfway through. When everyone is finished, report treatment (non)-compliance to the class.

> Example:　el paciente, tomar el medicamento hoy
> 　　　　　Student 1:　¿Tomó el paciente el medicamento hoy?
> 　　　　　Student 2:　Sí, el paciente tomó el medicamento hoy.

A. tú, tomar la aspirina esta mañana
B. su madre, tomar la codeína anoche
C. usted, usar la insulina
D. los niños, usar el inhalador
E. Maribel, comer frutas hoy

F. el señor Vega, tomar el antibiótico hoy
G. ustedes, tomar las vitaminas con el desayuno
H. la paciente, usar el oxígeno
I. Juan, comprar el jarabe
J. la doctora, escribir la receta para mi hermano

 9.4 Actividad

This is a *novela,* and you are the voice actors! In our *novela,* Rafalito takes an overdose of his medication, his girlfriend Isabela calls 911, and Pedro the *paramédico* saves the day by arriving in time to take him to the hospital. Volunteer to play Rafalito (*el paciente*); Isabela (*la novia de Rafalito*); and Pedro (*el paramédico*). Then exaggerate the emotions as you read the story aloud. You'll need to determine the subject of each verb in parentheses and conjugate it in the preterit mode of the past tense as you read.

> Isabela:　　Rafalito es mi novio y lo amo. Lo amo mucho pero es un hombre difícil y no puedo vivir con él.
> Rafalito:　　Isabela es mi novia y la amo. La amo muchísimo pero ella dice que no puede vivir conmigo. No puedo vivir sin ella. Quiero morir. Hace diez minutos que (tomar) una sobredosis de mis medicamentos.

Isabela: Ay, Rafalito, mi amor, mi vida, mi corazón. (Tomar) una sobredosis porque no quieres vivir sin mí. Pero Rafalito, no vas a morir, porque (llamar) al nueve-once y la ambulancia va a llegar pronto.

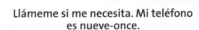

Llámeme si me necesita. Mi teléfono es nueve-once.

Pedro: [*Pedro enters the scene*] Soy Pedro, el paramédico. Estoy aquí y todo va a estar súper bien. ¿Quién (llamar) al nueve-once?

Isabela: Yo (llamar) porque mi novio (tomar) pastillas para quitarse la vida.

Pedro: Señor, ¿qué (tomar) usted?

Rafalito: Pastillas. Aquí está la botella. Son para los nervios.

Pedro: ¿Cuántas pastillas (tomar) usted?

Rafalito: (Tomar) todas. Como diez pastillas.

Pedro: ¿Cuánto tiempo hace que usted las (tomar)?

Rafalito: Hace media hora, más o menos.

Pedro: ¿(Tomar) bebidas alcohólicas también?

Rafalito: No. No bebo nunca.

Pedro: ¿(Vomitar)? ¿Tiene deseo de vomitar?

Rafalito: No. No (vomitar), pero tengo mucho sueño.

Pedro: Vamos a llevarlo al hospital. Usted va a estar súper bien.

Isabela: Pedro, tú (salvar) a mi novio. Eres buenísimo. ¿Cuál es tu número de teléfono?

Pedro: Llámeme si me necesita. Mi teléfono es nueve-once. Con su permiso, en este momento tengo que salvar una vida. Hasta luego.

 ## 9.5 Actividad

The following questions are incomplete. Choose from the list of familiar and new verbs to make lucid questions using the past tense. The context of the question should help you choose. Try them out on your partner, who will answer using complete sentences ad lib. Switch roles halfway through.

beber	to drink	salir	to leave
cuidar	to care for	tragar	to swallow
escribir	to write	ver*	to see
nacer	to be born	vivir	to live

A. ¿En qué año _____ usted?

B. ¿Le _____ la doctora una receta para un diurético?

C. ¿Por cuántos años _____ sus padres con usted?

D. ¿Cuántas botellas de vino _____ los enfermeros en la fiesta?

E. _____ tú el accidente ayer?

F. ¿A qué hora _____ de tu casa esta mañana?

G. ¿_____ bien a tu padre en el hospital?

H. ¿_____ doña María la pastilla de quinientos miligramos sin problema?

9.6 Actividad

With your partner, take turns being the visiting nurse and the patient. Review the patient's list of things to do today (*Quehaceres para hoy*) and ask what has been accomplished.

Example: tomar el antibiótico
Student 1:   ¿Tomó usted el antibiótico?
Student 2:   Sí, tomé el antibiótico.
(*or*) No, no lo tomé.

Quehaceres para hoy

Tomar el antibiótico	☑
Llamar a la farmacia	☑
Cambiar el vendaje	☑
Comer una banana	☐
Usar el oxígeno	☑
Leer el periódico	☐
Llamar a la clínica	☑
Comprar la medicina	☐
Medir la glucosa	☑

*When *ver* is used in the preterit, the accents are not written.

9.7 Reciclaje

Tell about the last time that you had an appointment with a doctor, physician's assistant, or nurse practitioner. Start your sentences with *primero* (first), *después* (afterwards), *luego* (later), and *finalmente* (finally). For example, *Primero, la enfermera me tomó la temperatura y la presión arterial. Después . . .*

 9.8 Reciclaje

You are a doting parent, and your partner is, well, tolerant. You are sure your grown child must be hungry and never eats enough. Ask "way too many" questions about what he or she ate today. Here are a couple of questions to get you started. Then share your findings with the class; for example, *José nunca come lo suficiente. Hoy comió pan y tomó café esta mañana para el desayuno.*

    A. ¿Comiste bien hoy?
    B. ¿Qué comiste esta mañana?
    C. ¿Comiste mucho?
    D. ¿A qué hora desayunaste?
    E. ¿Tienes hambre?

 ### Estructura: El pretérito de algunos verbos irregulares (The Preterit of Some Irregular Verbs)

- Recall that the verb *estar* (to be) is used to talk about location, feelings, and conditions. Here are the forms of *estar* in the preterit.

estuve	Estuve enfermo anoche.
estuviste	Estuviste en la clínica ayer.
estuvo	Mi esposa estuvo en el hospital el lunes.
estuvimos	Estuvimos en casa anoche.
estuvieron	Los niños estuvieron enfermos con gripe.

- The verb *tener* (to have) takes forms that are very similar to the verb *estar*. You will remember from chapter 6 that *tener que* + infinitive means "to have to." In the preterit, we can talk about things that we *had* as well as things that we *had to do* in the past.

tuve	Tuve fiebre anoche.
tuviste	Tuviste un ataque epiléptico.
tuvo	Ana tuvo que tomar la nitroglicerina para quitar el dolor.

tuvimos   Mi hermano y yo tuvimos que cuidar a nuestro padre.

tuvieron   Mis padres tuvieron que comprar un recordatorio de
            pastillas.

- The verbs *ser* and *ir* take the same form in the preterit. They are differentiated by the context of the sentence.

fui   Fui estudiante de medicina por un año. (Ser)

fuiste   ¿Fuiste a la clínica ayer? (Ir)

fue   Hoy es domingo. Ayer fue sábado. (Ser)

fuimos   Fuimos a la clínica para consultar con el neurólogo. (Ir)

fueron   Los niños no fueron pacientes de esta clínica. (Ser)

- The verb *decir* (to say, to tell) is irregular in the first person singular of the present tense (*digo*) and also in the preterit. It normally requires the indirect object pronoun, which indicates to whom something was said.

dije   Le dije a la enfermera que mi mamá sufre de azúcar.

dijiste   ¿Qué le dijiste a tu mamá anoche, Paquito?

dijo   El pediatra me dijo que el niño no tiene infección.

dijimos   Le dijimos a Rosa que ella debe ir al consultorio.

dijeron   Varios pacientes nos dijeron que la cafetería debe
            servir arroz.

 9.9 Actividad

"Active listening" exercises rehearse the switching between subjects of the verb in conversation. Choose a partner and practice active listening as in the example, using the past tense of the verbs *estar* and *tener*. Take turns being the practitioner and the patient, and vary your responses.

Example: dolor de cabeza
            Student 1:   Estuve enfermo/a.
            Student 2:   ¡Estuviste enfermo/a! ¿Qué tuviste?
            Student 1:   Tuve dolor de cabeza.
            Student 2:   Tuviste dolor de cabeza.
            Student 1:   Tuve un dolor horrible.

A. dolor de garganta   D. resfriado
B. escalofríos   E. alergias
C. dolor en la barriga   F. catarro

 9.10 Actividad

You are visiting your patient at home. Ask whether he or she had to do the following. Another way to ask the question is, *¿Fue necesario tomar la nitroglicerina?* Try it both ways.

Example: tomar la nitroglicerina
             Student 1:   ¿Tuvo que tomar la nitroglicerina?
             Student 2:   Sí, tuve que tomar la nitroglicerina.
                          (*or*) No, no tuve que tomar la
                          nitroglicerina.

A. usar insulina
B. usar el oxígeno
C. cambiar el vendaje
D. tomar una pastilla para el dolor
E. llamar a la compañía de seguros médicos

 9.11 Ejercicio

The following were plans that Doctor Aquino had last January. Make sentences about what he did on certain days. Ask questions of classmates.

Example: El tres de enero el doctor Aquino y Ana comieron en
             la casa de Javier.

3 de enero   comer en la casa de Javier con Ana
5 de enero   visitar a doña Mercedes en Boston
11 de enero   trabajar en la clínica desde las ocho hasta las
               cinco
13 de enero   ir a la clase de inglés con don Máximo
14 de enero   consultar con el anestesiólogo
15 de enero   no comer o beber nada después de la medianoche
16 de enero   tener una colonoscopia
17 de enero   ir donde la doctora Muñoz Domínguez para un
               examen físico
30 de enero   ir de vacaciones a Venezuela

 9.12 Actividad

Read the letter that Doña Silvestrina sent to her son in the United States, and answer the questions that follow.

A. ¿Cómo se llama la madre de Felipe, y cómo está ella?
B. ¿Qué le pasó a doña Silvestrina?
C. ¿Tuvo fiebre?
D. ¿Cuál fue la temperatura?
E. ¿Cuántos días duró en el hospital?
F. ¿Qué tratamiento le dieron?
G. ¿Quién cuidó a doña Silvestrina?

> 9 de enero del 2009
>
> Querido hijo Felipe,
>
> ¿Cómo estás? Espero que estés bien.
> Estoy un poco mejor. Estuve en el hospital
> interna por 3 días. Tu hermana llamó la
> ambulancia porque tuve una fiebre de 40
> grados. Tuve una pulmonía la cual dijo
> la doctora es una infección de los
> pulmones. Me dieron antibióticos por
> suero y eso ayudó a quitar la infección y
> la fiebre.
>
> Los doctores y enfermeros fueron muy
> amables y me cuidaron bien. Escríbeme
> pronto. Gracias por lo que me mandaste.
> Que Dios todopoderoso te bendiga.
>
> Tu madre que te quiere mucho,
>
> Silvestrina Robles de Jiménez

Give Test Results

 9.13 Ejercicio

To say "test results" in Spanish, use *el resultado*. Positive and negative are *positivo/a* and *negativo/a*. As adjectives, these must agree in gender and number with the noun they modify.

El resultado fue positivo.   Las placas fueron negativas.

Tell the patient about the following tests, as in the example. If everything is fine, you can add, *Todo está bien. Gracias a Dios.* If not, give reassurance. *Tenga confianza. Todo va a estar bien.*

Example: la placa del pecho (negativa)
Tenemos el resultado de la placa del pecho. Fue negativa.

A. la prueba de embarazo (pregnancy test)   (positiva)
B. el análisis de sangre   (negativo)
C. la prueba del SIDA (AIDS test)   (negativa)
D. el sonograma de la vesícula (gall bladder)   (negativo)
E. la biopsia   (positiva)
F. la tomografía computarizada   (negativa)
G. la prueba de tuberculosis   (positiva)

 ## 9.14 Drama imprevisto

Divide the class down the middle. Designate one group as the treatment
team and the other as the patient and his or her family. Choose one of the
tests from Ejercicio 9.13, and conduct a case conference in which the treatment team gives the test result and the patient's family asks questions.
When you ask a question, identify your relationship to the patient. When
you answer a question, identify your profession.

 ## 9.15 Reciclaje

Practice using indirect objects. Remember that the object pronoun may be
placed prior to a conjugated verb or attached to the end of an infinitive as
a suffix.

> Example: Dije que no necesita una cita. (a usted)
>   Le dije a usted que no necesita una cita.

A. La doctora dijo que tiene amigdalitis.   (a Juan)
B. El paciente dijo que tiene dolor.   (a mí)
C. Yo dije que debe tomar el medicamento.   (al paciente)
D. Voy a chequear la presión de sangre.   (a sus padres)
E. Voy a poner una inyección.   (a Magali)
F. El doctor dijo que Ana necesita cirugía.   (a nosotros)
G. Yo dije que todo está bien.   (a ustedes)

Conduct a Pre-Surgery Interview

Vocabulario: Antes de la cirugía (Pre-Surgery)

¿Cuándo fue la última vez que . . .	When was the last time that . . . ?
usar alcohol o drogas	to use alcohol or drugs
orinar	to urinate
evacuar, defecar	to move one's bowels
menstruar	to menstruate

empezar su período	to start your menses
beber algo	to drink something
comer algo	to eat something

¿Tiene/Usa usted . . .?	Do you have / Do you use . . .?
un aparato prostético	a prosthesis
una dentadura postiza	dentures
un diente flojo	a loose tooth
lentes o lentes de contacto	glasses or contact lenses
una peluca	a wig
problemas con el corazón	heart problems
problemas con los pulmones	lung problems

Preguntas útiles

¿Fuma? ¿Cuánto bebe? ¿Usa drogas?

¿Cuándo comenzó su último período?

¿Cuándo fue la última vez que el niño evacuó?

¿Está usted alérgico a algún medicamento?

 9.16 Actividad

Prepare and present to the class a brief pre-surgery dialogue. Your partner will be the hypothetical patient who has arrived for, say, *una colecistecto-mía*. Find out the last time that he or she ate, drank, and so on. One pair may interview a patient who is appropriate to have surgery today, and another may interview a patient who is not.

Vocabulario: Palabras tranquilizadoras (Words of Reassurance)

Todo va a estar bien.	Everything is going to be fine.
Por favor, cálmese.	Please calm down.
No tenga miedo.	Don't be afraid.
Tenga confianza.	Have trust.
No se preocupe.	Don't worry.
No te preocupes.	Don't worry (*informal*).
No va a doler.	It's not going to hurt.
Va a mejorar.	It's going to get better.
Hay que seguir adelante.	One must go on.

 9.17 Drama imprevisto

Divide into groups of two or three. Designate groups as victims or paramedics. Briefly prepare within groups, and then a group of victims and a group of paramedics face each other to improvise an ambulance call. When preparing, the victims should think of how to answer the following questions. Paramedics will have opportunities to practice words of reassurance.

> ¿Qué le pasó?
> ¿Perdió la conciencia?
> ¿Tiene dificultad para respirar?
> ¿Es usted alérgico/a a algún medicamento?
> ¿Toma algún medicamento todos los días?
> ¿Qué otros problemas de salud tiene usted?
> ¿Cuál es el nombre de su doctor?

 ## 9.18 Drama imprevisto

Look at the drawing of an emergency room. As a class, triage the characters to decide who should be seen first and why (*¿A quién debemos de atender primero?*). Next, in pairs, choose patients and demonstrate for the class unscripted conversations between patient and triage nurse to find out what happened and other necessary information. Present these in the order that they were triaged. As a special challenge, as one pair presents, another patient with a less serious problem may interrupt and question the order of triage. Be polite.

Video program: *Dolor terrible*

Watch the *Demostración* for chapter 9, in which Sra. Flores shares a recent health concern with Rosmery. Then do the activity that follows.

Rosmery:	Me gusta hablar de México.
Sra. Flores:	Ya lo veo. Es difícil estar lejos de nuestros seres queridos. Rosmery, perdona, pero tengo que hacerte una pregunta.
Rosmery:	Sí, como no.
Sra. Flores:	Hace un mes Francisco y yo fuimos a un restaurante argentino, para celebrar nuestro aniversario de bodas. Lo hacemos todos los años. Bueno, la noche comenzó bien. El restaurante era muy elegante. Francisco pidió chorizo asado y yo pedí carne asada. Sabes que el asado es famoso en los restaurantes argentinos. La carne tenía un poco de grasa. Después de la comida pedimos un café y de repente me dolió el estómago. Fue algo terrible. Tenía náusea. Fui al baño y vomité. Francisco tuvo que llevarme a la casa de una vez. La pregunta es, ¿Qué puede ser? No puedo estar embarazada.
Rosmery:	¿Fue la primera vez que te dio un dolor tan grande?
Sra. Flores:	Sí, pero, A-A-A-Y-Y-Y-Y.
Rosmery:	¿Qué te pasa?
Sra. Flores:	Me duele, qué dolor.
Rosmery:	¿Dónde? ¿Dónde te duele? Enséñame dónde.
Sra. Flores:	Me duele aquí.
Rosmery:	¿Desde cuándo que te duele?
Sra. Flores:	Hace más o menos un mes. Son como ataques.
Rosmery:	¿Cómo es el dolor?
Sra. Flores:	Ay, es punzante, como un cuchillo.

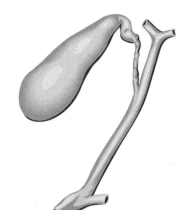

La vesícula bilar

Rosmery:	Cuando te duele, ¿cuánto tiempo dura el dolor?
Sra. Flores:	Más o menos de cinco a diez minutos, y a veces vomito.
Rosmery:	Vamos a ver. Voy a poner mi mano allí. Respira profundamente.
Sra. Flores:	A-y-y-y-y, allí me duele mucho.
Rosmery:	Tenemos que hacerte una cita con el doctor.

 9.19 Actividad

Working as a larger group, write on the board a clinical summary, in Spanish, of Sra. Flores's consultation with Rosmery. Include the following:

el motivo de la consulta	the chief complaint
el problema específico	the specific problem
la impresión diagnóstica	the diagnostic impression
el plan de tratamiento	the treatment plan

 ## Ask What Was Happening

 ## Estructura: El imperfecto del pasado
(The Imperfect Mood of the Past Tense)

- You have been practicing the preterit mood of the past tense, which is used to narrate actions that were completed in the past. In contrast, the imperfect describes past conditions and actions without freezing them in time. For example,

¿Qué pasó?	What happened?
¿Qué ocurría cuando eso pasó?	What was going on when that happened?

Habitual actions

Antes, fumaba dos paquetes de cigarrillos todos los días.	I used to smoke two packs of cigarettes a day.
Cuando me enfermaba mi abuela me preparaba un té.	Whenever I was sick, my grandmother prepared a tea for me.

Actions that were in progress or in the background

¿Qué hacía usted cuando el dolor empezó?	What were you doing when the pain began?

Mientras caminaba en el parque me dolían las rodillas.	While I walked in the park, my knees hurt.

Telling how things used to be

Mis padres eran estrictos con nosotros.	My parents were strict with us.
Antes, los doctores tenían más tiempo para hablar con los pacientes.	Before, doctors had more time to talk with patients.

Telling time and age in the past

Eran las cuatro de la mañana cuando tomé la nitro-glicerina.	It was four o'clock in the morning when I took the nitro-glycerine.
Cuando tenía cinco años me sacaron las amígdalas.	When I was five years old, they took out my tonsils.

- Here are the forms of the verbs in the imperfect. Verbs ending in *-er* and *-ir* share the same verb endings.

	tomar	*comer*	*vivir*
yo	tomaba	comía	vivía
tú	tomabas	comías	vivías
él, ella, usted	tomaba	comía	vivía
nosotros/as	tomábamos	comíamos	vivíamos
ellos, ellas, ustedes	tomaban	comían	vivían

Antes, yo tomaba una botella de cuarenta onzas de cerveza todas las noches.	I used to drink a 40-ounce bottle of beer every night.
Yo siempre comía fritura sin pensar en el colesterol.	I always would eat fried food without thinking about cholesterol.
Cuando vivíamos en Chile, tomábamos té de orégano para el estómago.	When we lived in Chile, we drank oregano tea for the stomach.

- Good news! There are very few irregular verbs in the imperfect. Here are two.

	ser	*ir*
yo	era	iba
tú	eras	ibas
él, ella, usted	era	iba
nosotros/as	éramos	íbamos
ellos, ellas, ustedes	eran	iban

Cuando era niño, mi abuela me hacía té de manzanilla.	When I was a child, my grand-mother made me chamomile tea.

- In the imperfect and combined with another verb, the verb *ir* can indicate past intentions.

Iba a darle aspirina al niño para el dolor, pero tenía fiebre también.	I was going to give aspirin to the child for pain, but he also had a fever.

9.20 Ejercicio

Use the imperfect to complete the following account.

Cuando _____ (ser) niño, _____ (vivir) en Puerto Rico. Mis

abuelos _____ (vivir) con nosotros. Abuela _____ (saber) mucho

de las plantas medicinales. Cuando _____ (tener) gripe, me _____

(hacer) té de hojas de limón y naranja. Cuando _____ (tener) gases

en la barriga, me _____ (preparar) té de anís. Mis padres no me

_____ (dar) remedios caseros. Ellos me _____ (llevar) a la

farmacia, y el farmacéutico nos _____ (vender) un jarabe o una

pastilla. No me _____ (gustar) los jarabes. _____ (preferir) las

tisanas de mi abuelita.

9.21 Actividad

Work in pairs. Ask your partner these questions, and then switch roles. Share your findings with the class.

A. Cuando tenías cinco años, ¿dónde vivías?
B. ¿Qué idiomas hablaban tus padres en casa?
C. ¿Te enfermabas mucho cuando eras niño?
D. ¿Qué te gustaba comer cuando eras niño?
E. ¿Tu abuela sabía mucho de remedios caseros?
F. Cuando eras joven, ¿te gustaban los jarabes para la tos?
G. Cuando eras estudiante, ¿te enfermabas de las enfermedades que estudiabas?

9.22 Actividad

The scene from the *Centro de rehabilitación cardiovascular* shows that one's actual behavior may be healthier than one's thoughts. These patients are thinking about

| leer | to read |
| *mirar televisión* to watch television | |

their old habits, despite their changed behavior. Assume the roles of specific patients, using the imperfect mode to tell what you used to do and the present tense to tell what you do now. For example, *Antes, tenía malos hábitos. Comía mucho. Ahora como poco.* As a variation, use the third person to tell stories about the characters in the drawing.

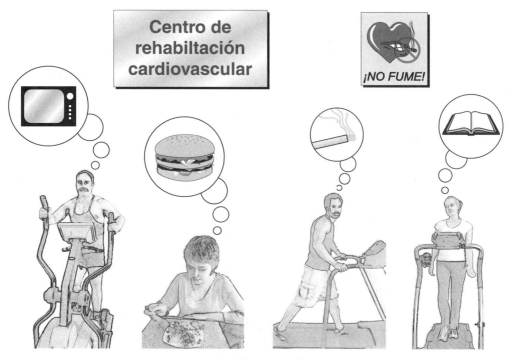

La rehabilitación cardíaca

 9.23 Drama imprevisto

Hold a cardiac rehabilitation group therapy session. Use the imperfect mode of the past tense to tell about your former life as a heart attack waiting to happen; the preterit mode to recount your heart attack; and the present tense to tell about your new habits. Here's an example.

> Antes, comía mucha fritura y no hacía ejercicio. En el 2007 tuve un ataque al corazón. Ahora como ensalada con vinagre, voy al gimnasio todos los días y tomo una aspirina por la mañana.

Here are some things that may be associated with heart health either for good or for bad.

estar sobrepeso, estar obeso/a	bajar de peso
comer más frutas y verduras	hacer ejercicio regularmente
dejar de fumar	tomar una aspirina todos los días
controlar la diabetes	controlar la hipertensión
comer fritura, comer dulces	cocinar con mucha sal
quitar la grasa de la carne	lidiar (cope) con el estrés

 ## 9.24 Drama imprevisto

Create a meeting of a self-help group like Alcoholics Anonymous. Use discretion. The actual membership of this revered treatment is anonymous, so you'll not know who in the room may be a member in real life. Use the imperfect mode to tell what your life was like before you made a commitment to sobriety, the preterit mode to say what happened to change your ways, and the present tense to describe your current behavior. Here is an example.

> Mi nombre es Barbara y soy alcoholica. Antes, bebía todas las noches y trasnochaba. No llegaba a mi casa hasta las cuatro de la mañana. No podía levantarme temprano para ir a trabajar. En el 2006 me enfermé de la diabetes y dejé de beber. Ahora voy a las reuniones de Alcohólicos Anónimos, paso más tiempo en la casa con mi familia y bebo café negro sin azúcar.

Here is a word bank to "scaffold" your communication.

trasnochar	to stay up all night
estar ebrio/a	to be intoxicated
estar borracho/a	to be drunk
manejar ebrio/a	to drive while intoxicated
sobrio/a	sober
pelear	to argue, fight
pasar tiempo en los bares	to spend time in bars
malgastar dinero	to spend money unwisely
dejar de beber	to give up drinking

 ## Video Program: *Memorias de México*

Watch the *Trama* for chapter 9, in which Rosmery and Sra. Flores reminisce about their grandmothers and countries of origin. Do the activity that follows.

Sra. Flores:	Rosmery, ¿piensas mucho en México?
Rosmery:	Ay, sí, y me hace mucha falta.
Sra. Flores:	¿Qué te hace falta?

Rosmery:	Cuando era niña vivíamos con mi abuela. Mi papá trabajaba aquí en los Estados Unidos. Mi mamá trabajaba en el Distrito Federal. Pasaba mucho tiempo con mi abuela. Ella siempre sabía qué hacer cuando estaba enferma. Es posible que por mi abuela decidiera ser enfermera.
Sra. Flores:	Interesante. Tu abuela sabía mucho de los remedios caseros.
Rosmery:	Sí. Por ejemplo, cuando no me podía dormir, ella me hacía un té de manzanilla. Cuando estaba resfriada, me hacía un té de hojas de naranja y limón con canela, jengibre y miel de abeja.
Sra. Flores:	Mi abuelita también sabía mucho de remedios caseros. Cuando me dolía el estómago me hacía un té de orégano o un té de anís.
Rosmery:	No me gusta mucho el té de orégano pero me encanta el té de anís. Mi abuela también me preparaba eso. Ay, es bueno para sacar los gases del estómago.
Sra. Flores:	En mi casa cuando nos enfermábamos no íbamos al doctor. Primero mi abuelita nos hacía un té. Si el té no funcionaba, íbamos a la farmacia y el farmacéutico nos recomendaba algo. Si el remedio de la farmacia no funcionaba, íbamos al doctor.
Rosmery:	Hasta ahora lo hacen así en muchos países. Y déjame decirte que en muchos países el farmacéutico recomienda los medicamentos que aquí en los Estados Unidos son controlados.
Sra. Flores:	¿Está viva tu abuela?
Rosmery:	No, mi abuela murió cuando yo tenía doce años.
Sra. Flores:	Lo lamento mucho.
Rosmery:	Gracias. Fue un tiempo muy difícil. Mi mamá dejó su trabajo en el Distrito Federal y vino a vivir con nosotros. Cada año celebrábamos el día de los muertos.

Sra. Flores: ¿El día de los muertos?

Rosmery: Íbamos a pasar la noche en el cementerio frente la tumba de mi abuela.

Sra. Flores: ¿No tenías miedo?

Rosmery: ¿Mande?

Sra. Flores: Que si no tenías miedo.

Rosmery: No, la verdad es que todo el mundo tiene miedo a la muerte, bueno, nadie se quiere morir antes de tiempo, pero cuando pasábamos la noche en el

Se celebra el día de los muertos el 2 de noviembre.

cementerio con mi abuela, nos sentíamos muy unidos como familia. Hacíamos la comida que a mi abuela le gustaba, chiles rellenos con queso, y llevábamos la comida al cementerio para comer. Llevábamos flores también, como ofrenda para mi abuela. No nos sentíamos tan solos, porque el espíritu de mi abuela estaba con nosotros. Hasta ahora creo que ella está siempre conmigo.

Sra. Flores: Es una tradición muy bonita. Acá en los Estados Unidos todo es diferente. Acá celebran el día de las brujas, tú sabes, Halloween, y no respetan de la misma manera a los muertos. Los niños van de casa en casa buscando dulces.

Rosmery: Los niños buscan dulces, y sus padres pagan al dentista.

Sra. Flores: Es verdad.

Rosmery: Ay, mis hijos están muy americaniza-dos. Tenemos que visitar México pronto.

Family members from places where tradition and ground conditions dictate above-ground burial may consider cremation disrespectful and below-ground burials eerie.

9.25 Actividad

Ask a partner the following questions that compare Rosmery and your partner.

A. ¿Dónde vivía Rosmery cuando era niña?
B. ¿Dónde vivías tú?
C. ¿Qué tomaba Rosmery cuando estaba resfriada?
D. ¿Qué tomabas tú?
E. ¿Iba Rosmery al doctor frecuentemente?
F. ¿Con qué frecuencia ibas al doctor?

UN CHISTE

Una mujer murió y su esposo, el viudo, estaba en la funeraria con un amigo. El hombre lloraba inconsolablemente. Tenía mucha baba (mucho moco) en la barbilla. Cuando llegó otra persona su amigo le dijo, «Mira, la baba». El hombre le respondió, «Sí, lavaba y cocinaba».

Cultural Note: *Remedios caseros*

Pythagoras said, "Before calling the doctor, call a friend." A Latino might advise, "*Antes que al médico llame a la abuelita o al farmacéutico.*" In the video for chapter 9, Rosmery and Sra. Flores reminisce about their grandmothers, who always knew what *remedio casero,* or home remedy, to recommend. When Abuela's *tisana* (tea) did not work, then the family would consult with the pharmacist, who might have recommended and sold a drug that in many countries would be controlled. If that did not work, the family would consult a physician. This particular pathway may spring from tradition, finances, or the availability of a health care provider.

Herbal remedies are available at open-air markets, neighborhood grocers, and botanical shops (*botánicas*), although travelers may bring remedies when returning from abroad. Dried plants pass customs in a way that live plants with soil do not. In the United States herbal remedies are not regulated by the Food and Drug Administration. Although a remedy that is made from a fresh or dried plant is commonly referred to as *un té,* this is a generalization of "tea," which is the name of a more specific group of plants. The proper name for such remedies is *una tisana* or *una infusión.*

The dawning of the age of antibiotics (which contributed significantly to longevity) and the widespread use of medications that either block or enhance (agonize) neurotransmitters led many to attribute illness to microbes or chemical imbalances. Another worldview attributes illness to an imbalance in the body or spirit. Forces that may be out of balance have been described as ying and yang and hot and cold among others. Many Latinos think of certain botanical remedies as being *hot* and others as *cold.* These are general terms that include a small percentage of botanical remedies. "Hot" remedies include ginger, cinnamon, and citrus leaves (*jengibre, canela y hojas de los árboles cítricos*) and help restore balance when we suffer from a cold or a depressed affect. "Cold" remedies include anise, chamomile, linden flower, and oregano (*anís, manzanilla, flor de tilo y orégano*) and help restore balance when we suffer from dyspepsia, "nerves," or insomnia.

In general, many home remedies are effective either for their own medicinal properties, for their placebo effect, for the comfort they conjure, or a combination of these. However, when there is a more effective agent available, the use of a home remedy as a first line of defense may delay medical care at the patient's risk. Although phytotherapy is generally considered safe and effective, it may be helpful to know what a patient is taking and to review a list of contraindications or possible herb-drug interactions. General knowledge of herb-drug interactions is sparse, although the World Health Organization has published monographs, and other books are becoming available in both traditional and alternative markets. Interactions may include the capacity of the herb to slow the absorption of a drug (suspected of fibrous herbs such as psyllium), to affect the drug's elimination, to synergize its effect (*sábila,* or aloe vera, may synergize another antihyperglycemic agent), or to add to its hepatotoxicity.

Chapter 10
Padecimientos e historia médica

By the end of this chapter you will know how to ask about medical history, including illnesses, surgeries, and immunizations. You will learn the names of internal organs, the most common illnesses and diseases, and various surgeries.

Ask About Current Medical Conditions

Vocabulario: Padecimientos y la historia abreviada
(Illnesses and the Abbreviated History)

A lot of vocabulary follows. To aid memorization, the terms are organized in some of the ways that they are elicited during a history and physical exam. For example, we begin with an abbreviated history and proceed to a review of systems and a list of infectious and tropical diseases. Then we provide opportunities for more elaborate practice. Let's begin with the conditions that are part of an abbreviated, or critical, history. Some practitioners consider these to be too dangerous to miss.

La historia abreviada (The Abbreviated History)

la enfermedad cardiovascular	cardiovascular disease
la angina de pecho	angina pectoris
el ataque al corazón	heart attack
el infarto cardíaco	coronary infarction
la trombosis cardíaca	coronary thrombosis
la hypertensión, la presión alta	hypertension
la insuficiencia cardíaca	congestive heart failure
el asma	asthma
el cáncer, metástasis a . . .	cancer, mestastasis to . . .
la diabetes	diabetes

la epilepsia	epilepsy
la convulsión, el ataque epiléptico	convulsion, seizure
la hepatitis	hepatitis
la herida en la cabeza	head injury
la ictericia, la piel amarillenta	jaundice, yellowish skin
los ojos amarillentos	yellowish eyes
problemas de los riñones	kidney problems
la insuficiencia renal	kidney failure
. . . aguda, crónica, grave	. . . acute, chronic, serious
la fiebre reumática	rheumatic fever
la tuberculosis	tuberculosis

Preguntas útiles

¿Padece del corazón?	Do you have heart problems?
¿Padece de los riñones?	Do you have kidney problems?
¿Ha tenido problemas con el hígado?	Have you had liver problems?
¿Tuvo alguna vez un golpe en la cabeza?	Have you had a head injury?

**Síntomas previos a
un derrame cerebral**

1. Entumecimiento o debilidad repentinos en la cara, un brazo o una pierna, particularmente en un lado del cuerpo.

2. Confusión y problemas para hablar, comprender, ver o caminar.

3. Dolor de cabeza severo.

**Si tiene alguno de
estos síntomas,
llame al 911 de inmediato.**

Estructura: Los verbos *padecer* y *sufrir* (To Suffer From)

- The verb *padecer* is used to speak of illnesses or conditions from which the patient suffers. In the present indicative tense *padecer* is irregular in only the first person singular (*yo*). It is used with the preposition *de.*
- These are the forms of the verb *padecer* in the present tense.

yo	padezco	Padezco de leucemia.
tú	padeces	¿Padeces de diabetes?
él, ella, usted	padece	¿De qué padece usted?
nosotros/as	padecemos	Mi hermano y yo padecemos de asma.
ellos, ellas, ustedes	padecen	Mis padres padecen del corazón.

- *Sufrir* can also be used to identify current medical conditions. Like *padecer,* it is used with the preposition *de.* However, *sufrir* is a regular verb ending in *-ir.*

¿Sufre de alguna enfermedad o problema médico?

Hace cinco años que sufro de artritis reumatoide.

 ## 10.1 Actividad

Make sentences that combine a person or people from column A, the correct form of either the verb *padecer* or *sufrir,* and an illness or condition from column B. Use complete sentences to say who suffers from what. You do not have to read straight across the lines.

Example: Los niños padecen de asma. / Los niños sufren de asma.

A	B
los niños	artritis
los pacientes	asma
la paciente	angina
mis padres	anemia
mi hijo	diabetes
yo	enfisema
Rosaura y Filomena	hepatitis C
usted	ataques epilépticos
mi hermana y yo	cáncer con metástasis al cerebro

 ## 10.2 Actividad

Cues may aid your memory. Take turns writing the name of a fictitious patient on the board and, under the name, write a brief list of diagnoses from the abbreviated history. When it is your turn, classmates will ask related questions, and you may answer ad lib. For example, if your patient suffers from *convulsiones,* classmates might ask, *¿Toma fenotoina para prevenir los ataques? ¿Cuándo fue la última vez que tuvo una convulsión?*

Vocabulario: Enfermedades y el repaso de sistemas
(Illnesses and Review of Systems)

Another way to aid the process of memorization is to organize the information to be memorized. Some well-known methods suggest using "pegs" to organize the list to be memorized. For this we'll use the "review of systems." To keep the size of this list manageable, we won't repeat conditions that were included in the abbreviated medical history.

El sistema neurológico

el aneurisma	aneurysm
la catarata	cataract
la ciática	sciatica
la espina bífida	spina bifida
la hemorragia cerebral, el derrame, el chorro	hemorrhage
el infarto cerebral	cerebral infarction
la jaqueca, la migraña	migraine
la parálisis cerebral	cerebral palsy
el tumor cerebral	brain tumor

El sistema respiratorio

la amigdalitis	tonsillitis
la bronquitis crónica	chronic bronchitis
la enfermedad pulmonar obstructiva crónica	COPD
el enfisema	emphysema
la pulmonía, la neumonía	pneumonia
la tuberculosis	tuberculosis

El sistema cardiovascular

la hipercolesterolemia	hypercholesterolemia
la hipertensión, la hipotensión	hypertension, hypotension
el soplo cardíaco	heart murmur

El sistema gastrointestinal

el cálculo biliar (la piedra biliar)	gallstone
la cirrosis hepática	cirrhosis of the liver
el cólico, el empacho	colic, indigestion

las hemorroides	hemorrhoids
el pólipo	polyp
el reflujo esofágico, la acidez	esophageal reflux
la úlcera	ulcer

El sistema genitourinario

el agrandamiento de la próstata	benign prostatic hypertrophy (BPH)
el cálculo (piedras) en el riñon	renal calculus (stones)
la endometriosis	endometriosis
la infección del aparato urinario	bladder infection (UTI)
la nefritis	nephritis

El sistema endocrinológico

la hiperglucemia, la hipoglucemia	hyperglycemia, hypoglycemia
el hipertiroidismo, el hipotiroidismo	hyperthyroidism, hypothyroidism
la obesidad	obesity

El sistema esqueletomuscular

la artritis reumatoide	rheumatoid arthritis
la ciática	sciatica
la distrofia muscular	muscular dystrophy
la esclerosis múltiple	multiple sclerosis
la osteoporosis	osteoporosis

La piel

el eczema	eczema
la irritación del pañal	diaper rash
los piojos	head lice
la psoriasis	psoriasis
la sarna	scabies

Problemas de la sangre

la anemia	anemia
la anemia drepanocítica	sickle cell anemia
la hemofilia	hemophilia
la leucemia	leukemia
el linfoma	lymphoma

Derrame refers to a leak or overflow. It is not a medical term, but is commonly used for hemorrhage. *Amígdala* is "tonsil" (the false cognate in English refers to a structure in the brain). A folk explanation attributes *empacho* to food sticking to the walls of the intestine. A parent may report,

El niño está empachado, and pinch and pull at the abdomen to help "dislodge" the food.

 ## 10.3 Actividad

Linking new vocabulary to memory cues will assist recall. To that end let's play a guessing game of associations. When it is your turn, say a word or phrase that you associate with one of the illnesses or conditions. Class members will guess which illness or condition you have in mind. If the guesses are not on target, give another clue. Here are some sample associations.

Es una inflamación del hígado.	la hepatitis
Póngase una nitroglicerina debajo de la lengua.	la angina del pecho
Uno en quinientos africano-americanos lo tiene.	la anemia drepanocítica

Vocabulario: Las enfermedades infecciosas y tropicales
(Infectious and Tropical Diseases)

To lead a more complete history-taking interview, you may want to ask about some of the following diseases. Venereal infectious diseases are included in chapter 12.

el cólera	cholera
la conjuntivitis	conjunctivitis
la culebrilla	herpes zoster, shingles
el dengue (clásico, hemorrágico)	dengue (classic, hemorrhagic)
la difteria	diphtheria
la disentería	dysentery
el estafilococo dorado	MRSA, golden staph
la fiebre tifóidea	typhoid fever
la frambesia, el pían*	yaws
la leptospirosis	leptospirosis
las lombrices	intestinal worms
la meningitis	meningitis
la mononucleosis	mononucleosis
el paludismo	malaria
la paperas	mumps
la pinta*	pinta

*Yaws and pinta are two nonvenereal forms of syphilis that are present in the Americas and can cause a VDRL test to be positive, although the VDRL test is less common now, and more-specific tests result in fewer false positives.

el sarampión

la paperas

la rubéola	rubella (German measles)
el sarampión	rubeola, measles
el tétano, el tétanos	tetanus
la tos ferina	pertussis, whooping cough
la varicela, las viruelas locas	chicken pox

 10.4 Actividad

Deep processing may be the most important mnemonic device. Thinking about the meaning of a word and using it in various contexts will help you to store it with cues for recall. As a classroom discussion, answer the following questions by identifying the illnesses and conditions that fit the following categories.

A. ¿Cuáles afectan el cerebro?
B. ¿Cuáles son de interés para un pediatra?
C. ¿Cuáles se mejoran con los antibióticos?
D. ¿Cuáles son de interés para un cardiólogo?
E. ¿Cuáles enfermedades no son contagiosas?
F. ¿Cuáles son de interés para un gerontólogo?
G. ¿Para cuáles enfermedades hay vacuna (*vaccine*)?
H. ¿Cuáles enfermedades están causadas por un virus?
I. ¿Cuáles son las enfermedades más comunes donde usted trabaja?
J. ¿Cuáles pueden ser transmitidas por vectores, como los mosquitos?

Lectura: El estafilococo dorado (MRSA) y la leptospirosis

Muchas personas saludables tienen la bacteria estafilococo dorado en la piel. En algunos casos la bacteria entra en el cuerpo y causa una infección en la sangre o una pulmonía. La meticilina es un antibiótico muy efectivo contra el estafilococo, pero algunos estafilococos son resistentes a la meticilina. Estos se llaman *estafilococo dorado* o *estafilococo resistente a la meticilina*. También se llama MRSA por su nombre en inglés.

Las infecciones serias son más comunes en los hospitales que en la comunidad. Una infección adquirida (acquired) en el hospital se llama *una infección nosocomial.* Para prevenir la infección es importante lavarse las manos. También es importante practicar las precauciones universales, no compartir toallas, lavar bien las sábanas y siempre cubrir las cortadas con un vendaje o una tirita (curita).

La leptospirosis es una infección contagiosa y grave causada por algunos tipos de la bacteria *leptospira.* No es muy común en los Estados Unidos. Hay más casos en lugares tropicales cuando el agua potable está contaminada con orine de ratas, ratones u otros animales. Los síntomas incluyen fiebre, escalofríos, dolor de cabeza y dolores en el cuerpo, una tos seca, náuseas, vómitos y/o diarrea. El tratamiento normalmente incluye tomar penicilinas, tetraciclinas, cloramfenicol o eritromicina.

Ask About Medical History

Estructura: El pretérito perfecto
(The Present Perfect Tense)

- Use the present perfect tense to speak about a past experience that is related to the present in some way. As in English, use the auxiliary verb "to have" (*haber*) and the past participle. To form the past participle of *-ar* verbs, add *-ado* to the stem. To form the past participle of *-er* and *-ir* verbs, add *-ido* to the stem.

He consultado con el neurólogo.	I have consulted with the neurologist.
¿Has tenido varicela?	Have you had chicken pox?
¿Ha tenido cirugía?	Have you had surgery?
Hemos llamado a la doctora.	We have called the doctor.
¿Han leído la radiografía?	Have they read the x-ray?

- This will be especially helpful during medical history-taking interviews, both for asking general questions and for asking about specific illnesses.

  ¿De qué enfermedades ha padecido usted?
  ¿Cuáles enfermedades ha tenido usted?
  ¿Ha padecido de paludismo?

- The patient may respond using the present perfect, but it is likely that he or she will use the preterit form of the verb *tener.*

He tenido varicela.	I have had chicken pox.
Tuve paperas cuando era niño.	I had mumps when I was a child.

- Recall that in chapter 3 we used the past participle as an adjective to say, *El tobillo está hinchado.* When used as an adjective, the past participle must agree with the noun in number and gender (*Las rodillas están hinchadas*). In the present perfect tense (when following the verb *haber*), it does not have number or gender, so it always ends in *-o*.
- The following verbs are irregular in the formation of the past participle. You are already familiar with *muerto* and *roto*.

decir	dicho	Yo le he dicho que sí.
escribir	escrito	¿Has escrito tu nombre?
hacer	hecho	He hecho planes para la cirugía.
morir	muerto	Dos de mis tíos han muerto del corazón.
poner	puesto	No me han puesto el suero.
romper	roto	¿Se ha roto usted un hueso?
ver	visto	No he visto a la doctora.

 10.5 Actividad

¿Ha tenido varicela? We'll bet you've never been on a disease scavenger hunt. Hold a soiree in the classroom in which all students circulate, asking the questions needed to fill their survey (*encuesta*). Then confirm the accuracy of your list by discussing findings and inter-rater reliability as a group. We'll restrict this to conditions that most people don't mind revealing.

Enfermedades	*Nombres de compañeros*		
la conjuntivitis	_____	_____	_____
el paludismo	_____	_____	_____
la rubéola	_____	_____	_____
la paperas	_____	_____	_____
la varicela	_____	_____	_____
una gripe mala	_____	_____	_____

 10.6 Actividad

Work with a partner to prepare a history-taking interview to present to the class. After eliciting the illnesses from which the patient has suffered, gather more specific information. Recall that the imperfect mode of the past tense may be used to tell background information such as age. For example, *¿Cuántos años tenía usted cuando tuvo varicela? ¿Dónde vivía?* Your interview should establish what illness the patient suffered from, how old he or she was at the time, where he or she was living, and so on.

 ## 10.7 Actividad

Prepare a similar presentation in which you ask your partner about a family member's history. This may be an interview with a sandwich-generation person concerning a child or an elderly parent. For example, *¿De qué enfermedades ha padecido el niño?* and *¿Tuvo varicela?*

 ## 10.8 Drama imprevisto

Play the game *afortunadamente, desafortunadamente.* One person suffers from an illness. The next student adds a statement that begins with *afortunadamente* and the following student adds a statement that begins with *desafortunadamente.* See how long you can carry a thread of conversation until you have to change topics. Here's an example.

> Padezco de diabetes. Afortunadamente, tengo una receta para la metformina. Desafortunadamente, la farmacia está cerrada. Afortunadamente, tengo metformina en la casa. Desafortunadamente, me gustan los dulces. Afortunadamente, no hay dulces en la casa. Desafortunadamente, hoy es Halloween.

 ## 10.9 Drama imprevisto

Play the television talk show *Hipocondríaco competitivo* (Competitive Hypochondriac). You'll need four students to sit in front of the classroom, an emcee, and a studio audience. As members of the studio audience ask contestants about their medical history (*historia médica*) and current conditions (*padecimientos actuales*), things get a little competitive, and dare we say, contagious. Audience members may add sympathetic comments such as, *¡Pobrecito! ¡Qué pena!* and *¡Qué calamidad!*

 ## Video Program: *La colecistitis*

Watch the *Trama* for chapter 10 and do the activity that follows.

Dr. Vargas:	Rosmery me dijo que tenía un fuerte dolor en el abdomen.
Sra. Flores:	Sí, doctor, es un dolor terrible, pero va y viene.

Dr. Vargas:	¿Con qué frecuencia le duele?
Sra. Flores:	Tres o cuatro veces por semana. Los ataques duran de cinco a diez minutos.
Dr. Vargas:	¿Cuándo empezó este problema?
Sra. Flores:	Hace un mes.
Dr. Vargas:	¿Hay algo que lo empeora?
Sra. Flores:	Sí, doctor. Está peor cuando como algo grasoso como los huevos o la carne de res.
Dr. Vargas:	Cuando le duele el abdomen, ¿tiene náusea o vómitos?
Sra. Flores:	Sí. Una vez estaba en un restaurante argentino con mi esposo, Francisco. Me sentí muy mal, y vomité, y él tuvo que llevarme a la casa.
Dr. Vargas:	Vamos a hablar de su historia médica. ¿Ha tenido cirugías?
Sra. Flores:	Tuve un parto por cesárea. Elsita nació por cesárea. Y cuando tenía diez años me sacaron las amígdalas.
Dr. Vargas:	Una cesárea y una tonsilectomía. ¿Ha tenido otras cirugías?
Sra. Flores:	No. Esas dos, nada más.
Dr. Vargas:	¿De qué enfermedades padece?
Sra. Flores:	No tengo nada. Estoy saludable. Sólo el dolor de estómago.
Dr. Vargas:	¿Tiene diabetes?
Sra. Flores:	No.
Dr. Vargas:	¿Ha tenido convulsiones o ataques epilépticos?
Sra. Flores:	No.
Dr. Vargas:	¿Ha tenido asma, hipertensión o dificultad para respirar?
Sra. Flores:	No.
Dr. Vargas:	¿Ha tenido problemas con el corazón?
Sra. Flores:	No, gracias a Dios.
Dr. Vargas:	Bien. Voy a tocarle el abdomen. Acuéstese por favor. Respira profundamente.
Sra. Flores:	A-y-y-y-y, eso me duele.
Dr. Vargas:	Lo siento. Perdone. Eso es un signo clásico de la colecistitis. La colecistitis es una inflamación de la vesícula biliar. La vesícula está al lado derecho,

debajo del hígado. Le duele cuando la toco con la mano. Tenemos que hacer una sonografía para confirmar el diagnóstico.

Sra. Flores: ¿Es algo muy serio, doctor?

Dr. Vargas: Primero vamos a hacer la cita para la sonografía. Rosmery le va a hacer la cita. Si usted tiene cálculos, o piedras, en la vesícula, vamos a hacer una cita con un cirujano.

Sra. Flores: ¿La cirugía es peligrosa?

Dr. Vargas: No se preocupe. Es un procedimiento común. Va a estar en el hospital uno o dos días, pero todo va a estar bien.

 ## 10.10 Actividad

Answer the following comprehension questions based on the chapter 10 *Demostración.*

A. ¿Quién refirió a la Sra. Flores al doctor Vargas?
B. ¿Cuál fue el motivo de la consulta?
C. ¿Qué historia médica tiene la Sra. Flores?
D. ¿Qué empeora a la Sra. Flores?
E. ¿Cuál es la historia de este problema?
F. ¿Cuál es la impresión diagnóstica del Dr. Vargas?
G. ¿Qué otra prueba quiere el doctor?
H. ¿Cree usted que la Sra. Flores va a necesitar cirugía? ¿Por qué cree eso?

 ## Estructura: Pronombres indefinidos y negativos
(Indefinite and Negative Pronouns)

• Indefinite pronouns refer to people and things that we either cannot specify or do not want to specify. Negative pronouns work alone or in conjunction with the word *no* to make a negative statement.

Pronombres indefinidos		*Pronombres negativos*	
algo	something	nada	anything, nothing
alguien	someone	nadie	no one
alguno/a/os/as	some, any	ninguno/a	none, not any

Here we also include useful positive and negative expressions that are not pronouns.

alguna vez	ever	nunca, jamás	never
algunas veces	sometimes	siempre	always
también	also, too	tampoco	neither

- Spanish often uses double negatives. *No necesito nada* means, "I don't need anything." The word *no* precedes the verb, and the negative pronoun follows it. The word *no* is omitted when the negative word precedes the verb.

¿Necesita algo para el dolor?	Do you need something for the pain?
No necesito nada.	I don't need anything.
¿Hay alguien en casa?	Is there someone at home?
No hay nadie.	There is no one.
¿Ha tenido cirugía alguna vez?	Have you ever had surgery?
No he tenido cirugía nunca.	I have never had surgery.
Nunca he tenido cirugía.	I have never had surgery.
¿Algunas veces le duele la mano?	Does your hand sometimes hurt?
No me duele nunca.	It never hurts.
Nunca me duele.	It never hurts.

- The pronouns *alguno* and *ninguno* drop their final *-o* when they are used before a masculine, singular noun. Then they become *algún* and *ningún.*

¿Toma usted algún medicamento?	Do you take any medicine?
No tomo ningún medicamento.	I don't take any medicine.
No tomo nada.	I do not take anything.
¿Le ayuda algún medicamento?	Does any medicine help you?
No me ayuda ningún medicamento.	No medicine helps me.
Ningún medicamento me ayuda.	No medicine helps me.

10.11 Ejercicio

Complete the following conversation, using the indefinite and the negative pronouns as needed.

Dra. Ávila: ¿Sufre usted de alguna enfermedad?

Doña Rosa: No, no sufro de _____ enfermedad.

Dra. Ávila: ¿_____?

Doña Rosa: No tomo _____ medicamento.

Dra. Ávila: ¿Es usted alérgica a _____ alimento?

Doña Rosa: No _____.

Dra. Ávila: En su familia, ¿_____ ha tenido cáncer?

Doña Rosa: No, en mi familia _____ ha padecido de cáncer.

Dra. Ávila: ¿Hay _____ en la casa para ayudarla?

Doña Rosa: Vivo sola. No hay más _____ en casa.

Ask About Symptoms

Vocabulario: Síntomas generales (General Symptoms)

Síntomas neurológicos

la confusión	confusion
el entumecimiento	numbness, tingling
el problema para hablar	problem with speaking
el problema para ver, caminar	problem with seeing, walking

Síntomas cardíacos

el desmayo	fainting
el dolor del pecho . . .	chest pain . . .
. . . que corre por el brazo	that radiates to the arm
las manos y los pies fríos	cold hands and feet
el mareo	dizziness
la taquicardia	tachycardia
los tobillos hinchados	swollen ankles (edema)

Síntomas respiratorios

la dificultad para respirar	difficulty breathing
la falta de aire	shortness of breath
la fatiga, el cansancio	fatigue
los silbidos	wheezing
los sudores nocturnos	night sweats
la tos, toser	cough, to cough

Síntomas del reumatismo

el dolor en las articulaciones	joint pain
la inflamación	inflammation
la hinchazón	swelling
la rigidez	stiffness

Síntomas gastrointestinales

el ardor	burning sensation
los calambres	cramps
la diarrea	diarrhea
el estreñimiento	constipation
el gas abdominal	abdominal gas
la náusea	nausea
la pérdida del apetito	loss of appetite
la pérdida de peso	weight loss
el vómito	vomiting

Síntomas genitourinarios

la dificultad para comenzar a orinar	difficulty starting to urinate
el flujo de orina débil	weak urine stream
la incontinencia de orina	urinary incontinence
la urgencia urinaria	urinary urgency

 10.12 Actividad

After reviewing the symptoms listed above, tell the common indications for the following medicines. For example, Dulcolax®. *Dulcolax® es para aliviar el estreñimiento.*

A. Mylanta®

B. Compazine®

C. la calamina

D. Benadryl®

E. la nitroglicerina

F. Proventil©

G. Prilosec®

H. Afrin®

I. Robitussin DM®

J. la aspirina

 10.13 Actividad

Relate some of the usual symptoms of the following illnesses or conditions.

Example: *¿Cuáles son algunos de los síntomas de la depresión?*
Algunos de los síntomas de la depresión son la
tristeza, la pérdida de peso y/o la pérdida del apetito.

A. el asma

B. la úlcera

C. la gripe

D. el hipotiroidismo

E. el enfisema

F. la artritis

G. la tuberculosis

H. el ataque al corazón

I. la hipertensión

J. la pulmonía

 10.14 Drama imprevisto

This is a guessing game. The instructor should hand each student an index card with one of the illnesses or conditions on it. The instructor should choose illnesses that have fairly common symptoms, such as *asma* or *bronquitis.* Students should move around the classroom asking questions about symptoms until they have guessed the illness or condition that other students have on their cards. Be prepared to share what you have learned with the class.

Example: Student 1:   ¿Qué síntomas tiene usted?
             Student 2:   Tengo mareos y desmayos.
             Student 1:   ¿Tiene la tensión baja?
             Student 2:   Sí, tengo la tensión baja.

 ## 10.15 Actividad

As a class exercise, write a brief patient-education piece about an illness that is common in your area of practice. Here is a sample.

> La pulmonía es una inflamación en los pulmones. Hay una infección bacteriana o un virus que afecta una parte de un pulmón o hasta los dos pulmones. Los síntomas son fiebre, tos, dolor en el pecho y/o dolor cuando respira. El tratamiento es tomar antibióticos o antivirales. A veces también el paciente necesita medicamentos por suero intravenoso y/o terapia respiratoria.

Educate a Patient About Tuberculosis

Lectura: La tuberculosis

La tuberculosis es una infección bacteriana. Usualmente afecta los pulmones y es contagiosa. Pasa de una persona a otra por medio del aire, por ejemplo cuando una persona con tuberculosis tose, estornuda o habla. Pero en un 15 por ciento de los casos es una infección que puede ocurrir en otras partes del cuerpo, tal como en el cerebro, los riñones, los huesos o la espina dorsal.

Hay una prueba para la tuberculosis. Para hacerla, un enfermero pone una inyección subcutánea en el antebrazo debajo de la piel usando una jeringuilla pequeña. Dentro de dos o tres días es necesario examinar el brazo para ver si hay una reacción. Si hay una reacción suficientemente grande y con hinchazón en la área afectada, el resultado es positivo. Si es positivo, la persona está infectada con la bacteria, pero la persona no está necesariamente enferma o contagiosa. Para determinar si tiene la enfermedad de tuberculosis de los pulmones hay que hacer una placa del pecho y/o análisis del esputo.

Cuando una persona tiene un resultado positivo, pero la placa del pecho es negativa, la persona no tiene la enfermedad de la tuberculosis, porque en su cuerpo la bacteria está inactiva o no está presente en cantidades suficientes. La bacteria a veces dura algunas semanas o hasta muchos años sin causar enfermedad. Un doctor a veces receta un medicamento que baja las posibilidades de tener una infección activa. Hay otras personas que nacieron en el exterior que han tenido la vacuna para la tuberculosis (la vacuna BCG, o Bacilo de Calmette-Guerin) y la vacuna causa el resultado positivo. La vacuna no es común en los Estados Unidos.

Algunos síntomas de la tuberculosis de los pulmones son cansancio, dolor del pecho, tos o tos con sangre, pérdida de peso, una fiebre leve y sudores nocturnos. Hay antibióticos que pueden curar la tuberculosis. Si toma los medicamentos para la tuberculosis es muy importante tomarlos por el tiempo indicado.

 ## 10.16 Actividad

Take turns with a partner asking and answering the following questions about tuberculosis.

A. ¿Es contagiosa la tuberculosis de los pulmones?
B. ¿Cómo pasa la tuberculosis de una persona a otra?
C. ¿Cuáles son los síntomas de la tuberculosis de los pulmones?
D. ¿Cómo se hace la prueba para la tuberculosis?
E. Si el resultado es positivo, ¿tiene tuberculosis el paciente?
F. ¿Cómo se confirma que el paciente tiene tuberculosis de los pulmones?
G. ¿Hay una vacuna para prevenir la tuberculosis?
H. ¿Hay tratamiento para curar la tuberculosis?

Ask About Surgical History

Like English-speaking laypeople, Spanish-speaking laypeople may be more likely to describe a surgery or procedure than to know its medical name. The doctor might say, *Usted tiene cálculos en la vesícula. Hay que operarlo/la,* rather than *Usted necesita una colecistectomía.* Likewise the patient, giving his or her *historia quirúrgica* (surgical history) might say, *Me sacaron la vesícula biliar.* Here we'll present the names for internal structures and the names for some common surgeries and procedures.

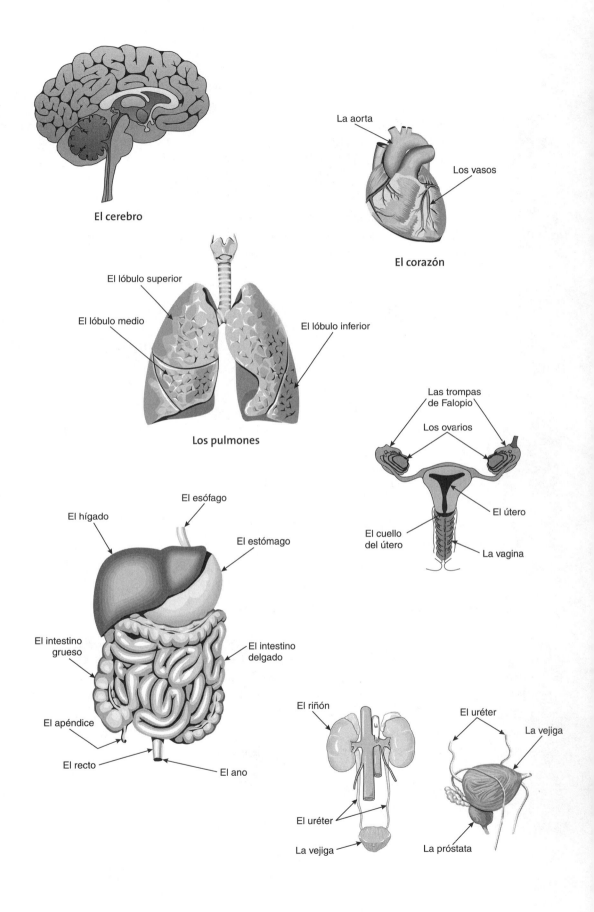

El cerebro

La aorta

Los vasos

El corazón

El lóbulo superior

El lóbulo medio

El lóbulo inferior

Los pulmones

Las trompas de Falopio

Los ovarios

El útero

El cuello del útero

La vagina

El esófago

El hígado

El estómago

El intestino grueso

El intestino delgado

El apéndice

El recto

El ano

El riñón

El uréter

La vejiga

El uréter

La vejiga

La próstata

Vocabulario: Los órganos internos y las glándulas
(Internal Organs and Glands)

el cerebro	brain
la amígdala	tonsil
la glándula tiroidea	thyroid
el ganglio linfático	lymph gland
el corazón	heart
el pulmón	lung
el esófago	esophagus
el estómago	stomach
el duodeno	duodenum
el apéndice	appendix
el páncreas	pancreas
la vesícula biliar	gallbladder
el bazo	spleen
el riñón	kidney
el hígado	liver
la vejiga	bladder
el intestino delgado	small intestine
el intestino grueso, el colon	large intestine, colon

Mujeres

la matriz	womb
el útero	uterus
el cuello del útero	cervix
la trompa de Falopio	Fallopian tube
el ovario	ovary

Hombres

la próstata	prostate gland
el testículo	testicle

Vocabulario: Algunas cirugías y procedimientos
(Some Surgeries and Procedures)

la anestesia local	local anesthesia
la anestesia general	general anesthesia
la artroscopia	arthroscopy
la cirugía ambulatoria	ambulatory surgery
la cirugía con hospitalización	inpatient surgery
la cirugía láser	laser surgery
la laparoscopia	laparoscopy
la sala de operaciones, el quirófano	operating room
la sala de recuperación	recovery room
el trasplante	transplant
la unidad de cuidado intensivo	intensive care unit

Los procedimientos (Procedures)

el amarre de las trompas	tubal ligation
la amígdalectomía, tonsilectomía	tonsillectomy
la apendectomía	appendectomy
el bypass de la arteria coronaria	coronary artery bypass
la cirugía de la arteria carótida	carotid artery surgery
la cirugía de bypass gástrico	gastric bypass surgery
la cirugía de cataratas	cataract surgery
la cirugía a corazón abierto	open-heart surgery
la cirugía exploratoria	exploratory surgery
la colecistectomía	cholecystectomy
la colostomía	colostomy
la histerectomía	hysterectomy
el marcapasos	pacemaker
la nefrectomía	nephrectomy
la neumonectomía	pneumonectomy
el reemplazo de rodilla, cadera	knee, hip replacement

Preguntas útiles

¿Ha tenido alguna cirugía?	Have you ever had surgery?
Enséñeme sus cicatrices.	Show me your scars.

Expresiones útiles

Me sacaron la matriz.	They took out my womb.
Me operaron de la próstata.	They operated on my prostate.

10.17 Ejercicio

Identify what it is that the following explanations describe.

A. _____ Es un procedimiento quirúrgico usado por los cirujanos ortopédicos para visualizar, diagnosticar y tratar problemas en las articulaciones.

B. _____ Es una operación que se hace sin hospitalizar (internar) al paciente.

C. _____ Es un procedimiento quirúrgico para sacar un riñón.

D. _____ El cirujano hace varias incisiones pequeñas para introducir una cámara pequeña que el cirujano usa para observar la cirugía e introducir los instrumentos que necesita para hacer la cirugía.

E. _____ Es un procedimiento quirúrgico para diagnosticar una enfermedad abdominal o para saber si la víctima de un trauma tiene heridas internas graves.

 10.18 Drama imprevisto

Play "tag team surgical consultation." Two volunteers role-play a surgeon and patient discussing a specific surgery. The rest of the class is divided down the middle, with one side designated to support the surgeon and the other designated to support the patient. Whenever the surgeon or patient is lost for words, a team member should step in.

A. Señor Peña has cancer in the left lung, which requires a lobectomy.
B. Señora Labredo has acute appendicitis and needs an appendectomy.
C. Señor del Rosario's son Tito has frequent tonsillitis and should have a tonsillectomy.
D. Señorita Garrido's father was in an accident today. He is positive for blood from the rectum and needs exploratory surgery.

 10.19 Drama imprevisto

With a partner, role-play a primary care doctor interviewing a new patient with an extensive surgical history. Demonstrate for the class an unscripted and unrehearsed interview to document the patient's surgical history. Include the name of the surgery, the year, and the surgeon. This may also be a fun variation of *Hipocondríaco competitivo* (p. 240).

Educate a Patient About Vaccinations

Vocabulario: Las vacunas (Vaccinations)

- "I am going to give you an injection" is *Voy a ponerle una inyección.* To ask about vaccination history, we will need the preterit of the verb *poner* (to put). The verb *poner* is irregular in the preterit. Here it is used with indirect objects.

yo	puse	Me puse la vacuna para el tétanos.
tú	pusiste	¿Te pusiste la vacuna para la hepatitis?
él, ella, usted	puso	La enfermera me puso una inyección.
nosotros/as	pusimos	Antes de viajar nos pusimos dos vacunas.
ellos, ellas, ustedes	pusieron	Mis padres se pusieron la vacuna antigripal.

- "Vaccination" in Spanish is *vacuna.* It is derived from the word for cow (*vaca*). This is because the vaccine that eradicated smallpox was made from cowpox vesicles obtained from healthy vaccinated bovine animals.

  ¿A usted le pusieron la vacuna para el tétanos?
  La enfermera me la puso ya.
- A booster shot is *una inyección de refuerzo.*

  Debe tener una inyección de refuerzo contra el tétanos, la difteria y la tos ferina cada diez años.

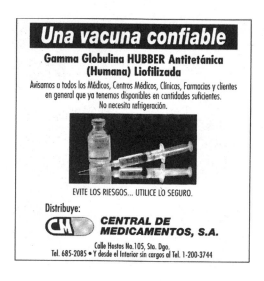

10.20 Actividad

Ask your partner whether he or she received the indicated vaccinations, as in the example. When you have finished, switch roles.

> Example: Student 1: ¿A usted le pusieron la vacuna para el tétanos?
>
> Student 2: Sí, me la pusieron. (*or*) No, no me la pusieron.

A. la meningitis   D. la pulmonía
B. la difteria   E. el sarampión
C. la varicela   F. la gripe

Lectura: La pandemia de gripe (The Pandemic Flu)

La gripe es una enfermedad de las vías respiratorias. Un virus la causa y la enfermedad es contagiosa. Los síntomas de la gripe incluyen todos los síntomas de un resfriado común, más una fiebre alta, dolores musculares, y posibles síntomas gastrointestinales como náusea, vómito y diarrea. Las complicaciones serias de la gripe incluyen la pulmonía, la deshidratación y la insuficiencia cardiaca congestiva.

Muchas personas se enferman con la influenza cada año y muchos de ellos se mejoran sin problema. Otras personas son hospitalizadas por varios días y algunas mueren de las complicaciones de la gripe. Hay ciertas personas que no se enferman con la gripe porque sus cuerpos la combaten o porque se han vacunado. La mejor manera para prevenir la gripe es lavarse las manos frecuentemente y recibir una vacuna contra la gripe todos los años.

La gripe pandémica es una gripe que no tiene vacuna para prevenirla. Para prevenir una pandemia de gripe, debe lavarse las manos frecuentemente y no debe poner las manos cerca de los ojos, la nariz o la boca. Si está enfermo con la gripe o si hay una pandemia de gripe en la comunidad, no debe salir de la casa para ir a lugares públicos como las escuelas o los mercados.

 10.21 Actividad

Make a poster that educates the Spanish-speaking public about how to prevent and to prepare for flu season and/or a possible pandemic flu. You may find it helpful to review the formal commands that you learned in chapter 6.

10.22 Actividad

Act out a brief consultation in which Señora Cruz sees a physician's assistant about a rather deep laceration. Find out when she had her last tetanus vaccination and explain the need for a booster shot and a few stitches. The record that follows may scaffold your conversation, or you may feel free to create another situation. For example, you may choose to discuss the meningitis vaccination with a family who is sending a child to college in September.

> Motivo de la consulta: «Abrí una lata de sopa y me corté la mano.»
> Impresión diagnóstica: Cortadura en la mano izquierda.
> Plan de tratamiento: Vacuna para el tétanos; cinco puntos; crema antibiótica; vendaje.

 ## 10.23 Drama imprevisto

Choose a patient and a practitioner. The practitioner must use the medical record in the illustration on page 256 as a guide to conduct a history and physical with the patient. The patient must decide the chief complaint, and the practitioner must ask questions to arrive at a more specific diagnostic impression and treatment plan. You may use a "tag team" style in which other class members may substitute as needed.

 ## 10.24 Reciclaje

Play "talk show." Two student "guests" sit in front, and the instructor roams with a microphone prop. Using only Spanish, "audience" members ask questions of the contestants, for example, *¿Ha tenido cirugía? ¿Ha fracturado un hueso?* (Answers to those questions may use the preterit or the present perfect.) Guests are free to invent a history, but audience members should take down details and then provide a case history summary concerning each guest.

 ## Video Program: *La sonografía*

Watch the *Demostración* for chapter 10 and do the activity that follows.

> Rosmery: Tú necesitas una cita para un ecograma abdominal.
> Sra. Flores: Perdón, el doctor me dijo que necesito una sonografía.

Rosmery:	Ecograma y una sonografía son lo mismo. Es una prueba que tiene muchos nombres. Se dice ecograma, ecografía, sonograma, sonografía y ultra-sonido. Son muchos nombres pero es lo mismo.
Sra. Flores:	Estoy un poco nerviosa.
Rosmery:	No te preocupes. La sonografía no duele. Tampoco es peligrosa. No usa rayos equis, y sí, podremos ver los órganos del cuerpo, para ver si tienes cálculos en la vesícula.

Sra. Flores:	¿Cómo debo prepararme para la prueba? ¿Puedo comer algo la noche anterior?
Rosmery:	Debes comer alimentos sin grasa la noche antes de la prueba.
Sra. Flores:	Es fácil evitar la comida grasosa, porque me duele mucho el estómago. Ahora como frutas, verduras y pan sin mantequilla.
Rosmery:	Muy bien. Pero no debes comer nada diez horas antes del examen. Te van a dar una bata para ponerte durante el examen. Luego te van a poner una gelatina clara en el abdomen y el técnico que te va a hacer el examen va a presionarte en el abdomen con una maquinita que se llama transductor. Es muy rápido. ¿Entiendes?
Sra. Flores:	Sí, gracias. Ahora me siento menos nerviosa.
Rosmery:	¿Está bien mañana a las nueve de la mañana para el examen?
Sra. Flores:	Sí. No trabajo mañana. Puedo llegar a las nueve de la mañana.
Rosmery:	Bien. Pero no olvides. No comas nada con grasa, y no comas nada después de las once de la noche.
Sra. Flores:	Entendido. Gracias.
Rosmery:	Nos vemos mañana, entonces.
Sra. Flores:	Hasta entonces.

Expediente Médico

Nombre del paciente_____ Número del expediente_____

Dirección_____ Teléfono_____

Fecha de nacimiento_____ Número de seguro social_____

Alergias_____ T._____ P._____ R._____ P.S._____

El problema:

La historia médica:

El examen:

El plan de tratamiento:

 10.25 Drama imprevisto

With a partner, present to the class your own (unscripted and unrehearsed) version of a pre-sonogram educational session like the chapter 10 *Demostración*. Challenge yourself by choosing one of the following variations.

A. The role of Rosmery is played by a manic nurse who moonlights as a chef and gives overly detailed instructions concerning what the patient may and may not eat the day before the test.

B. The role of Sra. Flores is played by a very anxious patient who asks a seemingly excessive number of questions.

C. The role of Rosmery is played by a nurse who asks the patient questions to quiz comprehension, and the part of Sra. Flores is played by a nonchalant patient who doesn't take the instructions seriously.

Cultural Note: Feeling at Home Somewhere Else

Think of another culture you have visited. Suppose you were living there and had to be institutionalized for a long convalescence. Considering your current cultural identity, what would help you to feel "at home"? Even if you were bilingual, would it be important for someone to speak with you in your primary language? What reading materials would you want to have available? Are there certain foods you would crave and others you would want to avoid? What sort of relationship would you want with your caretakers? How comfortable would you feel about being touched or bathed? How much of your personal information, treatment plan, and prognosis would you want caretakers to share with your family? Finally, how would you feel about caretakers writing in your medical record, "Patient unable to participate in treatment because of language barrier"?

Suppose a well-intentioned staff member were to treat you as a stereotypical person from your culture? For example, the dietitian arranges for you to have a special diet of hamburgers and hot dogs while the recreation therapist plays country and western music, but you actually have other preferences. Of course you'd be gracious about it, but would the stereotyping cancel the good intentions?

Now think about your current work setting. Does a receptionist greet patients and visitors in a familiar language? Do the magazines, newspapers, wall hangings, and dietary choices reflect the cultural diversity of the patients and their families? How diverse is the staff at various levels of the organization? Are health-education pamphlets and discharge instructions available in the languages that patients speak? How long does it usually take to find a qualified interpreter or translator when needed?

Of course Spanish-speakers themselves are culturally diverse to the extent that the large group is considered polycultural. They are heterogeneous with regard to cultural origin, religion, ethnicity, geographic origin, education, and socioeconomic position. We may describe North Americans that way, too, and acknowledge and celebrate the way diversity has enriched society. Such diversity challenges health care workers to learn the cultural traditions, worldviews, and practices of their own diverse patient population. However, even when you believe you are knowledgeable about a patient's culture of origin, you cannot safely assume that you are therefore knowledgeable about an individual's personal experience of his or her culture. General cultural knowledge must not promote the stereotyping of individuals.

In health care, there has been a tendency towards standardizing care along clinical pathways. This promotes consistent adherence to empirically proven methods. However, an obstetrician with volunteer experience abroad said about the delivery room, "The problem was that every time we turned our backs, the women would get out of the stirrups and squat in the corners of the room." There was apparent disagreement between care providers and patients about the best position in which to give birth. Health care workers are not necessarily trained to ask the patient his or her belief about treatment. Societies demonstrate varying degrees of expectation with regard to the extent to which newly arriving groups should assimilate.

Aside from the debate about the benefits of gravity-assisted childbirth, there are many areas in which a facility may work to become more "familiar-feeling" to a culturally diverse patient population. One hospital held a meeting between the chief cook, the dietitian, the owner of an ethnic restaurant, and hospital staff members who shared the cultural origins of many of the patients. Staff and patients contributed their favorite recipes from home. Then under the dietitian's guidance about what was nutritionally desirable, the cook was able to translate the recipes to prepare larger quantities of food. The restaurant owners shared information about suppliers of less common foods and spices. As a result, patients felt just a little more welcome, and perhaps some were able to draw upon emotional inner resources of comfort that had been instilled much earlier in life.

Chapter 11

Internamientos, odontología y la salud mental

By the end of this chapter you will know additional vocabulary to help you with hospital admissions and discharge planning. You will know the terms associated with dental prophylaxis and treatment. You will be able to ask about feelings. You will know some of the phrases and cultural considerations pertinent to a basic mental status exam.

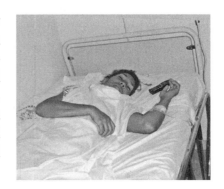

Announce a Hospitalization

Vocabulario: El internamiento (Hospital Admission)

dar de alta	to discharge
la estadía	stay, length of stay
la habitación privada	private room
la habitación semiprivada	semiprivate room
hospitalizar	to hospitalize
la hospitalización	hospitalization
internar	to admit to an institution
quedarse interno/a	to remain inpatient

11.1 Actividad

With a partner, prepare and present to the class a dialogue in which you inform a patient or patient's family member about the need for hospitalization and answer questions. Cover the diagnosis, the treatment needed, and the estimated length of stay. Here are some ideas for starters.

Nombre	*Diagnóstico*	*Procedimiento*	*Estadía estimada*
Señor Colón	colecistitis	colecistectomía	dos días
Juancito	amigdalitis	amigdalectomía	un día
Señora Méndez	apendicitis	apendectomía	dos días
Doña Olga	angina de pecho	angiograma	dos días
Señor Olivencia	artritis	reemplazo de cadera	cuatro días

 ## Video Program: *La laparoscopia*

Watch the *Trama* for chapter 11 and do the activity that follows. In the *Trama* Dr. Vargas explains a cholecystectomy to Sra. Vargas.

Dr. Vargas: Tenemos los resultados de la sonografía. Usted tiene cálculos en la vesícula biliar. Debemos hacer una cirugía para sacarle la vesícula.

Sra. Flores: ¿Una cirugía? Pero tengo que cuidar a mi hija, Elsita. ¿Cuánto tiempo voy a estar en el hospital, doctor?

Dr. Vargas: Uno o dos días. La colecistectomía es una cirugía común. Ahora, hacemos la colecistectomía laparoscópica. Hacemos cuatro pequeñas incisiones en el abdomen, y el paciente vuelve a su casa el próximo día.

Sra. Flores: ¿Por qué cuatro incisiones?

Dr. Vargas: Una es muy pequeña y debajo del ombligo, para introducir una pequeña cámara que el cirujano usa para ver la vesícula y observar la cirugía. Las otras tres son para introducir los instrumentos que el cirujano usa en la cirugía.

Sra. Flores:	Es increíble. La medicina está muy avanzada.
Dr. Vargas:	Gracias a la cirugía laparoscópica, los pacientes pueden volver a sus actividades normales más rápido.
Sra. Flores:	Pero, ¿no necesito la vesícula para nada?
Dr. Vargas:	Puede llevar una vida normal sin la vesícula. La cirugía, como cualquier procedimiento médico, tiene sus beneficios y riesgos. El primer beneficio es el quitar los síntomas, como el dolor, la náusea y los vómitos. El segundo beneficio es el evitar complicaciones con la vesícula, por ejemplo, sin tratamiento la inflamación se puede empeorar o puede tener infección.
Sra. Flores:	¿Cuáles son los riesgos, doctor?
Dr. Vargas:	Es una pregunta importante. En su caso, el riesgo de no hacer la cirugía es peor que los riesgos de la cirugía. Pocas personas tienen complicaciones con la cirugía, pero los riesgos incluyen la posibilidad de sangrar, la posibilidad de tener infección o las posibles complicaciones con la anestesia.
Sra. Flores:	Está bien, doctor.
Dr. Vargas:	El día después de la cirugía los pacientes se quitan los vendajes y se bañan. Normalmente toman líquidos por uno o dos días. Es importante caminar para evitar los coágulos de sangre en las piernas. Dentro de una semana resumen sus actividades normales.
Sra. Flores:	¿Cómo puedo saber si hay complicaciones?
Dr. Vargas:	Llame al consultorio del cirujano si tiene fiebre o tiene color amarillo en los ojos o en la piel. Llame si el dolor empeora, si el abdomen se hincha, o si tiene náusea o vómitos persistentes o secreción en las incisiones.
Sra. Flores:	Doctor, ¿usted me puede hacer la cirugía? Yo lo conozco, y me siento más cómoda con usted.
Dr. Vargas:	Gracias por la confianza, pero no soy cirujano. Hay una buena cirujana en la clínica. Ella se llama la doctora García. Ella la va a llamar para hacer una cita para hablar sobre la cirugía. En esa cita puede hablar con el anestesiólogo también.
Sra. Flores:	Gracias.
Dr. Vargas:	De nada. Suerte.

11.2 Drama imprevisto

In groups of three, spontaneously act for the class a family meeting after dinner that day at the Floreses' home. During the meeting, Sra. Flores discusses today's doctor's appointment and answers questions for Sr. Flores and Elsita, who give emotional support and help make plans for the household to run smoothly during her hospitalization.

Lectura: Las directivas avanzadas (Advance Directives)

Normalmente los hospitales hacen todo lo posible para curar a los pacientes. Cuando un paciente está gravemente enfermo y no hay posibilidad de recuperación, el paciente tiene derecho de aceptar o negar los tratamientos que no curan su enfermedad pero que lo mantienen con vida por más tiempo, por ejemplo, el ventilador

gravemente enfermo	terminally ill

derecho a negar	right to refuse

(máquina para respirar) y la reanimación cardiopulmonar. Hay personas que no les gusta la idea de mantenerse con vida usando máquinas u otros sistemas artificiales. La directiva avanzada es un documento legal que le permite al paciente dar instrucciones a los doctores con relación al uso de los sistemas artificiales. El documento se llama *directiva* porque el paciente le da instrucción al doctor con respeto a cuales son los tratamientos que quiere o que no quiere recibir. Se llama *avanzada* porque es importante firmarlo antes de estar enfermo gravemente o en coma y permanentemente inconsciente. Aunque una persona se niegue al uso del ventilador o a la reanimación cardiopulmonar, puede aceptar el uso de fluidos por suero intravenoso y/o medicamentos para el dolor que son designados solamente para mantenerlo confortable.

 ## 11.3 Actividad

In small groups, prepare and present to the class a skit in which one student interviews a patient and the patient's family to explain and answer questions about advance directives during the processing of a hospital admission. Add dynamics for more challenge. Include a family member who wants a guarantee of heroic measures for a patient who otherwise is eager to sign the advance directive document.

Discuss Activities of Daily Living

Estructura: Los verbos reflexivos (Reflexive Verbs)

- A verb is considered "reflexive" when a pronoun is used to indicate that an action is done to oneself. The subject and object of the verb are the same person. In a dictionary, the infinitive form of a reflexive verb appears with the pronoun *se* attached as a suffix. Thus the verb *bañar* means "to bathe," and *bañarse* means "to bathe oneself." Like the object pronouns, the reflexive pronouns are placed before a conjugated verb or a negative command, and they are attached to a verb infinitive or an affirmative command. When attached to the command as a suffix, they may necessitate a written accent to indicate the location of the spoken (prosodic) accent.

Baño al bebé por la tarde.	I bathe the baby in the afternoon.
Me baño por la mañana.	I bathe myself in the morning.
Tiene que bañarse hoy.	You have to bathe yourself today.
¡Báñese!	Take a bath!
No se bañe por dos días.	Don't bathe for two days.

- Here is the verb *lavarse,* which means "to wash oneself." Notice that the reflexive pronouns are *me, te, se, nos,* and *se.* Except for *se,* they are the same as the direct and indirect object pronouns.

me lavo	Me lavo las manos antes de examinar a los pacientes.
te lavas	¿Te lavas las manos después de toser o estornudar?
se lava	La enfermera se lava las manos frecuentemente.
nos lavamos	Cuando tenemos sueño nos lavamos la cara con agua fría.
se lavan	Los niños se lavan las manos antes de comer.

- In the sentence *Me lavo las manos,* the reflexive pronoun says whose hands are being washed. Spanish avoids redundancy by saying *las manos* instead of *mis manos.*

- Verbs may be used in their reflexive form—or not—to indicate an individual's level of independence in activities of daily living.

Baño a los pacientes.	I bathe the patients.
La Sra. Vega se baña.	Sra. Vega bathes herself.

Vocabulario: Actividades de la vida cotidiana
(Activities of Daily Living)

acostarse (o-ue)*	to lie down, to go to bed
afeitarse	to shave oneself
bañarse	to bathe oneself
cepillarse	to brush oneself
despertarse (e-ie)*	to awaken
ducharse	to shower oneself
levantarse	to get up
peinarse	to comb oneself
ponerse la ropa	to get dressed
quitarse la ropa	to take off one's clothes
vestirse (e-i)*	to get dressed
desvestirse (e-i)*	to take off one's clothes
virarse	to roll over

acostarse (o-ue)	*despertarse (e-ie)*	*vestirse (e-i)*
me acuesto	me despierto	me visto
te acuestas	te despiertas	te vistes
se acuesta	se despierta	se viste
nos acostamos	nos despertamos	nos vestimos
se acuestan	se despiertan	se visten

11.4 Ejercicio

Number the following phrases in the order that Juan might do them on a typical day. Then conjugate the verbs and tell the story. Following *antes de* or *después de,* a verb remains in its infinitive form: *Después de cenar, me cepillo los dientes.* Then tell it in the past tense.

_____ desayunar con huevos y pan

_____ mirar la televisión y acostarse tarde

_____ cenar

_____ llegar a la casa muy cansado

_____ despertarse muy temprano

*These are "stem-changing verbs," in which a vowel changes in all but the first person plural (*nosotros*). There are those in which an *o* changes to *ue,* those in which an *e* changes to *ie,* and those in which an *e* changes to *i.* In chapter 7 you learned the verb *preferir* (*e-ie*). These are treated as regular verbs in the preterit except for the verbs ending in -*ir,* which change only in the third person singular and plural.

_____ levantarse a las seis y media de la mañana

_____ cepillarse los dientes

_____ bañarse y vestirse

_____ salir a las ocho para trabajar en el hospital

 11.5 Actividad

Working in pairs, ask each other the following questions. Although it may now seem awkward to use the *usted* form when talking with a classmate, envision yourself talking to an adult patient with whom you are not on a first-name basis.

Example: Student 1: ¿Se baña usted por la mañana o por la noche?
Student 2: Me baño por la mañana.

A. ¿Se despierta usted antes de las seis de la mañana?
B. ¿Se ducha por la mañana o por la noche?
C. ¿Se afeita antes de bañarse o después?
D. ¿Se peina o se cepilla el cabello?
E. ¿Se cepilla los dientes antes del desayuno o después?
F. ¿Se viste antes de desayunar?
G. ¿Se acuesta temprano o tarde los domingos?
H. ¿Se quita la ropa antes de acostarse?

 11.6 Actividad

Ask a partner the following questions using the *tú* form of the verb, then switch places.

Example: Ask what time your partner goes to bed.
Student 1: ¿A qué hora te acuestas?
Student 2: Me acuesto a las diez de la noche.

A. Ask what time he or she wakes up in the morning.
B. Ask what time he or she gets up in the morning.
C. Ask if he or she is tired when he or she awakens.
D. Ask what time he or she gets dressed in the morning.
E. Ask if he or she is sleepy when he or she goes to bed.
F. Ask if he or she takes a bath every day.
G. Ask how many times a day he or she brushes his or her teeth.

11.7 Actividad

Statements describing a total care patient (except for falling asleep or waking up) do not require the reflexive form, while statements about an independent patient do require the reflexive form. After reading, provide additional information to further describe the differences between the following two patients.

> El señor Aquino Linares es inválido. Él necesita ayuda y depende completamente de un enfermero para cuidarlo. Por ejemplo, el enfermero baña al señor Linares. La señora Silva de Palma es independiente. Ella se baña sin ayuda.

 ## 11.8 Actividad

Relate your morning routine or your evening routine to your partner. Notice the use of the infinitive forms *despertarme* and *cepillarme* in the example. The infinitive form is used after *antes de* and *después de*.

> Example: Me despierto a las seis de la mañana. Después de despertarme, me cepillo los dientes. Desayuno antes de salir para el trabajo.

Afterwards, your partner should report your routine to the class, using the third person singular form of the verb.

 ## 11.9 Actividad

Tell a story based on the images that follow. Give a name to the protagonist and describe her morning routine. Add as much additional information as you can, making it up if necessary!

La rutina

11.10 Actividad

Practice the reflexive verbs in the preterit. Only those ending in *-ir* change stems in the preterit, and only in the third person singular and plural. Tell a partner the following information about yourself, and then ask about himself or herself, using the *tú* form, as in the example.

> Example: acostarse tarde anoche
> > Student 1:   Me acosté tarde anoche. ¿Te acostaste tarde anoche?
> > Student 2:   Anoche me acosté a las diez.

A. ducharse anoche antes de acostarse
B. despertarse temprano esta mañana
C. levantarse temprano esta mañana
D. peinarse esta mañana
E. afeitarse esta tarde
F. cepillarse después del desayuno
G. bañarse con agua tibia (lukewarm) esta tarde

 11.11 Drama imprevisto

Here's a good place for a game of "The Three-minute Date." With a partner, ask each other questions about personal hygiene habits. As for your own answers, you may choose to play the role of a slob, an insomniac, a clean freak, and so on, or you may choose to just answer as yourself. At announced intervals, switch partners and start over. Afterwards, share juicy tidbits with the class.

 ### Estructura: *Se* y eventos imprevistos
(*Se* and Unplanned Events)

- The pronoun *se* is used with reflexive verbs. It is also used when announcing an unplanned event that has no clear actor. Use the pronoun *se,* the indirect object (indicating to whom the event happened), and the third person singular or plural of the verb (as if what happened was the subject of the verb). For example,

> Se me hinchan los tobillos.   My ankles get swollen.
> Se le fracturó la pierna.   His/Her/Your leg fractured.

- Perhaps this constitutes a cultural-linguistic pardon that recognizes that some things just happen and are nobody's fault. *Rompí mi pierna* (I broke my leg) doesn't sound as much like an accident as *Se me rompió la pierna* (My leg broke).

- This construction is commonly used with verbs including *olvidar* (to forget), *perder* (*e-ie*) (to lose, to misplace), and *caer* (to drop, to fall), among others. For example,

Se me olvidó.	I forgot.
Se me olvidan las cosas.	I forget things.
Se me perdieron las recetas.	I lost the prescriptions.
Se me cayó la botella y se rompió.	I dropped the bottle and it broke.

 11.12 Ejercicio

Rephrase the following statements to emphasize the event more than the actor.

    Example: Olvidé la cita.   Se me olvidó la cita.

A. Rompí un hueso.   _____.

B. Olvidé ponerme la insulina.   _____.

C. Fracturaste el dedo.   _____.

D. Quemaste la mano.   _____.

E. ¿Perdió usted la receta?   _____.

 Estructura: Los verbos *dormir* y *poder*
(To Sleep; To Be Able)

- The verb *dormir* (to sleep) is an *o-ue* stem-changing verb in the present tense. In the preterit it has a stem change in the third person singular and plural (as do all stem-changing verbs that end in *-ir*).

El presente	*El pretérito*
duermo	dormí
duermes	dormiste
duerme	durmió
dormimos	dormimos
duermen	durmieron

- The reflexive form *dormirse* means "to nod off" or "to fall asleep."

¿Duerme bien por la noche?	Do you sleep well at night?
¿Durmió bien anoche?	Did you sleep well last night?
Me duermo aquí en la silla.	I'm falling asleep here in the chair.
¿A qué hora se durmió?	At what time did you fall asleep?

- The verb *poder* (to be able to), like *dormir,* is an *o-ue* stem-changing verb. It is often used before another verb in that verb's infinitive form.

puedo	Puedo respirar mejor ahora.
puedes	¿Me puedes decir qué pasó?
puede	Juan no puede caminar.
podemos	Podemos ayudar a su madre.
pueden	Los niños no pueden abrir la botella.

- After greeting your patient, a good way to start the examination is,

  ¿En qué le puedo ayudar?   How can I help you?

 ## 11.13 Actividad

Work with a partner to practice the new verbs. Take turns asking and answering the following questions.

   A. Ask if he or she slept well last night.
   B. Ask how long it has been that he or she has not slept well.
   C. Ask how many hours he or she sleeps at night (*por la noche*).
   D. Ask whether he or she needs something to sleep.
   E. Ask if he or she can open the pill bottle.
   F. Ask if he or she can swallow (*tragar*) the pill without problem.
   G. Ask if he or she can arrive at 7:00 on Monday morning.
   H. Advise that he or she cannot go home today because of a fever.

 ## 11.14 Actividad

You are a mental health professional, and your partner suffers from depression. Role-play an interview to explore sleep disturbance symptoms, such as insomnia and early morning awakening. To recycle material from chapter 7, ask about changes in weight and appetite, too.

 ## Plan a Hospital Discharge

The odd phrase *dar de alta* appears to have its origin in military service, where the terms *dar de baja* and *dar de alta* were used. When a soldier was injured, he was sent to the hospital with the orders *dar de baja,* because his movement reduced the number of soldiers. He was returned to the ranks with the orders *dar de alta,* because his arrival augmented the fighting force. In hospitals, the designation *dar de alta* refers to the doctor's order proclaiming the patient sufficiently cured to return home.

Vocabulario: Planear los cuidados posteriores
(Discharge Planning)

dar de alta	to discharge from the hospital
¿Cuándo me dan de alta?	When do they discharge me?
A usted le dan de alta hoy.	They discharge you today.
¿Necesita ayuda en la casa?	Do you need help at home?
¿Cocina usted para si mismo/a?	Do you cook for yourself?
¿En qué piso vive usted?	On what floor do you live?
¿Hay escalera?	Are there stairs?
¿Hay ascensor?	Is there an elevator?
¿Quién lo (la) va a llevar a la casa?	Who is going to take you home?
¿Tiene oxígeno en la casa?	Do you have oxygen at home?
¿Tiene usted familiares o amigos que lo (la) ayudan en la casa?	Do you have family members or friends who help you at home?
¿Tiene o ha tenido un enfermero que lo (la) visita en la casa?	Do you have or have you had a nurse who visits you at home?
¿De qué agencia es/fue el enfermero?	From what agency is/was the nurse?
¿Cuál es su número de teléfono?	What is his or her telephone number?

 11.15 Actividad

You are a discharge planning nurse, and your partner is a hospitalized patient. Present to the class a role play of a typical discharge planning interview. Here are some possible situations to get started.

A. Señora Soto is going to be discharged today. She will need a nurse to visit her at home tomorrow to check her blood pressure. Gather the information you'll need to make an interagency referral.

B. Señor López is going to be discharged tomorrow. Find out whether he has had visiting nurse services. He will need a nurse to visit him at home to check the incision (*la incisión*). He must call the doctor if he has a fever.

C. Doña Leomara goes home tomorrow. Find out whether she has a pill organizer at home. A nurse is going to visit her at home to change the bandage (*cambiar el vendaje*) on Mondays, Wednesdays, and Fridays.

11.16 Drama imprevisto

Role-play a meeting between an elderly patient, his or her adult child, and a hospital discharge planner. The discharge planner is gathering information about the patient's level of independence in activities of daily living; the adult child is concerned that the parent needs a lot of help; the patient is proud, values independence, and insists, among other things, «Voy para mi casa. Nadie me va a echar en un asilo.»

 ## Teach About Dental Hygiene

Vocabulario: El consultorio del dentista (The Dentist's Office)

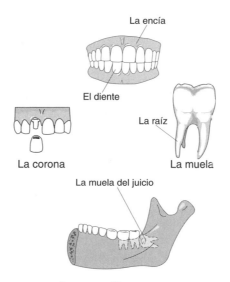

La encía

El diente

La corona

La raíz

La muela

La muela del juicio

Los dientes

La boca

la corona	crown
la dentadura postiza	false teeth
el diente	tooth
los dientes de leche	baby teeth
las encías	gums
la muela	molar
la muela del juicio	wisdom tooth

La higiene bucal (Oral Hygiene)

la crema dental	toothpaste
el enjuague	rinse
el fluoruro	fluoride
el/la higienista dental	dental hygienist
el hilo dental	dental floss
la limpieza	cleaning
prevenir	to prevent
el sarro, la placa	plaque

Los padecimientos y los tratamientos

la caries dental	dental cavity
el empaste	filling
la enfermedad periodontal	periodontal disease
enjuagarse la boca	to rinse one's mouth
la extracción de diente	tooth extraction
la gingivitis	gingivitis
el sellante	sealant
el tratamiento de canal	root canal treatment

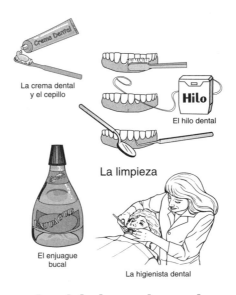

La crema dental
y el cepillo

El hilo dental

La limpieza

El enjuague
bucal

La higienista dental

La higiene bucal

Lectura: Las caries y la gingivitis (Cavities and Gingivitis)

Las bacterias que normalmente están en la boca pueden causar las caries.
Primero, las bacterias forman placa en los dientes. Las bacterias en la placa
transforman en ácidos el azúcar que comemos o bebemos. Estos ácidos

hacen las caries. Los bebés que duermen con el biberón pueden tener caries por el azúcar que hay en la leche. Por eso, los bebés no deben dormir con un biberón en la boca. Para prevenir las caries debe comer y beber menos dulces. También, hay que cepillarse los dientes dos veces al día y usar el hilo dental. Debe usar una crema dental que tiene fluoruro. El fluoruro protege los dientes. Hay suplementos de fluoruro en forma de tabletas, gotas y enjuagues. Debe de ir al consultorio del dentista dos veces al año para una limpieza profesional. El dentista puede ponerle sellantes en los dientes para prevenir las caries.

La gingivitis es una inflamación de las encías. Algunos de los síntomas de la gingivitis son las encías rojas e hinchadas, dolor cuando toma bebida o comida fría, caliente o dulce, y sangre en las encías cuando se cepilla. Sin tratamiento adecuado la gingivitis puede causar la enfermedad periodontal. El tratamiento incluye la limpieza diaria con hilo dental y cepillo, el uso de una crema dental con fluoruro y exámenes regulares por un dentista o higienista dental.

 ## 11.17 Actividad

Check your comprehension of the reading by taking turns with a partner asking each other the following questions.

A. ¿Qué causa las caries?
B. ¿Cómo se previenen las caries?
C. ¿Deben de dormir los bebés con un biberón en la boca?
D. Si quiero prevenir las caries, ¿cuál es la mejor merienda?
E. ¿Qué es la gingivitis y cuáles son los síntomas?
F. ¿Quién puede explicarme el uso correcto del hilo dental?

11.18 Actividad

With a partner, plan and present to the class an interview between a dental hygienist and a patient. The hygienist will want to know, for example, the last time the patient saw a dentist, the last time he or she had a

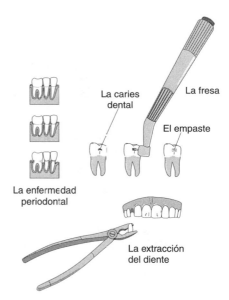

La caries dental

La fresa

El empaste

La enfermedad periodontal

La extracción del diente

Los padecimientos y los tratamientos

cleaning, and whether the patient has pain, hot or cold sensitivity, or bleeding when he or she brushes. The hygienist may then educate the patient about oral hygiene.

Conduct a Mental Status Exam

Estructura: El verbo *sentirse* (To Feel)

- Until now we have used the verb *estar* to talk about feelings and the verb *tener* to talk about drive states.

  Estoy muy molesto cuando tengo hambre.
- To talk about feelings we may use the reflexive verb *sentirse,* too.

¿Cómo se siente usted?	How do you feel?
Me siento cansado/a.	I feel tired.
- *Sentirse* is a stem-changing verb like *despertarse* because the *e* changes to *ie* except in the first person plural (*nosotros*).

me siento	Me siento cansado.
te sientes	¿Cómo te sientes?
se siente	Mi papá se siente solo.
nos sentimos	Nos sentimos bien aquí en México.
se sienten	Los niños se sienten mejor hoy.

Vocabulario: Los sentimientos (Feelings)

The following adjectives represent feelings. They must agree with their corresponding nouns in both gender and number. For example *Juan se siente dichoso,* and *Ana y Luisa se sienten contentas.*

aborrecido	disgusted	contento	content
agitado	agitated	culpable	guilty
agobiado	overwhelmed	deprimido	depressed
agotado	drained	descorazonado	disheartened
agradable	pleasant	desesperado	desperate
agradecido	thankful	dichoso	lucky
alegre	happy	disgustado	disgusted
aliviado	relieved	encantado	pleased
ansioso	anxious	enfadado	annoyed
asustado	frightened	enfermo	sick
avergonzado	ashamed	enfogonado	enraged (*slang*)
celoso	jealous	enojado	angry

frustrado	frustrated	rechazado	rejected
furioso	furious	satisfecho	satisfied
interesado	interested	solitario	lonely
molesto	uncomfortable	soñoliento	sleepy
nervioso	nervous	sorprendido	surprised
ofendido	offended	tímido	shy
orgulloso	proud	traicionado	betrayed
preocupado	worried	triste	sad

These are also used with the verb *estar,* as in *Estoy disgustado,* and *Marisol está ansiosa. La niña está tímida* means that the girl is feeling or acting shy at the moment, while *La niña es tímida* means that the girl is always shy. The reflexive verb *ponerse* may be used when a situation is perceived to cause an emotional response. For example, *Me pongo nervioso cuando estoy donde el dentista.* Now *there's* an opening for a cognitive behavioral therapist!

 11.19 Actividad

The preceding list is a lot of new vocabulary at once. Aid your memory by organizing some of the words into five basic affective states: joy, sadness, anger, fear, and shame. Choose the words that you feel best conceptualize each category. When you finish, the class may depict a version on a blackboard, and then do a "graffiti" exercise in which students write next to each category the cues and cures or triggers and treatments that they associate with each.

---

la alegría (joy)   la tristeza (sadness)

_____   _____

_____   _____

_____   _____

el enojo (anger)   el miedo (fear)   la vergüenza (shame)

_____   _____   _____

_____   _____   _____

_____   _____   _____

11.20 Actividad

Choose a partner and identify the feelings associated with various situations, as in the example. Answer ad lib. Remember that each adjective must agree with the subject in gender and number. Do not use the same *sentimiento* in more than one response. When you have finished, repeat this activity using the verb *estar*. For example, *¿Cómo estás? Estoy asustado.*

Example: Student 1:   Tengo un trabajo nuevo.
            Student 2:   ¿Cómo te sientes?
            Student 1:   Me siento *nervioso/a.*
            Student 2:   ¡Te sientes *nervioso/a!*

A. Tengo cáncer.   F. Tuve una biopsia ayer.
B. Me voy a casar.   G. Voy a tener cirugía.
C. Hablo español muy bien.   H. Tengo cien dólares.
D. El paciente está mejor.   I. Tengo el día libre mañana.
E. Necesito una inyección.   J. Mi amiga está muy enferma.

 11.21 Actividad

Look at the faces in the illustration and name the feeling that corresponds with the expression. There may be more than one correct answer for each. Remember the agreement of gender. Tell the class what happened or is happening to make the character feel this way. For example, *Ella se siente alegre. Su mamá está mejor.* Name the characters if you wish.

Las emociones

Vocabulario: Las enfermedades mentales y sus síntomas
(Mental Illnesses and Symptoms)

El retraso, el retraso mental	delay, mental retardation

Las enfermedades mentales

Los trastornos de ansiedad (Anxiety Disorders)

la fobia social	social phobia
el trastorno de estrés postraumático	post-traumatic stress disorder
el trastorno obsesivo compulsivo	obsessive-compulsive disorder
el trastorno de pánico	panic disorder

Los trastornos del estado de ánimo (Mood Disorders)

la depresión	depression
la enfermedad bipolar	bipolar disorder
la manía	mania

Los trastornos sicóticos (Psychotic Disorders)

la esquizofrenia	schizophrenia
la sicosis	psychosis
el trastorno esquizoafectivo	schizoaffective disorder

Los síntomas (Symptoms)

la alucinación	hallucination
el delirio	delusion
la falta de apetito	lack of appetite
el insomnio	insomnia
la irritabilidad	irritability
el llanto	weeping, crying jag
las palpitaciones	palpitations
la paranoia	paranoia
la tristeza	sadness
las voces	voices

El suicidio (Suicide)

hacerse daño	to harm oneself
suicidarse, quitarse la vida, matarse	to commit suicide

Preguntas útiles

¿Cómo está su estado de ánimo?	How is your mood?

¿Piensa en suicidarse?	Are you planning to commit suicide?
¿Piensa en quitarse la vida?	Are you planning to commit suicide?
¿Tiene deseo de hacerse daño?	Do you want to hurt yourself?
¿Hay voces que le molestan?	Are there voices that bother you?
¿Oye voces que otra persona no puede oír?	Do you hear voices that others cannot hear?

Oír (To hear)	
oigo	oímos
oyes	oyen
oye	

 ## 11.22 Actividad

Conduct these portions of a mental status exam with a partner. Switch roles halfway through. When you have finished, consider presenting a mental status exam to the class. One partner may play the role of a patient who suffers from anxiety, delirium, depression, bipolar disorder, or schizophrenia.

A. ¿Cómo se llama usted?

B. ¿Dónde estamos? (¿Cómo se llama el lugar donde estamos?)

C. ¿Qué día es? (¿En qué año estamos? ¿Cuál es la fecha de hoy?)

D. ¿Cóme se siente? ¿Cómo está su estado de ánimo?

E. ¿Duerme bien? (¿Cuánto tiempo hace que no duerme bien?)

F. ¿Come bien? (¿Tiene apetito?)

G. ¿Toma algún medicamento para los nervios?

H. ¿Estuvo usted alguna vez hospitalizado por problemas emocionales?

I. ¿Cuándo fue? ¿Dónde fue? (¿Tomó usted medicamento en el hospital?)

J. ¿Oye voces que otra persona no puede oír? (¿Qué dicen las voces?)

K. ¿Usa drogas (cocaína, heroína o marihuana)? ¿Toma bebidas alcohólicas?

L. ¿Tiene deseo de suicidarse?

M. ¿Tiene deseo de hacerse daño?

N. Voy a decirle tres palabras. Favor de repetirlas: *cama, manzana, brazo.*

O. Voy a decirle unos números. Favor de repetirlos. *2; 1 - 6; 5 - 6 - 3; 8 - 2 - 1 - 7.*

P. ¿Cuáles fueron las tres palabras que yo le dije y que usted me repitió?

11.23 Actividad

In groups of three, role-play an interview with Señor Peinado, his son Emilio, and a mental health professional. The family's chief complaint is, «Hace dos semanas que Emilio habla solo» (Emilio has been talking to himself for the past two weeks). Emilio has spoken of suicide, and he does not like the side effects of haloperidol.

 ## 11.24 Drama imprevisto

Look at the photo of Doña Isabella. Enact an interview between Doña Isabella, her family, and a mental health professional. Her adult children brought her to the United States to live, but she seems depressed. She feels useless (*inútil*) and wants to work. She cannot communicate with her grandchildren.

Doña Isabella

 ## Video Program: At the Drop of a Hat

Watch the *Atracción especial* for chapter 11 and do the activity that follows. That is when you'll get a chance to play, too.

Dr. Vargas: Okay, contestants. We are going to play "At the drop of a hat." Draw an emotion from the hat and then repeat a line while acting—or overacting—that emotion. Later we'll identify the emotions for points. The line is *Tengo una cita con el gastroenterólogo.*

Rosmery: Tengo una cita con el gastroenterólogo.

Marisol: Tengo una cita con el gastroenterólogo.

Francisco: ¿Qué quieres decir con eso?

Marisol: Relájate, mi amor, es un juego.

Francisco: Tengo una cita con el gastroenterólogo.

Dr. Vargas: Okay, for one thousand points, who can identify all the emotions?

Elsita:	¡Yo! ¡Yo! Rosmery estuvo asustada, Mamá estuvo enamorada, y Papá estuvo furioso.
Dr. Vargas:	¡Perfecto! Let's play another round. The line is, *La doctora va a volver pronto.*
Rosmery:	La doctora va a volver pronto.
Marisol:	La doctora va a volver pronto.
Francisco:	La doctora va a volver pronto.
Dr. Vargas:	Okay, for one thousand points, who can identify the emotions?
Elsita:	¡Yo lo sé! ¡Yo lo sé!
Dr. Vargas:	Okay, Elsita, ¿cómo se sintieron?
Elsita:	Rosmery estuvo deprimida, Mamá estuvo aliviada, y Papá estuvo preocupado.
Dr. Vargas:	¡Mil puntos para Elsita!

 ## 11.25 Drama imprevisto

Now it is your turn to play "At the drop of a hat," a game in which you draw an emotion from a hat and then overact a line of script demonstrating that emotion. The instructor will prepare a container with slips of paper identifying emotional states. Students take turns drawing an emotion and reading a line "in character." The "studio audience" then attempts to identify the emotions for points. Here are some possible lines, but feel free to make up your own.

A. Tengo que trabajar en el hospital mañana.
B. El profesor / La profesora va a cocinar esta noche.
C. Tenemos un examen en la clase de español esta noche.

Cultural Note: *Los nervios*

Mental health assessment and treatment are affected by language and by factors beyond language. A marginally bilingual patient who is being interviewed in his or her second language may demonstrate depressive symptoms of psychomotor retardation and thought blocking; or may use neologisms or have word-finding problems. The same patient may exhibit hypomanic symptoms of tangential speech or talk in a circumstantial rather than linear logic. Recall that in the chapter 9 *Demostración* video segment, Marisol set out to tell Rosmery about her cholecystitis pain. However, before arriving at a description of the pain, she spoke of the anniversary, the restaurant, and the food that she and Francisco ordered. Clinicians face the danger of mistakenly attributing artifacts of speaking a second language to psychopathology, and also the danger of confusing the cultural norm and the phychologically abnormal (type 1 and type 2 errors).

Beyond language, many patients have unique psychosocial stressors. For example, a few immigrants have mortgaged family homesteads to unscrupulous opportunists for money to pay a "coyote" for passage abroad. This greatly increases the pressure to work and send money home to repay the debt. Others may greatly miss their homeland but not have paperwork that permits round-trip travel. Some feel caught between the desire to return home and the embarrassment of not having achieved economic goals they had originally set off to accomplish.

Patients may have limited experience in describing psychiatric problems. When asked about his or her condition, the patient may say, *Padezco de los nervios* or *Sufro de los nervios,* terms related to traditional beliefs that nerves are central to psychiatric distress. When asked what medication he or she takes, the patient may respond, *Tomo una pastilla para los nervios.* Furthermore, while some Latinos may "psychologize" stressors and emotional problems, others may attribute them to physical or spiritual causes. Some patients retain folk explanations for their problems, including a belief in *el espiritismo,* which is related to communication with spirits. Auditory hallucinations may be attributed to *seres,* or "beings."

It is important to assess the degree to which a patient has retained original and traditional cultural beliefs and values. Some clues are elicited by asking whom the patient has consulted about the problem: *¿Con quién ha consultado usted?* This may include a doctor, a priest (*sacerdote*), a pastor (*pastor*), or even a folk healer (*espiritista, santero, curandero*). It is helpful to know what the helpers have said about the problem (*¿Qué le dijo el sacerdote?*). Because of the primacy of family in a patient's support system, it is beneficial to know how the family interprets the meaning of the distress. Considering the influence of religion,

The *sábila* (aloe vera) was hung on this door to keep evil spirits away. Its use in treating burns is well known, and studies have shown that aloe juice can produce an additive effect with other antihyperglycemic agents.

it will be advantageous to discover what the priest, pastor, or church believes about taking medications. One must assess and respect the current values and beliefs of the patient as a starting point before suggesting another approach. Would you be willing to ally with a folk healer?

There are aspects of the mental status exam that are not helpful when literally translated from English. Clinicians sometimes assess the patient's general fund of knowledge in order to get a sense of the patient's overall intelligence and store of information. It would be unfair to ask a recent immigrant to name the past five United States presidents, the distance from New York to California, or the accomplishments of Samuel Clemens. It may be more appropriate to ask, *¿Quién fue Cristóbal Colón?*, *¿Cuál es la capital de su país?*, or *¿Quién es presidente de los Estados Unidos?*

Sometimes the higher mental functions are tested by assessing the patient's capacity for abstract thinking. This is done by asking the patient to interpret proverbs. There is some controversy over whether a proverb should be one with which the patient is expected to be familiar. Even so, it is probably not as helpful to translate "Men who live in glass houses should not throw stones" as it would be to provide a saying that is more commonly known in the patient's community. Here are several of the more common Spanish proverbs:

1. De tal palo, tal astilla (similar to "A chip off the old block").
2. Casa de herrero, cuchillo de palo (The blacksmith's house has a wooden knife).

3. Todo lo que brilla no es oro (All that shines is not gold).
4. Más vale pájaro en mano que cien volando (A bird in hand is worth a hundred flying).
5. No hay rosa sin espinas (There is no rose without thorns).
6. El día más claro llueve (It rains on the clearest day).
7. No hay mal que por bien no venga (similar to "Every cloud has a silver lining").

For an interpretation, ask: *¿Qué significa eso?* (What does that mean?), or *¿Qué quiere decir eso?* (What does that express?).

Ataque de nervios is a culture-bound syndrome that constitutes an accepted—and sometimes expected—behavioral reaction to overwhelming psychosocial distress such as loss, bereavement, or sudden bad news. It appears in some non-Latino cultures as well. The symptoms resemble those of panic attack, except that unlike panic, *ataque de nervios* has an easily identifiable precipitant. In addition to panic symptoms, sufferers may complain of a sensation of heat rising to the head, may fall to the floor as if having a seizure, or may become aggressive. Although sometimes sufferers are brought to medical attention, *ataque de nervios* is primarily dealt with in the community and without medical intervention. In some cases, herbal remedies and brief, intensive family support may rival the efficacy of benzodiazepines. Often, the sufferer will resume his or her premorbid level of functioning within a day. When the *ataque* takes place outside of the cultural context, medical intervention is more likely. If the practitioner determines that hospitalization is indicated, care should be taken not to isolate the patient from his or her primary support system.

Chapter 12
Maternidad y el sexo más seguro

By the end of this chapter you will know vocabulary that is helpful in labor and delivery. You will be able to use informal commands to make direct requests on a more personal basis. You will have had some practice educating patients about safer sex and sexually transmitted diseases.

Confirm a Pregnancy

Vocabulario: El embarazo (Pregnancy)

La menstruación (Menstruation)

menstruar	to menstruate
el período, la regla	period
la ovulación	ovulation
el calambre	cramp
el coágulo	clot
la menopausia, el cambio	menopause, the change

El embarazo (Pregnancy)

estar embarazada*	to be pregnant
embarazo ectópico	ectopic pregnancy
el aborto provocado	abortion
el aborto natural, el aborto espontáneo	miscarriage

Las pruebas (Tests)

la prueba del embarazo	pregnancy test

*Although you may hear the slang term *preñada,* it is generally reserved for animals.

la sonografía	ultrasound
la prueba de Papanicolaou	Pap smear test

Preguntas y expresiones útiles

¿Menstrua usted?	Do you menstruate?
¿Menstrua usted todavía?	Do you still menstruate?
¿Cuántos años tenía cuando menstruó por primera vez?	How old were you when you had your first period?
¿Cuándo comenzó su último período?	When did your last period start?
¿Son regulares sus períodos?	Are your periods regular?
¿Por cuántos días duran sus períodos?	For how many days do your periods last?
¿Cuántos días hay entre un período y otro?	How many days are there between periods?
¿Sangra más que lo normal?	Do you bleed more than usual?
¿Tiene relaciones sexuales?	Are you sexually active?
¿Ha estado embarazada anteriormente?	Have you been pregnant before?
¿Cuántos embarazos ha tenido?	How many pregnancies have you had?
¿Ha perdido un embarazo?	Have you lost a pregnancy?
¿Ha subido de peso?	Have you gained weight?
Su fecha de parto es . . .	Your due date is . . .

 12.1 Actividad

Work with a partner or in small groups to formulate the questions you would use to elicit the indicated information from a patient. When you have finished, each person should write a question on the board as a "graffiti exercise." The class as a whole will then edit the written expressions.

A. Her gynecologist's name
B. When her last period was
C. How long her periods last
D. Whether her periods are regular
E. Whether she has much pain with her periods
F. How long it has been that (*¿Qué tiempo hace que. . . ?*) she does not have her menses
G. How much weight she has gained during this pregnancy
H. Whether she uses drugs, including cocaine, heroin, and/or marijuana
I. Whether she has had a Pap smear

J. When her last Pap smear test was

K. Whether she has had an ultrasound

12.2 Actividad

You are an obstetric nurse in an outpatient clinic. Your classmate is a patient who came for a pregnancy test, and the result was positive. Present to the class a role play in which you inform her that she is pregnant and ask any pertinent questions. Here are some ideas.

A. How does she feel about this news?

B. When did her last menstrual period begin?

C. Has she been pregnant before?

D. How many pregnancies has she had?

E. How many children does she have?

F. Has she had abortions or miscarriages?

G. When was her most recent pregnancy?

H. What type of deliveries has she had?

12.3 Drama imprevisto

Three students role-play an unscripted meeting between a nervous husband, his wife, and an obstetrician. The husband reports changes in his wife that have given him reason to believe that she may be pregnant. The wife believes that her husband is misguided because *¡No puede ser!*

12.4 Actividad

Form groups of three and prepare a skit in which Señora Peña brings her daughter Marisol to the clinic after discovering that Marisol is six or seven months pregnant but has concealed the pregnancy from the family until today.

Teach About Possible Complications

Vocabulario: Posibles complicaciones (Possible Complications)

las contracciones del útero	uterine contractions
el dolor cuando orina	painful urination
el dolor de cabeza severo	severe headache

la fiebre	fever
la hinchazón	swelling
los problemas con la vista	vision problems
el sangramiento vaginal	bleeding from the vagina
la secreción vaginal, el flujo vaginal	vaginal secretions
los tobillos o los pies hinchados	swollen ankles or feet
el vómito persistente	persistent vomiting

Preguntas útiles

¿Dónde está el dolor?	Where is the pain?
Señale dónde le duele.	Point to where it hurts.

 ## 12.5 Actividad

You are an obstetrician at an outpatient clinic. Teach a pregnant patient what symptoms should prompt her to telephone the clinic to request an urgent appointment and how to make the call.

 ## 12.6 Actividad

Role-play a crisis call from a pregnant patient who has called to report one or more of the possible complications of pregnancy. Provide reassurance. Ask whether she currently has or has experienced the other symptoms. (For example, *¿Ha tenido o tiene usted secreciones o sangramiento vaginal?*) Make an urgent care arrangement or a follow-up appointment.

 ## Coach a Delivery

Vocabulario: El parto (Delivery)

nacer	to be born
romper fuente, romper la bolsa de agua	to break water
las contracciones del útero	uterine contractions
el monitoreo fetal	fetal monitor
dar a luz, parir, alumbrar	to deliver
el parto, el alumbramiento	delivery
el parto vaginal, el parto espontáneo	vaginal delivery, spontaneous delivery (NSVD)
la operación cesárea	cesarean section
los dolores del parto	labor pains

la episiotomía	episiotomy
la placenta	placenta
el medicamento epidural para el dolor	epidural medication for the pain
el medicamento para adelantar el parto	medication to advance the delivery
dar el seno, dar el pecho, amamantar*	to breast-feed
la unidad para cuidados intensivos neonatales	neonatal intensive care unit (NICU)
¡Es hembra! ¡Es varón!	It's a girl! It's a boy!
¡Felicidades!	Congratulations!

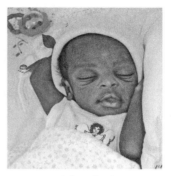

¡Es hembra!

Estructura: El imperativo informal (Informal [*Tú*] Commands)

- In chapter 6 you learned to make requests using *favor de, hay que,* and *tener que* and you learned formal (*usted*) commands, and in chapter 7 you used the verb *deber* to say what a person ought to do. Here you'll learn to make direct requests of persons with whom you may relate on a less formal basis. Use the informal (*tú*) form when addressing children and persons with whom you are on a first-name basis. This includes younger patients and pregnant families with whom you have an ongoing relationship.

| tutear | to address informally |

- Affirmative (Do it!) commands are formed by using the third person singular.

| comer | ¡Come más vegetales! | Eat more vegetables! |
| tomar | ¡Toma el medicamento! | Take the medicine! |

- Negative (Don't do it!) commands are formed like the formal (*usted*) commands, and an *-s* is added. That is, remove the *-o* from the first person singular form of the present tense and add *-es* for verbs that end in *-ar* and *-as* for verbs that end in *-er* and *-ir*.

---

* *La mamadera, el biberón, la mamilla,* and *la tetera* are all words for the baby's bottle, depending on the country of origin.

comer	¡No comas nada!	Don't eat anything!
tomar	¡No tomes el medicamento!	Don't take the medicine!

- Commands express imperative when instructions are direct and to the point, as may be appropriate in settings such as the labor and delivery room.

empujar	¡Empuja!	Push!
	¡No empujes!	Don't push!
mirar	¡Mira!	Look!
	¡No mires!	Don't look!
respirar	¡Respira!	Breathe!
	¡No respires!	Don't breathe!

- When reflexive or object pronouns are used with commands, the pronouns are attached to the end of the verb when the command is affirmative and placed before the verb when the command is negative.

acostarse	¡Acuéstate!*	Lie down!
bañarse	¡No te bañes!	Don't bathe!
lavarse	¡Lávate las manos!	Wash your hands!
levantarse	¡No te levantes!	Don't get up!
moverse	¡No te muevas!	Don't move!
virarse	¡Vírate!	Roll over!

When the use of a pronoun results in the spoken stress being prior to the penultimate syllable, an accent mark is written.

- Here are eight commonly used irregular verbs.

decir (to say, to tell)	¡Di!	¡No digas!
hacer (to do, to make)	¡Haz!	¡No hagas!
ir (to go)	¡Ve!	¡No vayas!
poner (to put)	¡Pon!	¡No pongas!
salir (to leave, to go out)	¡Sal!	¡No salgas!
ser (to be)	¡Sé!	¡No seas!
tener (to have)	¡Ten!	¡No tengas!
venir (to come)	¡Ven!	¡No vengas!

 12.7 Ejercicio

Say the informal commands that best complete the following affirmative and negative sentences.

A. (hacer)   No _____ la cita para hoy. _____ la cita para mañana.

*With *¡Acuéstate!* you may wish to specify *boca arriba* for "face up" or *boca abajo* for "face down."

B. (salir) _____ temprano de la casa. No _____
tarde.

C. (ir) _____ al consultorio. No _____ al hospital.

D. (bañar) No _____ al bebé hoy. _____ al bebé
mañana.

E. (bañarse) No _____ hoy. _____ mañana.

F. (ponerse) _____ la bata del hospital. No _____
ropa interior.

G. (comer) No _____ nada después de las once. _____
bien mañana.

 12.8 Ejercicio

The instructor will read each of the following commands. Change them to
the affirmative or the negative form.

A. ¡No te muevas!   E. ¡Come!
B. ¡Levántate!   F. ¡Acuéstate!
C. ¡No te vires!   G. ¡No levantes el brazo!
D. ¡No te bañes ni hoy ni mañana! H. ¡Respira profundamente!

 12.9 Ejercicio

The following commands might be heard in the labor and delivery area.
Say each of them in Spanish.

A. Don't worry (preocuparse)!
B. Relax (relajarse)!
C. Don't eat anything (Literally, "Don't eat nothing!")!
D. If you are thirsty, don't drink anything; eat ice chips (pedacitos
   de hielo)!
E. Push!
F. Don't push!
G. Breathe!
H. Don't breathe!

12.10 Actividad

Let's translate the game *Simon Says.* The leader will say—or not say— *Simón dice* prior to giving a command. Take turns being the leader. Here are some sample commands for starters. Note that *¡Muévete!* means "Move!" but *¡Mueve el brazo!* does not use the reflexive pronoun.

A. ¡Levántate!	E. ¡Abre la boca!
B. ¡No te levantes!	F. ¡Cierra los ojos!
C. ¡Siéntate!	G. ¡No muevas el dedo!
D. ¡Mueve la mano derecha!	H. ¡Levanta el pie izquierdo!

 12.11 Reciclaje

Let's relate this to other medical specialties. For example, the orthopedist may wish to say,

Mantén la pierna elevada.	Keep your leg up.
No le hagas peso.	Don't bear weight on it.

What other commands do you think the orthopedist may need? What commands do you think that an x-ray technician would use frequently? Share with the class those you are likely to use at work. As a class activity, write various medical specialties as headings on the board. Then write associated commands beneath each. Edit these as a larger group.

Lectura: Después del parto

Después del parto es normal sangrar por la vagina por dos o hasta tres semanas. Pero si sangra mucho o la sangre es muy roja, acuéstese con los pies elevados por dos o tres horas. Si la sangre continua, llame a su médico. No tenga relaciones sexuales por las primeras seis semanas después del parto o hasta que su obstetra, ginecólogo o partera le dé el permiso. Aunque no tiene su período todavía, puede quedar embarazada otra vez.

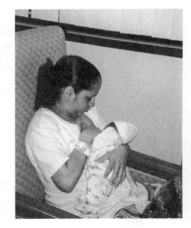

Si amamanta al bebé debe de amamantarlo en el principio de ocho a doce veces en veinticuatro horas. No se ponga a dieta. Necesita calorías y fluidos para hacer leche. Coma una dieta balanceada y siga tomando las vitaminas prenatales.

🗨 **Promote Safer Sex**

Vocabulario: Las enfermedades transmitidas sexualmente (Sexually Transmitted Diseases)

Las enfermedades

la clamidia	chlamydia
la gonorrea	gonorrhea
la hepatitis B	hepatitis B
la hepatitis C	hepatitis C
el herpes	herpes
el SIDA	AIDS
la sífilis	syphilis
la verruga venérea	genital wart, papilloma
el virus del papiloma humano	human papilloma virus

Los síntomas

las ampollas	blisters
el ardor	burning sensation
el dolor al orinar	painful urination
el goteo	dripping
las lesiones	lesions
la orina oscura	dark-colored urine

Las prevenciones

abstenerse	to abstain (conjugated like *tener*)
el condón de látex	latex condom
la educación	education
el examen pélvico	pelvic exam

La abstinencia es la única forma de evitar las enfermedades de transmisión sexual. Si no puede abstenerse, debe tener una relación sexual monógama con un compañero o una compañera que no tiene enfermedades. Los condones de látex con espermicida son efectivos contra el VIH, el virus que causa el SIDA.

Lectura: El SIDA (AIDS)

El Síndrome de Inmunodeficiencia Adquirida (SIDA) es una enfermedad muy grave que daña las defensas del cuerpo. Daña la capacidad que tiene el cuerpo para combatir infecciones. Hay

> *dañar* to damage

un virus llamado VIH (ve-i-hache) que causa el SIDA. Una persona puede tener el virus por muchos años sin estar enfermo o tener los síntomas del SIDA. Una persona infectada que no tiene síntomas del SIDA puede transmitir el virus a otra persona. Esta persona es *un portador sano* del SIDA. Algunos de los síntomas del SIDA son inflamación de los ganglios linfáticos, fiebre persistente sin explicación, sudores nocturnos, una pérdida rápida de peso, fatiga constante, diarrea persistente y manchas blancas

ganglios linfáticos	lymph glands

en la boca (infección por hongos, o *thrush* en inglés). Hay otras enfermedades que pueden causar estos síntomas y no es necesariamente el SIDA. Si tiene algunos de estos síntomas sin una buena explicación, llame al médico.

La educación es la mejor defensa contra el SIDA. Es importante saber cómo defenderse del SIDA. La manera más segura es abstenerse, o no tener relaciones sexuales. Si tiene relaciones, es importante tenerlas con una sola persona y saber que esa persona es una persona sana. La comunicación entre parejas es esencial. Hay que hablar con la pareja acerca del SIDA y acerca de su historia sexual. Es muy peligroso tener relaciones sexuales con una persona que se inyecta drogas, o con varias personas. Es importante usar un condón de látex. Debe tener una prueba del VIH antes de planear el embarazo. Una madre infectada puede transmitir el virus al bebé.

Es peligroso inyectarse con drogas. Para estar saludable, es necesario dejar de usar las drogas. Si no puede dejar de usar las drogas, no use las jeringuillas de otra persona y no comparta las jeringuillas. Si va a usar una jeringuilla más de una vez, lávela con una solución de cloro (Clorox®) y agua y después enjuáguela con agua. Hágalo cada vez que la usa.

1. Es muy importante hablar con la pareja sobre el SIDA.
2. Es importante usar un condón de látex cada vez que tiene contacto sexual.
3. No use drogas. Si usa drogas, no comparta jeringuillas. Lave las jeringuillas con una solución de cloro y agua y después enjuáguelas con agua.

El SIDA no puede ser transmitido por contacto casual. Es decir que el compartir comida, usar baños públicos, o abrazarse con una persona infectada no es peligroso.

abrazarse	to hug

No hay todavía cura para el SIDA. Hay tratamiento. Hay drogas antivirales que pueden extender la vida de algunas personas. Si tiene síntomas del SIDA, es muy importante hablar con el médico o ir a una clínica.

 12.12 Actividad

Check your reading comprehension with a partner. Take turns asking each other the following questions. Answer in complete sentences.

A. ¿Qué es el SIDA, y qué lo causa?

B. ¿Cuáles son los síntomas del SIDA?

C. ¿Cuál es la mejor defensa contra el SIDA?

D. ¿Con quién se debe hablar sobre el SIDA?

E. ¿Por qué se debe usar un condón de látex?

F. Si se inyecta drogas, ¿cómo debe lavar la jeringuilla?

G. ¿Se puede transmitir el SIDA al usar baños públicos?

H. ¿Hay cura para el SIDA?

I. ¿Cuándo debe consultarse con un doctor?

 12.13 Actividad

Ask a partner the following questions. This exercise is good practice for educating patients about safer sex. You must answer in complete sentences. When you have finished, switch roles.

A. ¿Cuál es la manera más segura de evitar las enfermedades de transmisión sexual?

B. ¿Tienen siempre síntomas las enfermedades transmitidas sexualmente?

C. ¿Cuáles son algunos de los síntomas de las enfermedades de transmisión sexual?

D. ¿Qué debe hacer si se tiene algunos de los síntomas?

E. ¿Quién debe ir al médico o a una clínica regularmente para hacerse un análisis de sangre?

F. Si tengo relaciones sexuales con varias personas, ¿qué protección debo usar?

 12.14 Actividad

You are a nurse in a community health clinic. Your partner is a patient who has asked for an HIV test. Demonstrate an educational session. The Spanish word for antibodies is *anticuerpos.*

 12.15 Actividad

In groups of three, spontaneously role-play a Spanish-speaking couple in a medical consultation concerned about whether they are in danger of getting AIDS.

12.16 Drama imprevisto

One student plays the part of Victor L. Virus, and the class conducts an interview that features his exciting life. This can be naughty fun. Here are a few possible questions, but feel free to invent your own. Victor answers ad lib.

Victor L. Virus

A. ¿Eres introvertido o extrovertido?
B. ¿Conoces a mi hermano?
C. ¿Tienes una personalidad contagiosa?
D. ¿Qué te gusta hacer?
E. ¿Te gustan las personas que beben? ¿Por qué?
F. ¿Con qué frecuencia te lavas las manos? ¿Debo lavarme las manos frecuentemente?
G. Dicen que tu primera novia no era lo que esperabas. ¿Qué pasó?
H. Si tú y yo salimos una noche, ¿qué debo esperar? ¿Hay algo que no debemos usar?

 ## Video Program: *Mi hermano tiene SIDA*

Watch the *Trama* for chapter 12 and do the exercise that follows. In the *Trama* Marisol and Francisco Flores talk about caring for Marisol's brother who suffers from HIV disease and can no longer live alone.

Francisco: Marisol, me siento muy contento. Tu cirugía salió bien. Pero me dijiste que querías hablar algo conmigo.

Marisol: Sí. Quiero hablar contigo sobre mi hermano Raúl. Francisco, estoy muy preocupada por él. Ya no puede vivir solo. Él necesita ayuda. Creo que tiene que venir a vivir con nosotros ahora.

Francisco: ¿Qué ayuda necesita?

Marisol: Sabes que él vive en un quinto piso y no puede subir la escalera. Siempre se siente cansado. Y a veces no se toma el medicamento.

Francisco: Mi amor, Raúl tiene SIDA.

Marisol:	Sí, yo entiendo que Raúl tiene SIDA, y la hepatitis B también.
Francisco:	Raúl usa drogas.
Marisol:	Raúl *usaba* drogas. Él está limpio hace dos años. Tú lo sabes.
Francisco:	Tienes razón. *Usaba* drogas. Usó drogas por varios años, hasta que le diagnosticaron con el virus VIH. Dejó de usar drogas hace dos años. Es verdad. No le fue fácil, pero lo hizo. Mira, no quiero discutir contigo. Simplemente estoy preocupado por Elsita. Tenemos que pensar en Elsita primero.
Marisol:	Yo siempre pienso en Elsita. Creo que podemos cuidar a mi hermano sin ponerla en riesgo.
Francisco:	¿Dijiste sin ponerla en el riesgo? El SIDA es contagioso, ¿no?
Marisol:	He leído mucho acerca del SIDA. Y hablé con el trabajador social de Raúl. El SIDA es contagioso, sí, pero no puede ser transmitido por contacto casual. Se puede vivir juntos, compartir la comida, hasta usar el mismo baño. El SIDA se transmite de una persona a otra a través de la sangre, el semen, las secreciones vaginales y por amamantar. Para protegernos, si tenemos una cortada, tenemos que cubrirla con un curita, y tenemos que lavarnos las manos frecuentemente.
Francisco:	Y la hepatitis, ¿no es contagiosa también?
Marisol:	Raúl tiene la hepatitis B. Como el SIDA, la hepatitis B se transmite a través de la sangre y otros fluidos del cuerpo. La diferencia es que hay una vacuna que nos puede proteger de la hepatitis B. Nos podemos vacunar.
Francisco:	Es mucho trabajo, trabajar, cuidar a Elsita y cuidar a tu hermano. ¿Por qué Raúl no va a un asilo? En los asilos saben cuidar a las personas con SIDA.
Marisol:	No me hables de un asilo. Él es mi hermano. En el asilo muy pocas personas hablan español. No le hacen la comida que a él le gusta. No hacen arroz todos los días. Tratan a los enfermos como números, o como pacientes; no como personas.
Francisco:	Sí, tienes razón. Va a cambiar nuestra rutina, pero él va a sentirse mejor. Estoy de acuerdo contigo. Él puede vivir con nosotros.

Marisol:	¿Sabes por qué te amo, Francisco?
Francisco:	Dímelo.
Marisol:	Porque siempre sabes qué debemos hacer.

 ## 12.17 Drama imprevisto

Form appropriately sized groups to improvise the following situations. You may take a few moments to plan your role play, but your skit should be unscripted.

A. Enact a Flores family meeting in which Marisol and Francisco explain to Elsita just what she needs to know about tío Raúl coming to live with them.

B. Enact a meeting between Marisol, Francisco, and Raúl in which Marisol and Francisco attempt to convince Raúl, who is an independent person with medical and home-care needs, that he should live with them.

C. Enact a home-care evaluation conducted by a visiting nurse at the Floreses' home with Raúl, Marisol and Francisco present.

 ## Video Program: What's My Line—What's Your Temperature?

Watch the *Atracción especial* for chapter 12. Afterwards, you'll have an opportunity to play the game "What's My Line—What's Your Temperature?" too.

Dr. Vargas:	Okay, contestants. We are going to play "What's My Line—What's Your Temperature?" Draw a medical specialty from the hat and then act that role by asking about symptoms. Later, we'll identify the specialties for points. Have fun! To begin this round, everyone draw a card from the hat, and then circulate asking questions and performing examinations.
Rosmery:	Déjame ver la boca. ¿Te cepillaste hoy? ¿Usas hilo dental todos los días? Dos veces por día, ¿ah? Tienes muchas caries. Aparte de eso, una sonrisa muy bonita.
Marisol:	¿Te sientes triste? ¿Escuchas voces? ¿Cómo te sientes cuando estás enojado?
Francisco:	¿Evacuaste hoy? ¿Tienes diarrea? ¿Estás estreñida? Tengo que introducir una cámara por el ano.
Dr. Vargas:	Okay, for one thousand points, who can identify all the specialties?

Elsita:	¡Yo! ¡Yo! Rosmery es odontóloga, Mamá es psicóloga y Papá es gastroenterólogo.
Dr. Vargas:	¡Ah, perfecto! Let's play another round. All players draw another card.
Rosmery:	Vamos a escucharte el corazón. U-u-y-y, estás enamorado. Está latiendo mucho. Vamos a ver los tobillos si están hinchados. Están hinchados. Te voy a dar una receta para la nitroglicerina.
Marisol:	¿Cuánto pesas? ¿Usas drogas? ¿Tomas alcohol?
Francisco:	¿Me oyes bien? ¿Tienes una tos seca? ¿Te duele la garganta?
Dr. Vargas:	Okay, for ten thousand points, who can identify all the specialties?
Elsita:	¡Yo lo sé! ¡Yo lo sé!
Dr. Vargas:	¿Quiénes son, Elsita?
Elsita:	Rosmery es cardióloga. Mamá es anestesióloga, y Papá es otorrinolaringólogo.
Dr. Vargas:	¡Diez mil puntos para Elsita!

 2.18 Drama imprevisto

Now it is your turn to play "What's My Line—What's Your Temperature?" The instructor will prepare a container with slips of paper identifying medical specialties. Several students will take a paper and then ask each other the questions that a person with that role would likely ask during an examination. The "studio audience" then attempts to identify the medical specialties for points. Have fun!

Consolidate your learning. Make an algorithm that integrates many of your new skills and will be useful for medical assessment in a variety of settings. (The number of the corresponding chapter appears in parentheses.) Order your questions in the way that is most appropriate for you.

¿Qué la pasa? (3)
¿Toma algún medicamento o remedio casero todos los días? (6)
¿Es usted alérgico/a a algún medicamento? (6)
¿Qué enfermedades hay en su familia? (5)
¿Ha tenido / Ha padecido de / Ha sufrido de . . . ? (10)
¿Con quién ha consultado? (10)
¿Qué le dijo? (9)
¿Con qué frecuencia . . . ? ¿Desde cuándo . . . ? (8)
¿Cuánto tiempo hace que . . . ? ¿Cuánto tiempo dura . . . ? (8)
¿Qué le ayuda? ¿Qué le mejora? ¿Qué le empeora? (8)
¿Cuándo fue la última vez que . . . ? (9)

Now apply your algorithm to the following *reciclaje.*

 ## 12.19 Reciclaje

You are a doctor in an outpatient clinic. A classmate is a patient who has come to the clinic with this chief complaint: «Tengo sudores nocturnos». Use your algorithm to investigate.

Cultural Note: Fathers and Childbirth

The birthing process has changed greatly in the United States during the past two generations. Most hospitals teach childbirth classes to couples using techniques designed by the French physician Fernand Lamaze. These include training the father or a friend to give support to the mother during childbirth. Through these changes over recent decades we have practically eradicated the medicated birth, especially the use of twilight and general anesthesia during birth. Latinos are generally eager to participate as couples in this preparation as well as in the actual delivery. However, not all do so because the classes are not always available in Spanish when needed, and because the practice is not yet as widespread in many of the countries from which the patients have emigrated. In poorer areas the presence of several deliveries in one room contraindicates the participation of fathers because of modesty.

Some Latinas do not communicate to their partner the expectation that he will take part in the delivery, and some men do not feel comfortable with the idea. Sexual topics are not traditionally discussed in the home. One man standing outside the room in which his wife was in labor admitted that he wanted to be in the room but would not enter because there were female relatives inside who would presumably know more about what to do.

At times the difference in participation between non-Latino and Latino men is not fully understood by health care providers as a difference in tradition. Assessing and understanding the individual family's cultural norms will enable the health care provider to begin the educational process from the perspective of the patient, her partner, and the family. This increases empathy, eliminating negative perceptions about fathers and alleviating their discomfort in the delivery room.

Cultural Note: The Prevention of Sexually Transmitted Diseases

At times, patients do not easily embrace the goals of health professionals in their teaching about safer sex. Many Latino families do not speak openly about sexual matters. The Catholic Church has disapproved of most forms of contraception. When educating patients about sex, the health care provider should assess and then respect the values of the patient prior to presenting new information in a nonjudgmental manner. Such respect is crucial.

Discussion of sexual roles can uncover conflict in the individual and in his or her family. Many adults heard during childhood the refrain *La mujer es de la casa y el hombre de la calle* (the woman is of the house and the man is of the street). This traditional double standard may pressure women to live at home until marriage, to remain chaste, and to value childbearing more than higher education and a career. The first- or second-generation female immigrant may feel caught between her traditional values and what she perceives to be a different norm in North America. She may feel guilty over seeking sexual fulfillment as a single woman and insecure about asserting herself in business. She may not speak openly about being sexually active, except when confidentiality is assured. Other required yet sometimes taboo topics in sex education include homosexual behavior, alcoholism, and substance abuse. Raise these in a private setting, and do so only after establishing rapport with the patient.

Cultural Note: The Joy of Language

S peaking about *confianza* in an earlier cultural note, we suggested that one might not achieve this level of confidence without crossing the language boundary. Beyond this, a benefit of learning Spanish is to be able to appreciate the genuine enjoyment that people have of their language and their culture. Listening to music can help the non-Hispanic clinician develop more appreciation of the culture. Music and language are mediums that communicate the delight of life itself.

A group of teenagers in a small village of the Dominican Republic were teaching riddles to a group of North American tourists. Such word games are traditional fun in Latin America. Here is one of the *adivinanzas,* or riddles.

> Oro no es. Plata no es. Abre la cortina y verás lo que es.

It's not gold. It's not silver. Open the curtain and you shall see what it is. The answer is contained in the riddle itself: *plata no es . . . ¡plátano es!* Here is another.

> Cajita redonda, blanca como la nieve.
> Todo el mundo sabe abrir, y nadie puede cerrar.

Let's see. "Little round box, white as snow. Everyone knows how to open it, but nobody can close it." Do you give up? *¡El huevo!* Here's one more.

> Fui al mercado, y me enamoré de ella.
> La llevé a casa, y lloré con ella. ¿Quién es?

"I went to the market and fell in love with her. I brought her home and cried with her." *¡La cebolla!*

Words with double meaning (*doble significado*) are often the substance of jokes. If a male duck is a *pato,* then a female duck must be a *pata,* but *pata* is also an animal's leg!

> Si hay un pato con una pata en una caja (box), ¿cuántas patas hay?

Whatever answer you receive, you can call it wrong. There is either one leg, one female duck, or four legs! Now you can answer this: *¿Cuál es el animal que hace sus hijos con las patas?* Here's another: *¿Qué hace un pato con una pata? Cojear* (to limp). But can you answer the next one?

¿Qué tienen en común un tren y una manzana?

What do a train and an apple have in common? This may lose a little in translation. *La manzana no es pera y el tren no espera.*

This type of fun is in danger of being forgotten by some immigrants, who like too many of us have traded conversation for television. It is part of a culture. If you truly enjoy having fun with words and with people, you have already crossed boundaries.

Appendix 1
El abecedario (The Spanish Alphabet)

Knowing the alphabet in Spanish (also called *el alfabeto*) will help you spell words aloud and conduct vision exams. To ask how the name Baldemira is spelled, use *¿Cómo se escribe Baldemira?* or *¿Cómo se deletrea Baldemira?*

Letra	Nombre	Letra	Nombre	Letra	Nombre
a	a	j	jota	r	ere
b	be	k	ka	s	ese
c	ce	l	ele	t	te
d	de	m	eme	u	u
e	e	n	ene	v	ve
f	efe	ñ	eñe	w	doble ve
g	ge	o	o	x	equis
h	hache	p	pe	y	i griega
i	i	q	cu	z	zeta

Some grammars include *rr* in the alphabet. The fourth edition of the *Diccionario académico* (1803) included *ch* and *ll* in the alphabet. Although these are digraphs (comprised of two letters each), they are considered letters because each represents a single sound. Words beginning with these two letters occupied their own sections in Spanish dictionaries until 1994, when La Asociación de Academias de la Lengua Española reordered those words into their places in the universal Latin alphabet. Now, words beginning with *ch* are found between words that begin with *ce* and those that begin with *ci,* and words beginning with *ll* are placed between words that begin with *li* and those that begin with *lo.*

Appendix 2
A Guide to Some Irregular and Stem-Changing Verbs

Most of these verbs and morphologies have been introduced in the text. They are included here as a reference and for further study. The future tense expresses action that will happen in the future, as in *Me acostaré temprano el domingo* (I will go to bed early on Sunday).

acostarse (o-ue)—to lie down, go to bed

present	me acuesto, te acuestas, se acuesta, nos acostamos, se acuestan
preterit	me acosté, te acostaste, se acostó, nos acostamos, se acostaron
imperfect	me acostaba, te acostabas, se acostaba, nos acostábamos, se acostaban
future	me acostaré, te acostarás, se acostará, nos acostaremos, se acostarán
usted command	¡Acuéstese! ¡No se acueste!
tú command	¡Acuéstate! ¡No te acuestes!
past participle	acostado

almorzar (o-ue)—to eat lunch

present	almuerzo, almuerzas, almuerza, almorzamos, almuerzan
preterit	almorcé, almorzaste, almorzó, almorzamos, almorzaron
imperfect	almorzaba, almorzabas, almorzaba, almorzábamos, almorzaban
future	almorzaré, almorzarás, almorzará, almorzaremos, amorzarán
usted command	¡Almuerce! ¡No almuerce!
tú command	¡Almuerza! ¡No almuerces!
past participle	almorzado

comenzar (e-ie)—to begin

present	comienzo, comienzas, comienza, comenzamos, comienzan
preterit	comencé, comenzaste, comenzó, comenzamos, comenzaron
imperfect	comenzaba, comenzabas, comenzaba, comenzábamos, comenzaban
future	comenzaré, comenzarás, comenzará, comenzaremos, comenzarán
usted command	¡Comience!　　¡No comience!
tú command	¡Comienza!　　¡No comiences!
past participle	comenzado

dar—to give

present	doy, das, da, damos, dan
preterit	di, diste, dio, dimos, dieron
imperfect	daba, dabas, daba, dábamos, daban
future	daré, darás, dará, daremos, darán
usted command	¡Dé!　　¡No dé!
tú command	¡Da!　　¡No des!
past participle	dado

decir—to say, to tell

present	digo, dices, dice, decimos, dicen
preterit	dije, dijiste, dijo, dijimos, dijeron
future	diré, dirás, dirá, diremos, dirán
imperfect	decía, decías, decía, decíamos, decían
usted command	¡Diga!　　¡No diga!
tú command	¡Di!　　¡No digas!
past participle	dicho

despertarse (e-ie)—to wake up

present	me despierto, te despiertas, se despierta, nos despertamos, se despiertan
preterit	me desperté, te despertaste, se despertó, nos despertamos, se despertaron
imperfect	me despertaba, te despertabas, se despertaba, nos despertábamos, se despertaban
future	me despertaré, te despertarás, se despertará, nos despertaremos, se despertarán
usted command	¡Despiértese!　　¡No se despierte!
tú command	¡Despiértate!　　¡No te despiertes!
past participle	despierto

dormir (o-ue)—to sleep

present	duermo, duermes, duerme, dormimos, duermen
preterit	dormí, dormiste, durmió, dormimos, durmieron
imperfect	dormía, dormías, dormía, dormíamos, dormían
future	dormiré, dormirás, dormirá, dormiremos, dormirán
usted command	¡Duérmase! ¡No se duerma!
tú command	¡Duérmete! ¡No te duermas!
past participle	dormido

estar—to be

present	estoy, estás, está, estamos, están
preterit	estuve, estuviste, estuvo, estuvimos, estuvieron
imperfect	estaba, estabas, estaba, estábamos, estaban
future	estaré, estarás, estará, estaremos, estarán
usted command	¡Esté! ¡No esté!
tú command	¡Está! ¡No estés!
past participle	estado

hacer—to do, to make

present	hago, haces, hace, hacemos, hacen
preterit	hice, hiciste, hizo, hicimos, hicieron
imperfect	hacía, hacías, hacía, hacíamos, hacían
future	haré, harás, hará, haremos, harán
usted command	¡Haga! ¡No haga!
tú command	¡Haz! ¡No hagas!
past participle	hecho

ir—to go

present	voy, vas, va, vamos, van
preterit	fui, fuiste, fue, fuimos, fueron
imperfect	iba, ibas, iba, íbamos, iban
future	iré, irás, irá, iremos, irán
usted command	¡Vaya! ¡No vaya!
tú command	¡Ve! ¡No vayas!
past participle	ido

poder (o-ue)—to be able

present	puedo, puedes, puede, podemos, pueden
preterit	pude, pudiste, pudo, pudimos, pudieron
imperfect	podía, podías, podía, podíamos, podían
future	podré, podrás, podrá, podremos, podrán
past participle	podido

poner—to put, to place

present	pongo, pones, pone, ponemos, ponen
preterit	puse, pusiste, puso, pusimos, pusieron
imperfect	ponía, ponías, ponía, poníamos, ponían
future	pondré, pondrás, pondrá, pondremos, pondrán
usted command	¡Ponga! ¡No ponga!
tú command	¡Pon! ¡No pongas!
past participle	puesto

preferir (e-ie)—to prefer

present	prefiero, prefieres, prefiere, preferimos, prefieren
preterit	preferí, preferiste, prefirió, preferimos, prefirieron
imperfect	prefería, preferías, prefería, preferíamos, preferían
future	preferiré, preferirás, preferirá, preferiremos, preferirán
usted command	¡Prefiera! ¡No prefiera!
tú command	¡Prefiere! ¡No prefieras!
past participle	preferido

querer (e-ie)—to want, to like

present	quiero, quieres, quiere, queremos, quieren
preterit	quise, quisiste, quiso, quisimos, quisieron
imperfect	quería, querías, quería, queríamos, querían
future	querré, querrás, querrá, querremos, querrán
past participle	querido

saber—to know

present	sé, sabes, sabe, sabemos, saben
preterit	supe, supiste, supo, supimos, supieron
imperfect	sabía, sabías, sabía, sabíamos, sabían
future	sabré, sabrás, sabrá, sabremos, sabrán
usted command	¡Sepa! ¡No sepa!
tú command	¡Sabe! ¡No sepas!
past participle	sabido

sentarse (e-ie)—to sit down

present	me siento, te sientas, se sienta, nos sentamos, se sientan
preterit	me senté, te sentaste, se sentó, nos sentamos, se sentaron
imperfect	me sentaba, te sentabas, se sentaba, nos sentábamos, se sentaban
future	me sentaré, te sentarás, se sentará, nos sentaremos, se sentarán

usted command	¡Siéntese!	¡No se siente!
tú command	¡Siéntate!	¡No te sientes!
past participle	sentado	

sentirse (e-ie)—to feel

present	me siento, te sientes, se siente, nos sentimos, se sienten
preterit	me sentí, te sentiste, se sintió, nos sentimos, se sintieron
imperfect	me sentía, te sentías, se sentía, nos sentíamos, se sentían
future	me sentiré, te sentirás, se sentirá, nos sentiremos, se sentirán

usted command	¡Siéntase!	¡No se sienta!
tú command	¡Siéntete!	¡No te sientas!
past participle	sentido	

ser—to be

present	soy, eres, es, somos, son
preterit	fui, fuiste, fue, fuimos, fueron
imperfect	era, eras, era, éramos, eran
future	seré, serás, será, seremos, serán

usted command	¡Sea!	¡No sea!
tú command	¡Sé!	¡No seas!
past participle	sido	

tener—to have

present	tengo, tienes, tiene, tenemos, tienen
preterit	tuve, tuviste, tuvo, tuvimos, tuvieron
imperfect	tenía, tenías, tenía, teníamos, tenían
future	tendré, tendrás, tendrá, tendremos, tendrán

usted command	¡Tenga!	¡No tenga!
tú command	¡Ten!	¡No tengas!
past participle	tenido	

venir—to come

present	vengo, vienes, viene, venimos, vienen
preterit	vine, viniste, vino, vinimos, vinieron
imperfect	venía, venías, venía, veníamos, venían
future	vendré, vendrás, vendrá, vendremos, vendrán

usted command	¡Venga!	¡No venga!
tú command	¡Ven!	¡No vengas!
past participle	venido	

vestirse (e-i)—to dress oneself

present	me visto, te vistes, se viste, nos vestimos, se visten
preterit	me vestí, te vestiste, se vistió, nos vestimos, se vistieron
imperfect	me vestía, te vestías, se vestía, nos vestíamos, se vestían
future	me vestiré, te vestirás, se vestirá, nos vestiremos, se vestirán
usted command	¡Vístase! ¡No se vista!
tú command	¡Vístete! ¡No te vistas!
past participle	vestido

English to Spanish Glossary

The translations in this glossary are generally limited to the context in which the words are used in the book. The abbreviation (*v*) indicates a verb.

a

abdomen **el abdomen**

able (to be able) (*v*) **poder** (o-ue)

abortion **el aborto (provocado; espontáneo)**

about **sobre**

abrasion **la abrasión**

accident **el accidente**

acetaminophen **el acetaminofén**

ache (*v*) **doler** (o-ue)

active **activo/a**

acute **agudo/a**

addict **el/la adicto/a**

address **la dirección**

adrenaline **la adrenalina**

advance (*v*) **adelantar**

aerosol **el aerosol**

after **después de**

afternoon **la tarde**

afterward **después**

age **la edad**

agitated **agitado/a**

AIDS **el SIDA**

ailment **el padecimiento, la enfermedad**

air **el aire**

air pollution **la contaminación de aire**

alcohol **el alcohol**

alive **vivo/a**

allergic **alérgico/a**

allergy **la alergia**

also **también**

always **siempre**

ambulance **la ambulancia**

American **americano/a**

americanized **americanizado/a**

amount **la cantidad**

analgesic **el analgésico, el calmante**

analysis **el análisis**

anaphylactic shock **el shock anafiláctico**

anaphylaxis **la anafilaxis**

and **y**

anemia **la anemia**

anesthesia **la anestesia**

aneurysm **el aneurisma**

anger (*v*) **enojar(se), enfadar(se)**

anger **el enojo, el enfado**

angina pectoris **la angina de pecho**

angiogram **el angiograma**

angry **enojado/a, enfadado/a**

animal **el animal**

animal dander **la caspa de animal**

anise **el anís**

ankle **el tobillo**

annoy (*v*) **molestar**

annoyance **la molestia**

annoyed **enfadado/a**

answer (*v*) **contestar**

antacid **el antiácido**

antibiotic **el antibiótico**

antibody **el anticuerpo**
anticholinergic **el anticolinérgico**
anticoagulant **el anticoagulante**
anticonvulsant **el anticonvulsante**
antidepressant **el antidepresivo**
antidiarrheal **el antidiarreico**
antihistamine **el antihistamínico**
anti-inflammatory **el antiinflamatorio**
antispasmodic **el antiespasmódico**
anus **el ano**
anxiety **la ansiedad**
anxious **ansioso/a, nervioso/a**
anyone **alguien**
apoplexy **la apoplejía**
appendectomy **la apendectomía**
appendicitis **la apendicitis**
appendix **el apéndice**
appetite **el apetito**
apple **la manzana**
appointment **la cita**
April **abril**
area **la área**
argue (*v*) **discutir, pelear**
arise (*v*) **levantar(se)**
arm **el brazo**
arrive (*v*) **llegar**
arthritis **la artritis**
arthroscopy **la artroscopia**
as, like **como**
ashamed **avergonzado/a**
ask (*v*) **preguntar**
ask for (*v*) **pedir** (e-i)
aspirin **la aspirina**
asthma **el asma** (*feminine*)
attack **el ataque**
audiologist **el/la audiólogo/a**
August **agosto**
aunt **la tía**
avocado **el aguacate**
avoid (*v*) **evitar**
awake **despierto/a**
awaken (*v*) **despertar(se)** (e-ie)

b

baby **el/la bebé**
baby teeth **los dientes de leche**
back **la espalda**
bacterial **bacteriano/a**

bacterium **la bacteria**
bad **malo/a**
badly **mal**
banana **la banana, el plátano, el guineo**
bandage **el vendaje, la tirita, la curita**
barbiturate **el barbitúrico**
bath **el baño**
bathe (*v*) **bañar(se)**
bathroom **el cuarto de baño**
be (*v*) **ser** (*irregular*), **estar** (*irregular*)
bean **el frijol, la habichuela, la judía**
because **porque**
bed **la cama**
bedpan **la silleta, el pato de cama**
beef **la carne de res**
beer **la cerveza**
before **antes de**
behind **detrás de**
believe (*v*) **creer**
benefit **el beneficio**
betrayed **traicionado/a**
better **mejor**
better (to get better) (*v*) **mejorar**
beverage **la bebida**
bilingual **bilingüe**
biopsy **la biopsia**
birth **el nacimiento, el parto,**
    el alumbramiento
black **negro/a**
bladder **la vejiga**
blanket **la frazada**
bleed (*v*) **sangrar**
blind **ciego/a**
blister **la ampolla**
blond, blonde **rubio/a**
blood **la sangre**
blood pressure **la presión sanguínea,**
    la presión arterial, la presión de la
    sangre, la tensión arterial
board **la tabla**
body **el cuerpo**
bone **el hueso**
bore (*v*) **aburrir**
bottle **la botella, el frasco; el biberón,**
    la tetera (baby's bottle)
brain **el cerebro**
bread **el pan**
break (*v*) **quebrar, romper**
break water (*v*) **romper fuente**

breakfast (*v*) **desayunar**
breakfast **el desayuno**
breast **el seno**
breast-feed (*v*) **amamantar, dar el seno, dar el pecho**
breathe (*v*) **respirar**
breathing **la respiración**
broccoli **el brócoli**
bronchia **el bronquio**
bronchial **bronquial**
bronchoscopy **la broncoscopia**
broth **el caldo**
brother **el hermano**
brother-in-law **el cuñado**
bruise **el moretón**
bruit **el soplo**
brunette **moreno/a**
brush (*v*) **cepillar(se)**
brush **el cepillo**
bump (*v*) **golpear(se)**
bump **el golpe**
burn (*v*) **quemar(se)**
burn **la quemadura**
burned **quemado/a**
burning sensation **el ardor**
butter **la mantequilla**
buttock **el gluteo, la nalga, la pompis**
buy (*v*) **comprar**

C

cake **la torta, el bizcocho, el pastel**
calcium **el calcio**
call (*v*) **llamar**
call **la llamada**
calorie **la caloría**
can **la lata**
can (to be able) (*v*) **poder** (o-ue)
cancer **el cáncer**
candy **el dulce**
canned **enlatado/a**
capsule **la cápsula**
car **el coche, el carro, el automóvil**
carbohydrate **el carbohidrato**
card **la tarjeta**
cardiac **cardíaco/a**
cardiologist **el/la cardiólogo/a**
cardiology **la cardiología**

cardiovascular disease **la enfermedad cardiovascular**
care **el cuidado**
care for (*v*) **cuidar**
carpet **la alfombra**
carrier (asymptomatic) **el portador (sano)**
carrot **la zanahoria**
carry (*v*) **llevar**
cast **el yeso**
cataract **la catarata**
catheter **la sonda, el catéter**
catheter (urinary) **la algalia, la sonda**
cavity **la caries, la caries dental**
cereal **el cereal**
cerebral **cerebral**
cerebral palsy **la parálisis cerebral**
cervix **el cuello del útero, el cuello de la matriz**
cesarean section **la operación cesárea**
chair **la silla**
cheek **la mejilla, el cachete**
cheekbone **el pómulo**
cheese **el queso**
chest **el pecho**
chest pain **el dolor del pecho**
chicken **el pollo**
chicken pox **la varicela, la viruela loca**
child **el/la niño/a, el/la muchacho/a**
chills **los escalofríos**
chin **la barbilla**
Chinese **el chino** (*lang.*)
chlamydia **la clamidia**
chocolate **el chocolate**
cholecystectomy **la colecistectomía**
cholera **el cólera**
chronic **crónico/a**
cigarette **el cigarrillo**
cinnamon **la canela**
cirrhosis **la cirrosis, la cirrosis hepática**
city **la ciudad**
class **la clase**
classic **clásico/a**
clavicle **la clavícula**
clean **limpio/a**
cleaning **la limpieza**
clear **claro/a**
clinic **la clínica**
close (*v*) **cerrar** (e-ie)
closed **cerrado/a**

clot **el coágulo**

clothes **la ropa**

clothing **la ropa**

cocaine **la cocaína**

coccyx **el cóccix**

cockroach **la cucaracha**

coconut **el coco**

codeine **la codeína**

cold **frío/a**

cold (common cold) **el resfriado, el resfrío, el catarro, la monga** (*slang*)

colic **el cólico, los cólicos**

collide (*v*) **chocar**

collision (*n*) **el choque**

colon **el colon**

colonoscopy **la colonoscopia**

color **el color**

colostomy **la colostomía**

comb (*v*) **peinar(se)**

comb **el peine**

come (*v*) **venir** (*irregular*)

comfortable **cómodo/a, confortable**

common **común**

complication **la complicación**

condom **el condón, el preservativo**

confine (*v*) **internar**

confinement **el internamiento**

confirm (*v*) **confirmar**

congestion **la congestión, el catarro**

congestive heart failure **la insuficiencia cardíaca**

congratulations **felicidades**

conscious **consciente**

constant **constante, continuo/a**

constipation **el estreñimiento**

consult (*v*) **consultar**

consult **la consulta**

content **contento/a**

contraceptive **el contraceptivo, el anticonceptivo**

contraction **la contracción**

convulsion **la convulsión**

cook (*v*) **cocinar**

cook **el/la cocinero/a**

COPD **la enfermedad pulmonar obstructiva crónica, el enfisema**

cough (*v*) **toser**

cough **la tos**

cough suppressant **el antitusígeno**

counselor **el/la consejero/a**

CPR **la reanimación cardiopulmonar**

cramp **el calambre**

cranium **el cráneo**

crash (*v*) **chocar**

crash **el choque**

crazy **loco/a**

cream **la crema, el ungüento**

crisis **la crisis**

crown **la corona**

crush (*v*) **polvorizar**

crushing **pesado/a**

crutch **la muleta**

cry (*v*) **llorar**

crying jag, weeping **el llanto**

CT scan **la tomografía computarizada**

culture (laboratory) **el cultivo**

curious **curioso/a**

current **actual**

custodian **el/la tutor/a**

custody **la tutoría, la custodia**

cut (*v*) **cortar(se)**

cut **la cortada, la cortadura, el tajo**

cyst **el quiste**

d

damage (*v*) **dañar**

dangerous **peligroso/a**

dark **oscuro/a**

date **la fecha**

daughter **la hija**

daughter-in-law **la nuera, la yerna**

day **el día**

dead **muerto/a**

deaf **sordo/a**

death **la muerte**

decaffeinated **descafeinado/a**

December **diciembre**

decongestant **el descongestionante**

deep **profundo/a**

dehydration **la deshidratación**

deliver (a baby) (*v*) **dar a luz, parir, alumbrar**

delivery (of a baby) **el parto, el alumbramiento**

delusion **el delirio**

demonstrate (*v*) **demostrar**

dengue **el dengue**

dental floss **el hilo dental**
dental hygienist **el/la higienista dental**
dentist **el/la dentista, el/la odontólogo/a**
dentistry **la odontología**
denture **la dentadura postiza**
depressed **deprimido/a**
depression **la depresión**
dermatologist **el/la dermatólogo/a**
description **la descripción**
desk **el escritorio**
desperate **desesperado/a**
dessert **el postre**
diabetes **la diabetes**
diagnosis **el diagnóstico**
dialysis **la diálisis**
diarrhea **la diarrea**
die (v) **morir** (o-ue)
diet **la dieta, el plan de alimentación**
dietician **el/la dietista**
dine (v) **cenar**
dinner **la comida, la cena**
diphtheria **la difteria**
disabled **discapacitado/a, inválido/a**
discover (v) **descubrir**
disease **la enfermedad**
disgusted **disgustado/a**
disheartened **descorazonado/a**
disorder **el trastorno**
distressed **angustiado/a**
diuretic **el diurético**
divorce (v) **divorciarse**
divorce **el divorcio**
divorced **divorciado/a**
dizziness **el mareo**
dizzy **mareado/a**
do, make (v) **hacer** (*irregular*)
doctor **el doctor, la doctora, el/la médico/a**
doctor's office **el consultorio**
doll **la muñeca**
door **la puerta**
drain (v) **drenar**
drain **el drenaje**
drained, exhausted **agotado/a**
draw blood (v) **sacar sangre**
drill **la fresa dental, el taladro**
drink (v) **beber**
drink **la bebida**
drip (v) **gotear**
dripping **el goteo**

drive (v) **manejar**
drop **la gota**
drug **la droga**
drunk **borracho/a, ebrio/a**
dust **el polvo**
dust mite **el ácaro del polvo**
dysentery **la disentería**

e

each, every **cada**
ear **el oído** (inner), **la oreja** (outer)
early **temprano**
eat (v) **comer**
echogram **el ecograma**
ectopic pregnancy **el embarazo ectópico**
eczema **el eczema**
egg **el huevo**
eighth **el/la octavo/a**
elbow **el codo**
electrocardiogram **el electrocardiograma**
electroencephalogram **el electro-encefalograma**
elevator **el ascensor**
eliminate (v) **eliminar**
elixir **el elíxir**
embolism **la embolia**
emergency **la emergencia, la urgencia**
emergency room **la sala de emergencia, la sala de urgencias**
emphysema **el enfisema**
enchanted **encantado/a**
endocrinologist **el/la endocrinólogo/a**
endometriosis **la endometriosis**
endoscopy **la endoscopía**
English **el inglés** (*lang.*)
enrage (v) **enojar(se), enfadar(se), enfo-gonar(se)** (*slang*)
enraged **enojado/a, enfadado/a, enfo-gonado/a** (*slang*)
ENT doctor **el/la otorrinolaringólogo/a**
epilepsy **la epilepsia**
epinephrine **la epinefrina**
episiotomy **la episiotomía**
esophageal reflux **el reflujo esofágico**
esophagus **el esófago**
ever **alguna vez**
exam **el examen**
examination **la examinación**

examine (*v*) **examinar**
exhale (*v*) **exhalar**
expectorant **el expectorante**
exploratory **exploratorio/a**
extraction **la extracción**
eye **el ojo**
eyeglasses **los lentes, los anteojos**

f

face **la cara**
faint (*v*) **desmayar(se)**
fall (*v*) **caer**
Fallopian tube **la trompa de Falopio**
false teeth **los dientes postizos,
   la dentadura, la caja de dientes,
   el puente** (bridge)
fan **el abanico, el ventilador**
far **lejos**
fascinate (*v*) **fascinar**
fast (*v*) **ayunar**
fast **rápido/a**
fat **gordo/a**
fat **la grasa**
fat-free **descremado/a**
father **el padre**
father-in-law **el suegro**
fatigue **el cansancio, la fatiga**
fear **el miedo**
February **febrero**
feces **la materia fecal, las heces,
   el excremento**
feed (*v*) **alimentar, dar de comer**
feel (*v*) **sentir(se)** (e-ie)
female **hembra, femenino/a**
femur **el fémur**
fetus **el feto**
fever **la fiebre**
fiber **la fibra**
fibula **el peroné**
fifth **el/la quinto/a**
fight (*v*) **luchar, pelear**
filling (dental) **el empaste**
film **la placa**
find (*v*) **encontrar** (o-ue)
fine **bien**
finger **el dedo**
fingernail **la uña**
first **el/la primero/a**

fish (*v*) **pescar**
fish **el pescado**
floor **el piso**
flow **el flujo**
flu **la gripe, la influenza**
fluid **el fluido**
fluoride **el fluoruro**
foam **la espuma**
follow (*v*) **seguir** (e-ie)
food **el alimento, la comida**
foot **el pie**
forearm **el antebrazo**
forehead **la frente**
forget (*v*) **olvidar**
foster child **el/la hijo/a de crianza**
fourth **el/la cuarto/a**
fracture **la fractura**
   —compound **la fractura compuesta**
   —multiple **la fractura múltiple**
   —simple **la fractura simple**
French **el francés** (*lang.*)
french fries **las papas fritas**
frequency **la frecuencia**
frequent **frecuente**
frequently **frecuentemente**
Friday **el viernes**
friend **el/la amigo/a**
frightened **asustado/a**
from **de**
(in) front of **delante de, enfrente de**
fruit **la fruta**
frustrated **frustrado/a**
furious **furioso/a**

g

gallbladder **la vesícula biliar**
gallstone **el cálculo en la vesícula**
gasp (*v*) **jadear**
gasping **el jadeo**
gastritis **la gastritis**
gel **el gel**
gelatin **la gelatina**
general practitioner **el/la médico/a
   general / generalista / de cabecera**
generous **generoso/a**
genital wart **la verruga venérea**
geriatric **geriátrico/a**
geriatrician **el/la geriatra**

geriatrics **la geriatría**
German **el alemán** (*lang.*)
ginger **el jengibre**
gingivitis **la gingivitis, la enfermedad periodontal**
give (*v*) **dar** (*irregular*)
gland **la glándula**
glass **el vaso**
glaucoma **la glaucoma**
glove **el guante**
go (*v*) **ir** (*irregular*)
go to bed (*v*) **acostarse** (o-ue)
God **Dios**
godchild **el/la ahijado/a**
godfather **el padrino**
godmother **la madrina**
gold **el oro**
golden **dorado/a**
gonorrhea **la gonorrea**
good **bueno/a**
good-bye **adiós**
gout **la gota**
grain **el grano**
grandchild **el/la nieto/a**
grandparent **el/la abuelo/a**
grape **la uva**
grapefruit **la toronja**
grease **la grasa**
great-aunt **la tía abuela**
great-grandchild **el/la bisnieto/a**
great-grandfather **el bisabuelo**
great-grandmother **la bisabuela**
great-uncle **el tío abuelo**
green **verde**
greenish **verdoso/a**
grind (*v*) **moler** (o-ue)
ground **molido/a, majado/a**
guilt **la culpa**
guilty **culpable**
gum (anatomy) **la encía**
gynecologist **el/la ginecólogo/a**
gynecology **la ginecología**

h

hair **el cabello**
half-brother **el hermano de madre, el hermano de padre**

half-sister **la hermana de madre, la hermana de padre**
hallucination **la alucinación**
hallway **el pasillo**
hand **la mano**
handsome **guapo/a**
happen (*v*) **pasar**
happiness **la felicidad, la alegría**
happy **feliz, contento/a, alegre**
hard **duro/a**
harm (*v*) **dañar**
harm **el daño**
have (*v*) **tener** (*irregular*)
he **él**
head **la cabeza**
head injury **la herida en la cabeza**
headache **el dolor de cabeza**
health **la salud**
hear (*v*) **oír**
hearing **el oído**
heart **el corazón**
   —attack **el ataque al corazón**
   —murmur **el soplo en el corazón**
height **la altura**
helicopter **el helicóptero**
hello **hola**
help (*v*) **ayudar**
help **la ayuda**
hemophilia **la hemofilia**
hemorrhage **la hemorragia**
hemorrhagic **hemorrágico/a**
hemorrhoids **las hemorroides**
hepatitis **la hepatitis**
here **aquí**
hernia **la hernia**
heroin **la heroína, la manteca** (*slang*)
herpes **el herpes**
herpes zoster **la culebrilla**
hip **la cadera**
history **la historia**
HIV **el VIH**
hives **las ronchas, el sarpullido, la urticaria**
Holter monitor **la supervisión Holter**
honey **la miel de abeja**
hope (*v*) **esperar**
hope **la esperanza**
hopeless **desesperado/a**
hopelessness **la desesperación**

hospital **el hospital**
hospitalization **la hospitalización,**
  el internamiento
hour **la hora**
how **cómo**
how many **cuántos/as**
how much **cuánto/a**
humerus **el húmero**
hunger **el hambre**
hurt (*v*) **doler** (o-ue)
hypercholesterolemia **la hipercolesterol-**
  emia
hyperglycemia **la hiperglucemia**
hypertension **la hipertensión, la presión**
  alta
hyperthyroidism **el hipertiroidismo**
hypoglycemia **la hipoglucemia**
hypotension **la hipotensión, la presión**
  baja
hypothyroidism **el hipotiroidismo**
hysterectomy **la histerectomía**

i

I **yo**
ice cream **el helado, el mantecado**
ilium **el íleon**
ill **enfermo/a**
illness **la enfermedad, el padecimiento**
implant (*v*) **implantar**
implant **el implante**
in front of **delante de, enfrente de**
inch **la pulgada**
incontinence **la incontinencia**
infarct **el infarto**
infect (*v*) **infectar**
infection **la infección**
inflame (*v*) **inflamar**
inflammation **la inflamación**
influenza **la influenza**
inhale (*v*) **inhalar**
inhaler **el inhalador, la pompa** (*slang*)
inject (*v*) **inyectar**
injection **la inyección**
injure (*v*) **lastimar, herir**
injury **la herida**
insomnia **el insomnio**
insufficiency **la insuficiencia**
insurance **el seguro, el plan médico**

intelligent **inteligente, listo/a**
intensive care **el cuidado intensivo**
intensive care unit **la unidad de cuidados**
  intensivos
interest (*v*) **interesar**
interested **interesado/a**
interesting **interesante**
internist **el/la médico/a internista**
intestinal worm **la lombriz intestinal**
intestine **el intestino**
  —large **el intestino grueso**
  —small **el intestino delgado**
intravenous **intravenoso/a**
IV fluid **el suero**
iron (Fe) **el hierro**
irritability **la irritabilidad**
Italian **el italiano** (*lang.*)
itch (*v*) **picar, sentir comezón, sentir**
  picazón
itch **la picazón, la comezón**

j

January **enero**
Japanese **el japonés** (*lang.*)
jaundice **la ictericia**
jaundiced **amarillento/a**
jaw **la mandíbula**
jealous **celoso/a**
job **el trabajo**
joint **la articulación, la coyuntura**
July **julio**
June **junio**

k

kidney **el riñón**
kidney stone **el cálculo en el riñón,**
  la piedra en el riñón
kill (*v*) **matar**
kilogram **el kilogramo**
kind **amable, simpático/a**
kitchen **la cocina**
knee **la rodilla**
kneecap **la patela, la rótula**
know (*v*) **saber** (*irregular*), **conocer**
  (*irregular*)
knuckle **el nudillo**

l

labor **trabajo de parto**
labor pain **el dolor del parto**
laboratory **el laboratorio**
laceration **la laceración**
language **el idioma, la lengua, el lenguaje**
laparoscopy **la laparoscopia**
lard **la manteca**
large **grande**
large intestine **el intestino grueso**
laser **el láser**
late **tarde**
later **luego**
latex **el látex**
laxative **el laxante**
learn (*v*) **aprender**
left **el/la izquierdo/a**
leg **la pierna**
lemon **el limón**
length of stay **la estadía**
leptospirosis **la leptospirosis**
leukemia **la leucemia**
lice **los piojos**
like, as **como**
like (*v*) **gustar, querer** (e-ie)
like this **así**
lime **el limón**
lip **el labio**
liquid **el líquido**
listen (*v*) **escuchar**
listen with a stethoscope (*v*) **auscultar**
lithium **el litio**
live (*v*) **vivir**
liver **el hígado**
lonely **solitario/a**
long **largo/a**
look (*v*) **mirar**
lose (*v*) **perder** (e-ie)
luck **la suerte;** good luck **la buena suerte**
lucky **dichoso/a**
lukewarm **tibio/a**
lump **la bolita, la pelotita**
lumpectomy **la lumpectomía**
lunch (*v*) **almorzar** (o-ue)
lunch **el almuerzo**
lung **el pulmón**
lymph gland **el ganglio linfático**

m

machine **la máquina**
make, do (*v*) **hacer**
malaise **el malestar general**
malaria **el paludismo**
male **el varón**
man **el hombre**
mania **la manía**
manic-depressive **el/la maníaco-depresivo/a**
March **marzo**
married **casado/a**
marry (*v*) **casar(se)**
mash (*v*) **majar**
maternal **materno/a**
matter (*v*) **importar**
May **mayo**
meal **la comida**
measles **el sarampión;** German measles **la rubéola**
meat **la carne**
medical record **el expediente médico, la historia médica**
medication **el medicamento, la medicina**
medicine **la medicina**
meningitis **la meningitis**
menopause **la menopausia, el cambio de vida**
menstruate (*v*) **menstruar**
menstruation **la menstruación, la regla, el período**
mental illness **la enfermedad mental**
mental retardation **el retraso mental**
metacarpal **el metacarpiano**
metastasis **el metástasis**
midwife **la comadrona, la partera**
migraine **la jaqueca, la migraña**
milk **la leche**
milligram **el miligramo**
millilitre **el mililitro**
mine **mío/a/os/as**
miscarriage **el aborto natural, la pérdida**
miss (*v*) **hacer falta** (*irregular*)
molar **la muela**
mold **el moho**
mole **el lunar**
Monday **el lunes**

money **el dinero, la plata**
monitor (*v*) **monitorear**
monitor **el monitor**
mononucleosis **la mononucleosis**
month **el mes**
monthly **mensual, mensualmente**
more or less **más o menos**
morning **la mañana**
mother **la madre**
mother-in-law **la suegra**
mouth **la boca**
move (*v*) **mover (o-ue)**
move up (*v*) **adelantar**
MRI **las imágenes por resonancia magnética**
MRSA **el estafilococo resistente a la meticilina**
mucus **el moco**
multiple sclerosis **la esclerosis múltiple**
mumps **la paperas**
muscle **el músculo**
my **mi, mis**

n

name (*v*) **nombrar**
name **el nombre; el apellido** (surname)
natural **natural**
nausea **la náusea**
nebulize (*v*) **nebulizar**
neck **el cuello**
need (*v*) **necesitar**
need **la necesidad**
needle **la jeringuilla, la aguja**
negative **negativo/a**
neither **tampoco**
neonatal intensive care **el cuidado intensivo neonatal**
nephrectomy **la nefrectomía**
nephritis **la nefritis**
nerve **el nervio**
nervous **nervioso/a**
neurologist **el/la neurólogo/a**
neurology **la neurología**
never **nunca, jamás**
night **la noche**
night sweats **los sudores nocturnos**
ninth **el/la noveno/a**
nitroglycerine **la nitroglicerina**

nobody, no one **nadie**
none, not any **ningún, ninguno/a**
nose **la nariz**
nosocomial **nosocomial**
nothing **nada**
noun **el sustantivo**
November **noviembre**
numbness **el entumecimiento**
nurse **el/la enfermero/a, la norsa** (*slang*)
nurse practitioner **enfermero/a con licencia para diagnosticar y tratar padecimientos y recetar medicamentos**
nurse's aide **el/la ayudante de enfermero**
nursing **la enfermería**
  —home **el asilo, el hogar de ancianos**
nutritionist **el/la nutricionista**

o

oatmeal **la avena**
obese **obeso/a**
obesity **la obesidad**
obstetrician **el/la obstetra**
obstetrics **la obstetricia**
October **octubre**
odor **el olor**
offend (*v*) **ofender**
offended **ofendido/a**
offer (*v*) **ofrecer** (*irregular*)
offering **la ofrenda**
office **la oficina;** doctor's office **el consultorio**
oil **el aceite**
ointment **el ungüento, la crema**
old **viejo/a, anciano/a**
on (top of) **encima de**
oncologist **el/la oncólogo/a**
open (*v*) **abrir**
open **abierto/a**
operating room **la sala de operaciones, el quirófano**
ophthalmologist **el/la oftalmólogo/a**
ophthalmology **la oftalmología**
or **o**
oral **oral**
orange **la naranja, la china**
  —juice **el jugo de naranja, el jugo de china**
oregano **el orégano**

orthopedic **ortopédico/a**

orthopedic surgeon **el/la cirujano ortopédico/a**

orthopedics **la ortopedia**

orthopedist **el/la ortopedista**

osteoporosis **la osteoporosis**

otorhinolaryngologist (ENT) doctor **el/la otorrinolaringólogo/a**

otorhinolaryngology **la otorrino-laringología**

ought (*v*) **deber**

our **nuestro/a**

ovary **el ovario**

overdose **la sobredosis**

overweight **sobrepeso/a**

overwhelmed **agobiado/a**

ovulate (*v*) **ovular**

ovulation **la ovulación**

owe (*v*) **deber**

oxygen **el oxígeno**

p

pacemaker **el marcapasos**

pain (*v*) **doler** (o-ue)

pain **el dolor**

  —burning **quemante**

  —dull **latente, sordo**

  —sharp **agudo, punzante**

pale **pálido/a**

palpate (*v*) **palpar, tocar**

palpitation **la palpitación**

palsy **la parálisis**

pancreas **el páncreas**

pandemic **la pandemia**

pandemic **pandémico/a**

pant (*v*) **jadear**

panting **el jadeo**

Pap smear **la prueba de Papanicolau, el examen de Papanicolau**

paper **el papel**

papilloma **la papiloma**

paralysis **la parálisis**

paramedic **el/la paramédico/a**

paranoia **la paranoia**

paranoid **paranoico/a**

parents **los padres**

patch **el parche**

paternal **paterno/a**

patient **el/la paciente**

peanut butter **la manteca de cacahuate, la manteca de maní**

pediatric **pediátrico/a**

pediatrician **el/la pediatra**

pediatrics **la pediatría**

pen **el bolígrafo, la pluma, el lapicero**

penis **el pene**

percuss (*v*) **percutir, dar golpecitos**

period **el período, la regla, la menstruación**

permission **el permiso**

persistent **persistente**

personal **personal**

pertussis **la tos ferina**

phalange **la falange**

pharmacist **el/la farmacéutico/a**

pharmacy **la farmacia**

phlegm **la flema**

phobia **la fobia**

physical exam **el examen físico**

physical therapist **el/la terapeuta físico/a**

physician **el/la médico/a, el/la doctor/a**

physician's assistant **el/la asociado/a médico/a**

piece **el pedazo**

pill **la pastilla, la píldora**

pillow **la almohada**

pinta **la pinta**

place **el lugar**

placenta **la placenta**

plain **sencillo/a**

plaque (dental) **el sarro**

plastic surgeon **el/la cirujano/a plástico/a**

pleasant **agradable**

please (*v*) **gustar, encantar**

please **por favor**

pleasure **el placer**

pneumonectomy **la neumonectomía, la pulmonectomía**

pneumonia **la pulmonía, la neumonía**

pole **el palo**

polio **la polio, la poliomelitis**

pollen **el polen**

polyp **el pólipo**

poor **pobre**

porcelain **la porcelana**

portion **la porción**

Portuguese **el portugués** (*lang.*)

positive **positivo/a**
potato **la papa**
pound **la libra**
precaution **la precaución**
pregnancy **el embarazo**
pregnant **embarazada, encinta**
prescribe (*v*) **recetar**
prescription **la receta**
press (*v*) **palpar, presionar, oprimir**
pressure **la presión**
prevent (*v*) **prevenir** (*irregular*)
preventative **preventivo/a**
prevention **prevención**
private **privado/a**
procedure **el procedimiento**
prognosis **el pronóstico**
prostate **la próstata**
prostatitis **la prostatitis**
protein **la proteína**
proud **orgulloso/a**
provoke (*v*) **provocar**
prune **la ciruela**
psoriasis **la psoriasis**
psychiatric **psiquiátrico/a**
psychiatrist **el/la psiquiatra**
psychiatry **la psiquiatría**
psychologist **el/la psicólogo/a**
psychology **la psicología**
psychosis **la psicosis**
psychotic **psicótico/a**
pulmonologist **el/la neumonólogo/a**
pulsating **latente**
pulse **el pulso**
punctual **puntual**
puree **el puré**
push (*v*) **empujar**
put (*v*) **poner** (*irregular*)
pyramid **la pirámide**

q

quarter **cuarto/a**
question (*v*) **preguntar** (to ask), **cuestionar** (to doubt, wonder)
question **la pregunta**
quick **rápido/a**
quinine **la quinina**

r

radio **el radio**
radiologist **el/la radiólogo/a**
radiology **la radiología**
rash **la erupción, la irritación**
reach **el alcance**
reaction **la reacción**
read (*v*) **leer**
receive (*v*) **recibir**
receptionist **el/la recepcionista**
record (*v*) **grabar**
recorder **la grabadora**
recovery room **la sala de recuperación, la sala de restablecimiento**
rectum **el recto**
red **rojo/a, colorado/a**
refrigerator **el refrigerador, la nevera**
regular **regular**
reject (*v*) **rechazar**
rejected **rechazado/a**
rejection **el rechazo**
relieved **aliviado/a**
remain (*v*) **quedar(se)**
remedy **el remedio;** home remedy **el remedio casero**
remember (*v*) **recordar** (o-ue)
remove (*v*) **sacar, quitar(se)**
renal calculus **el cálculo en el riñón, las piedras en el riñón**
renal failure **la insuficiencia renal**
replacement **el reemplazo**
resistant **resistente**
respiratory therapist **el/la terapeuta respiratorio/a**
rest (*v*) **descansar**
rest **el descanso**
result **el resultado**
resuscitate (*v*) **resucitar**
resuscitation **la resucitación**
return (*v*) **volver** (o-ue)
rheumatic fever **la fiebre reumática**
rib **la costilla**
rice **el arroz**
rich **rico/a**
right **el/la derecho/a**
right **derecho/a**

rinse (*v*) **enjuagar**
rinse **el enjuague**
risk **el riesgo**
robe **la bata**
roll over (*v*) **virar(se)**
room **el cuarto, la habitación**
root canal **el tratamiento de canal**
rubella **la rubéola**
rum **el ron**
run (*v*) **correr**

S

sacrum **el sacro**
sad **triste**
sadness **la tristeza**
salad **la ensalada**
salt **la sal**
same **igual**
sample **la muestra**
satisfied **satisfecho/a**
Saturday **el sábado**
sausage **la salchicha, el chorizo**
say (*v*) **decir** (*irregular*)
scabies **la sarna**
scapula **el omóplato**
scare (*v*) **asustar**
scare **el susto**
scared **asustado/a**
schizophrenia **la esquizofrenia**
schizophrenic **el/la esquizofrénico/a**
school **la escuela**
sciatic **ciático/a**
sciatica **la ciática**
scrotum **el escroto**
sealant **el sellante**
seat belt **el cinturón de seguridad**
second **segundo/a**
secretary **el/la secretario/a**
secretion **la secreción**
sedative **el sedante, el calmante**
see (*v*) **ver** (*irregular*)
sensation **la sensación**
September **septiembre**
seventh **el/la séptimo/a**
severe **severo/a**
sew (*v*) **coser**

sexually transmitted disease **la enfermedad transmitida sexualmente**
shake (*v*) **agitar**
shame **la vergüenza**
share (*v*) **compartir**
shave (*v*) **afeitar(se)**
she **ella**
sheet **la sábana**
shingles **la culebrilla**
shoe **el zapato**
shop (*v*) **hacer compras** (*irregular*)
shop **la tienda**
short **bajo/a** (height), **corto/a** (length)
shortness of breath **falta de aire, la fatiga**
should (*v*) **deber**
shoulder **el hombro**
shy **tímido/a**
sick **enfermo/a**
sickness **la enfermedad**
side **el lado**
side effect **el efecto secundario**
sight **la vista**
single **soltero/a**
sister **la hermana**
sister-in-law **la cuñada**
sit (*v*) **sentar(se)** (e-ie)
sixth **el/la sexto/a**
skeleton **el esqueleto**
skin **la piel**
skinny **flaco/a**
sleep (*v*) **dormir** (o-ue)
sleeping pill **la pastilla para dormir**
slow **despacio, lento/a**
small **pequeño/a, chiquito/a**
small intestine **el intestino delgado**
smallpox **la viruela**
smell (*v*) **oler** (*irregular*)
smell (*sense of*) **el olfato**
smell **el olor**
smoke (*v*) **fumar**
smoke **el humo**
smoke detector **el detector de humo**
snack **la merienda**
sneeze (*v*) **estornudar**
sneeze **el estornudo**
sober **sobrio/a**
social **social**
social work **el trabajo social**

social worker **el/la trabajador/a social**
soda pop **el refresco**
soft **blando/a**
soft drink **el refresco**
some **algún/o/a**
someone **alguien**
something **algo**
sometimes **a veces**
son **el hijo**
son-in-law **el yerno**
sonogram **el sonograma, el ecograma**
sonograph **la sonografía, el ecograma**
soup **la sopa**
Spaniard **el/la español/a**
Spanish **el español** (*lang.*)
speak (*v*) **hablar**
specialty **la especialidad**
speech therapist **el/la terapeuta de lenguaje, el/la terapeuta del habla**
spend (money) **gastar**
spend (time) **pasar**
spice **la especia**
spina bifida **la espina bífida**
spine **la espina dorsal**
spirit **el ánimo, el espíritu**
spirometry **la espirometría**
spit (*v*) **escupir**
spleen **el bazo**
spontaneous **espontáneo/a**
sprain (*v*) **torcer(se)** (o-ue)
sprain **la torcedura**
sprained **torcido/a**
spray (*v*) **rociar**
sputum **el esputo**
squash **la calabaza**
stain (*v*) **manchar**
stain **la mancha**
staphylococcus **el estafilococo**
starch **el almidón**
start (*v*) **empezar** (e-ie)
start **el principio, el comienzo**
stepbrother **el hermanastro**
stepfather **el padrastro**
stepmother **la madrastra**
stepsister **la hermanastra**
sternum **el esternón**
steroid **el esteroide**
stiffness **la rigidez**
stitch (*v*) **coser**

stitch **el punto**
stomach **el estómago**
straight **derecho/a**
street **la calle**
stress **el estrés**
stretcher **la camilla**
stroke **la apoplejía, la embolia cerebral, la hemorragia vascular**
strong **fuerte**
student **el/la estudiante**
study (*v*) **estudiar**
study **el estudio**
sudden **repentino/a**
suffer (*v*) **sufrir**
suffer (from an illness) (*v*) **padecer**
sugar **el azúcar** (f)
suicide (*v*) **suicidarse, matarse, quitarse la vida**
suicide **el suicidio**
Sunday **el domingo**
supper **la cena**
suppository **el supositorio**
surgeon **el/la cirujano/a**
surgery **la cirugía**
surname **el apellido**
suspension **la suspención**
swallow (*v*) **tragar**
swallow **el trago**
sweat (*v*) **sudar**
sweat **el sudor**
sweet **dulce**
swell (*v*) **hinchar**
swelling **la hinchazón**
swollen **hinchado/a**
symptom **el síntoma**
syndrome **el síndrome**
syphilis **la sífilis**
syringe **la jeringa, la jeringuilla**
syrup **el jarabe** (medicine), **el almíbar**

t

tablespoon **la cuchara**
tablespoonful **la cucharada**
tachycardia **la taquicardia**
take (*v*) **tomar**
take out (*v*) **sacar**
talk (*v*) **hablar**
tall **alto/a**

taste (*v*) **probar** (o-ue)
taste **el gusto, el sabor**
tea **el té, la infusión, la tisana**
tear (secretion) **la lágrima**
teaspoon **la cucharita**
teaspoonful **la cucharadita**
technician **el/la técnico/a**
telephone **el teléfono**
tell (*v*) **decir** (*irregular*)
temperature **la temperatura**
tenth **el/la décimo/a**
test **la prueba**
testicle **el testículo**
tetanus **el tétano, el tétanos**
thankful **agradecido/a**
thank you **gracias**
that **ese, esa, aquel, aquella**
the **el, la**
therapist **el/la terapeuta**
there **allí, allá**
thermometer **el termómetro**
they **ellos, ellas**
thigh **el muslo**
thin **delgado/a**
third **tercero/a**
thirst **la sed**
this **este, esta**
those **esos, esas, aquellos, aquellas**
throat **la garganta**
thrombosis **la trombosis**
thrush **una infección producida por hongos**
Thursday **el jueves**
thus **así**
thyroid **la glándula tiroidea, el tiroides**
time **el tiempo, la hora**
tibia **la tibia**
tire (*v*) **cansar**
tired **cansado/a**
toast (*v*) **tostar**
toast **la tostada, el pan tostado**
today **hoy**
toe **el dedo del pie**
tomato **el tomate, el jitomate**
tomorrow **mañana**
tongue **la lengua**
tongue twister **el trabalengua**
tonsil **la amígdala**
tonsillectomy **la tonsilectomía, la amigda-**
   lectomía

tonsillitis **la amigdalitis**
too **también**
tooth **el diente**
toothpaste **la crema dental**
(on) top of **encima de**
topical **tópico/a**
tormented **mortificado/a**
touch (*v*) **tocar**
touch **el tacto**
towel **la toalla**
tradition **la tradición**
tranquilizer **el calmante**
transplant (*v*) **trasplantar**
transplant **el trasplante**
treat (*v*) **tratar**
treatment **el tratamiento**
triglyceride **el triglicérido**
true **verdadero, cierto**
truth **la verdad**
tuberculosis **la tuberculosis**
Tuesday **el martes**
tumor **el tumor**

u

ulcer **la úlcera**
ulna **el cúbito**
ultrasound **la sonografía, el ecograma**
uncle **el tío**
under **debajo de**
unit **la unidad**
United States **los Estados Unidos**
until **hasta**
urgency **la urgencia**
urinate (*v*) **orinar**
urine **la orina**
urine sample **la muestra de orina**
us **nosotros, nosotras**
useful **útil**
useless **inútil**
uterus **el útero, la matriz**

v

vaccinate (*v*) **vacunar**
vaccination **la vacuna**
vagina **la vagina**
vaginal **vaginal**
varicela **la varicela**

vegetable **el vegetal, la verdura,
   la legumbre**
vehicular **automovilístico/a**
vein **la vena**
vertebra **la vértebra**
very **muy**
victim **la víctima**
virus **el virus**
visit (*v*) **visitar**
visit **la visita**
visitor **el/la visitante**
vitamin **la vitamina**
voice **la voz**
vomit (*v*) **vomitar**
vomit **el vómito**

W

wait (*v*) **esperar**
walk (*v*) **caminar**
want (*v*) **querer** (e-ie)
wash (*v*) **lavar(se)**
we **nosotros, nosotras**
weak **débil**
weakness **la debilidad**
wear (*v*) **llevar**
Wednesday **el miércoles**
week **la semana**
weekly **semanal, semanalmente**
weeping, crying jag **el llanto**
weigh (*v*) **pesar**
weight **el peso**
well **bien, sano/a**
what **qué, cuál**
wheelchair **la silla de ruedas**
wheeze **el silbido**
where **¿dónde?**
   to where? **¿adónde?**
   from where? **¿de dónde?**
which **cuál**
white **blanco/a**
who **quién**
whole **entero/a**
whole grain **integral**
whom **a quién**

whooping cough **la tos ferina**
why **por qué**
widow **la viuda**
widower **el viudo**
wife **la esposa, la mujer**
window **la ventana**
wine **el vino**
wisdom **la sabiduría**
wisdom tooth **la muela del juicio**
withdraw (*v*) **retirar**
woman **la mujer**
womb **la matriz**
work (*v*) **trabajar**
worse **peor**
worsen (*v*) **empeorar**
wound **la herida**
wrist **la muñeca**
write (*v*) **escribir**
written **escrito/a**

X

x-ray **la radiografía, los rayos equis,
   la placa**
x-ray technician **el/la técnico/a de radiografía**

Y

yaws **el pían, la frambesia**
year **el año**
yellow **amarillo/a**
yellowish **amarillento/a**
yesterday **ayer**
yogurt **el yogur**
you **tú, usted, ustedes**
young **joven**
your **tu, su**
yours **tuyo/a, suyo/a**
yucca **la yuca**

Z

zero **el cero**

Spanish to English Glossary

The translations in this glossary are generally limited to the context in which the words are used in the book.

a

el abanico fan
el abdomen abdomen
el aborto espontáneo miscarriage
el aborto natural miscarriage
el aborto provocado abortion
la abrasión abrasion
abril April
abrir to open
la abuela grandmother
el abuelo grandfather
aburrido bored, boring
aburrir to bore
el ácaro del polvo dust mite
el accidente accident
el aceite oil
el acetaminofén acetaminophen
acostar(se) (o-ue) to lie down, to go to bed
activo/a active
actual current
adelantar to advance, to move up
el/la adicto/a addict
adiós good-bye
adónde to where
la adrenalina adrenaline
el aerosol aerosol
afeitar(se) to shave
agitar to agitate
agitado/a agitated

agobiado/a overwhelmed
agosto August
agotado/a drained, exhausted
agradable pleasant
agradecido/a thankful
el aguacate avocado
agudo/a acute
la aguja needle
el/la ahijado/a godson, goddaughter
el alcance reach
el alcohol alcohol
alegre happy
la alegría happiness
el alemán German
la alergia allergy
alérgico/a allergic
la alfombra rug, carpet
la algalia urinary catheter
algo something
alguien someone, anyone
algún/o/a some
alguna vez ever
algunas veces sometimes
alimentar to feed
el alimento food
aliviado/a relieved
el alivio relief
allá there
allí there
el almíbar syrup
el almidón starch

la almohada pillow
almorzar (o-ue) to eat/have lunch
el almuerzo lunch
alto/a tall
la alucinación hallucination
el alumbramiento birth
alumbrar to give birth
amable kind, nice
amamantar to breast-feed
amarillento/a yellowish, jaundiced
amarillo/a yellow
la ambulancia ambulance
la amígdala tonsil
la amigdalitis tonsillitis
el/la amigo/a friend
la ampolla blister
la anafilaxis anaphylaxis, anaphylactic shock
el analgésico analgesic
el análisis analysis
la anemia anemia
la anestesia anesthesia
el aneurisma aneurysm
la angina de pecho angina pectoris
el angiograma angiogram
angustiado/a distressed
el animal animal
el ánimo spirit
el anís anise
el ano anus
anoche last night
la ansiedad anxiety
ansioso/a anxious
el antebrazo forearm
antes de before
el antiácido antacid
el antibiótico antibiotic
el anticoagulante anticoagulant
el anticonvulsante anticonvulsant
el anticuerpo antibody
el antidepresivo antidepressant
el antidiarreico antidiarrheal
el antiespasmódico antispasmodic
el antihistamínico antihistamine
el antiinflamatorio anti-inflammatory
el antitusígeno antitussive
el año year
el apellido surname
la apendectomía appendectomy

el apéndice appendix
la apendicitis appendicitis
el apetito appetite
la apoplejía apoplexy
aprender to learn
aquel, aquella that
aquellos, aquellas those
aquí here
el ardor burning sensation
la área area
el arroz rice
la articulación joint
la artritis arthritis
la artroscopía arthroscopy
el ascensor elevator
así thus, in this way, like this
el asilo asylum, nursing home
el asma (*feminine*) asthma
el/la asociado/a médico/a physician's assistant
la aspirina aspirin
asustado/a scared, frightened
asustar to scare, to frighten
atacar to attack
el ataque attack
el/la audiólogo/a audiologist
auscultar to listen with a stethoscope
automovilístico/a vehicular
la avena oatmeal
avergonzado/a ashamed
ayer yesterday
la ayuda help
el/la ayudante assistant, helper
ayudar to help
ayunar to fast
el azúcar sugar
azucarado/a sugar-added

b

la bacteria bacterium
bacteriano/a bacterial
bajo/a short (*height*)
bañar(se) to bathe
el baño bath, bathroom
la barbilla chin
el barbitúrico barbiturate
la bata robe, hospital gown
el bazo spleen

el/la bebé baby
beber to drink
la bebida beverage
el beneficio benefit
el biberón baby's bottle
bien well
bilingüe bilingual
la biopsia biopsy
el/la bisabuelo/a great-grandfather, great-grandmother
el/la bisnieto/a great-grandson, great-granddaughter
blando/a soft
la boca mouth
el bolígrafo pen
la bolita lump
borracho/a drunk
la botella bottle
el brazo arm
el brócoli broccoli
la broncoscopia bronchoscopy
bronquial bronchial
el bronquio bronchial tube
buenmozo handsome
bueno/a good

C

el cabello hair
la cabeza head
cada each, every
la cadera hip
caer to fall
la calabaza squash
el calambre cramp
el calcio calcium
el cálculo en el riñón kidney stone
el caldo broth
la calle street
el calmante tranquilizer, analgesic
calmar(se) to calm, to calm down
el calor heat
la caloría calorie
la cama bed
la camilla stretcher, gurney
caminar to walk
el cáncer cancer
la canela cinnamon
cansado/a tired

el cansancio fatigue
cansar to tire, to grow tired
la cantidad amount
la cápsula capsule
la cara face
cardíaco/a cardiac
la cardiología cardiology
el/la cardiólogo/a cardiologist
la caries cavity
la carne meat
la carne de res beef
casado/a married
casar(se) to marry
la caspa dandruff
la caspa de animal animal dander
la catarata cataract
el catarro congestion, common cold
el catéter catheter
celoso/a jealous
la cena supper
cenar to eat/have supper
cepillar(se) to brush
el cereal cereal
  —cocido cooked cereal
  —seco dry cereal
cerebral cerebral
el cerebro brain
el cero zero
la cerveza beer
el chino Chinese
chiquito/a small
chocar to collide, to crash
el chocolate chocolate
el choque a collision, a crash
la ciática sciatica
ciático/a sciatic
la cicatriz scar
ciego/a blind
el cinturón de seguridad seat belt
la cirrosis cirrhosis
la ciruela plum, prune
la cirugía surgery
el/la cirujano/a surgeon
  —ortopédico/a orthopedic surgeon
  —plástico/a plastic surgeon
la cita appointment
la ciudad city
la clamidia chlamydia
la clase class

clásico/a classic
la clavícula clavicle
la clínica clinic
clínico/a clinical
el coágulo clot
la cocaína cocaine
el cóccix coccyx
el coche car
la cocina kitchen
cocinar to cook
el/la cocinero/a cook
el coco coconut
la codeína codeine
el codo elbow
la colecistectomía cholecystectomy
la colecistitis cholecystitis
el cólera cholera
el cólico, los cólicos colic
el colon colon
la colonoscopia colonoscopy
el color color
colorado/a red
la colostomía colostomy
la comadrona midwife
combatir to fight
comer to eat
la comezón itch, itching
la comida meal
cómo how
como like, as
cómodo/a comfortable
compartir to share
la complicación complication
comprar to buy
común common
el condón condom
confirmar to confirm
la congestión congestion
congestionado/a congested
consciente conscious
el/la consejero/a counselor
constante constant
consultar to consult
el consultorio doctor's office
la contaminación contamination
  —del aire air pollution
contento/a happy, contented
contestar to answer

la contracción contraction
el contraceptivo contraceptive
la convulsión convulsion
el corazón heart
la corona crown
  —de oro gold crown
  —de porcelana porcelain crown
correr to run
corriente regular, everyday
la cortadura cut
cortar(se) to cut
cortés polite
la cortesía politeness
corto/a short (length)
coser to sew
la costilla rib
la coyuntura joint
el cráneo cranium
creer to believe
la crema cream, ointment
  —dental toothpaste
la crisis crisis
crónico/a chronic
cuál which
cuándo when
cuánto/a how much
cuántos/as how many
cuarto/a quarter part
el cuarto room
el cúbito ulna
la cuchara tablespoon
la cucharada tablespoonful
la cucharadita teaspoonful
la cucharita teaspoon
el cuello neck
  —del útero, —de la matriz cervix
el cuerpo body
el cuidado intensivo intensive care
  —neonatal neonatal intensive care
cuidar to care for
la culebrilla herpes zoster, shingles
la culpa guilt
culpable guilty
el cultivo culture (laboratory)
el/la cuñado/a brother-in-law, sister-in-law
curioso/a curious
la curita small bandage
la custodia custody

d

dañar to damage, to harm
el daño damage, harm
dar (*irregular*) to give
dar a luz to give birth
dar de alta to discharge
de of, from
de dónde from where
debajo de under
deber ought, should, to owe
débil weak
la debilidad weakness
el/la décimo/a tenth
decir (*irregular*) to say, to tell
el dedo finger
el dedo del pie toe
defecar to move one's bowels
dejar to leave behind
delante de (in) front of
delgado/a thin
el delirio delusion
demasiado/a too much
demostrar (o-ue) to demonstrate
el dengue dengue
la dentadura teeth, set of teeth
   —**postiza** dentures, false teeth
el/la dentista dentist
la depresión depression
deprimido/a depressed
derecho/a right, straight
el/la dermatólogo/a dermatologist
el derrame leak, spill; used for stroke, cerebral hemorrhage
desayunar to eat/have breakfast
el desayuno breakfast
descafeinado/a decaffeinated
descansar to rest
el descanso rest
el descongestionante decongestant
descorazonado/a disheartened
descremado/a fat-free
la descripción description
descubrir to discover
desesperado/a hopeless, desperate
la deshidratación dehydration
desmayar(se) to faint
despacio slow, slowly

despertar(se) (e-ie) to awaken
despierto/a awake
después afterward
después de after
detrás de behind
el día day
la diabetes diabetes
el diagnóstico diagnosis
la diálisis dialysis
la diarrea diarrhea
dichoso/a lucky
diciembre December
el diente tooth
   —**de leche** baby tooth
la dieta diet
el/la dietista dietician
la difteria diphtheria
el dinero money
la dirección address
la disentería dysentery
disgustado/a disgusted
el diurético diuretic
divorciado/a divorced
divorciar(se) to divorce, to get divorced
el divorcio divorce
el doctor, la doctora doctor
doler (o-ue) to ache, to hurt
el dolor pain
   —**del parto** labor pain
   —**latente/sordo** dull ache
   —**punzante/agudo** sharp pain
   —**quemante** burning pain
el domingo Sunday
dónde where
dorado/a golden
dormir (o-ue) to sleep
el drenaje drain, drainage
drenar to drain
la droga drug
duchar(se) to shower
dulce sweet
el dulce candy
durar to last, endure
duro/a hard

e

ebrio/a drunk
el ecograma sonogram, sonograph

ectópico/a ectopic
la eczema eczema
la edad age
el efecto secundario side effect
el the
él he
el electrocardiograma electrocardiogram
el electroencefalograma electroencephalogram
eliminar to eliminate
el elíxir elixir
ella she
ellos/as they
embarazada pregnant
el embarazo pregnancy
la embolia embolism
la embolia cerebral stroke
la emergencia emergency
el empacho indigestion
el empaste filling (dental)
empeorar to worsen
empezar (e-ie) to start, begin
empujar to push
encantado/a pleased
encima de on top of
encinta pregnant
encontrar (o-ue) to find
el/la endocrinólogo/a endocrinologist
la endocrinología endocrinology
la endometriosis endometriosis
la endoscopía endoscopy
enero January
enfadado/a annoyed
enfadar(se) to become annoyed
la enfermedad sickness, illness
la enfermedad cardiovascular cardiovascular disease
la enfermedad pulmonar obstructiva crónica COPD
la enfermedad transmitida sexualmente sexually transmitted disease
el/la enfermero/a nurse
enfermo/a sick, ill
la enfisema emphysema
enfogonado/a enraged (*slang*)
enfogonar(se) to enrage (*slang*)
el enjuague rinse
enjuagar to rinse
enlatado/a canned

enojado/a angry
enojar to anger
enojar(se) to get angry
el enojo anger
la ensalada salad
enseñar to teach, to show
entero/a whole
el entumecimiento numbness
la epilepsia epilepsy
la epinefrina epinephrine
la episiotomía episiotomy
la erupción rash
esa that
los escalofríos chills
la esclerosis múltiple multiple sclerosis
escribir to write
escrito/a written
el escritorio desk
el escroto scrotum
escuchar to listen
la escuela school
escupir to spit
ese that
el esófago esophagus
la espalda back
el español Spanish, Spaniard
la especia spice
la especialidad specialty
la esperanza hope
esperar to wait, to hope
la espina bífida spina bifida
la espina dorsal spine
el espíritu spirit
la espirometría spirometry
espontáneo/a spontaneous
la espuma foam
el esputo sputum
el esqueleto skeleton
la esquizofrenia schizophrenia
el/la esquizofrénico/a schizophrenic
esta this
la estadía length of stay
los Estados Unidos the United States
el estafilococo staphylococcus
el estafilococo dorado MRSA (golden staph)
estar (*irregular*) to be
la estatura height
este this
el esternón sternum

el esteroide steroid
el estómago stomach
estornudar to sneeze
el estornudo sneeze
el estreñimiento constipation
el estrés stress
el/la estudiante student
estudiar to study
el estudio study
evacuar to move one's bowels
evitar to avoid
el examen exam
la examinación examination
examinar to examine
exhalar to exhale
el expectorante expectorant
el expediente médico medical record
exploratorio/a exploratory
la extracción extraction

f

la falange phalange
la falta de aire shortness of breath
el/la farmacéutico/a pharmacist
la farmacia pharmacy
fascinar to fascinate
la fatiga fatigue, shortness of breath
febrero February
la fecha date
las felicidades congratulations
feliz happy
el fémur femur
el feto fetus
la fibra fiber
la fiebre fever
la fiebre reumática rheumatic fever
firmar to sign
flaco/a skinny
la flema phlegm
el fluido fluid
el flujo flow, liquid discharge
el fluoruro fluoride
la fobia phobia
la fractura fracture
la frambesia yaws
el francés French
el frasco bottle
la frazada blanket

la frecuencia frequency
frecuente frequent
frecuentemente frequently
la frente forehead
la fresa dental drill; strawberry
el frío cold (temperature)
frío/a cold
frustrado/a frustrated
la fruta fruit
fuerte strong
fumar to smoke
furioso/a furious

g

el ganglio linfático lymph gland
la garganta throat
gastar to spend money
la gastritis gastritis
el gel gel
la gelatina gelatin
generoso/a generous
el/la geriatra geriatrist
la geriatría geriatrics
geriátrico/a geriatric
la ginecología gynecology
ginecológico/a gynecologic
el/la ginecólogo/a gynecologist
la gingivitis gingivitis
la glándula gland
la glándula tiroidea thyroid gland
la glaucoma glaucoma
el gluteo buttock
el golpe bump
golpear(se) to bump, hit
el golpecito tap
la gonorrea gonorrhea
gordo/a fat
la gota drop, gout
gotear to drip
el goteo dripping
la grabadora recorder
grabar to record
gracias thank you
el grano grain
la grasa fat, grease
la gripa common cold
la gripe flu, common cold
el guante glove

guapo/a handsome (with *ser*); angry (with *estar*)
el guineo banana
gustar to please
el gusto taste

h

la haba, la habichuela bean
hablar to talk, to speak
hacer (*irregular*) to do, to make
hacer falta to miss
el hambre hunger
hambriento/a hungry
hasta until
hay there is, there are
las heces fecales feces
el helado ice cream
el helicóptero helicopter
la hembra female
la hemofilia hemophilia
la hemorragia hemorrhage
hemorrágico/a hemorrhagic
las hemorroides hemorrhoids
la hepatitis hepatitis
la herida wound, injury
herir to injure
el/la hermanastro/a brother-in-law, sister-in-law
el/la hermano/a brother, sister
el/la hermano/a de madre/padre half-brother, half-sister
la hernia hernia
la heroína heroin
el herpes herpes
el hierro iron (Fe)
el hígado liver
higiénico/a hygienic
el/la higienista dental dental hygienist
el/la hijastro/a stepson, stepdaughter
el/la hijo/a son, daughter
el/la hijo/a de crianza foster child
el hilo dental dental floss
hinchado/a swollen
hinchar to swell
la hinchazón swelling
la hipercolesterolemia hypercolesterolemia
la hiperglucemia hyperglycemia

la hipertensión hypertension
el hipertiroidismo hyperthyroidism
la hipoglucemia hypoglycemia
la hipotensión hypotension
el hipotiroidismo hypothyroidism
la histerectomía hysterectomy
la historia history
hola hello
el hombre man
el hombro shoulder
la hora hour
el hospital hospital
la hospitalización hospitalization
hospitalizar hospitalize
hoy today
el hueso bone
el huevo egg
el húmero humerus
el humo smoke

i

la ictericia jaundice
el idioma language
igual equal, same
igualmente equally, same here, same to you
el íleon ilium
implantar to implant
el implante implant
importar to matter
incapacitado/a disabled
incluir (*irregular*) to include
la incontinencia incontinence
el infarto infarct
la infección infection
infectar to infect
la inflamación inflammation
inflamado/a inflamed
inflamar to inflame
la influenza influenza
la infusión infusion, tea
el inglés English
el inhalador inhaler
el insomnio insomnia
la insuficiencia insufficiency
   —cardíaca congestive heart failure
   —renal renal failure
integral whole-grain
inteligente intelligent

interesado/a interested
interesante interesting
interesar to interest
el internamiento hospitalization
internar to admit (to an institution)
el intestino intestine
   —delgado small intestine
   —grueso large intestine
inútil useless
la inyección injection
ir (*irregular*) to go
la irritabilidad irritability
la irritación rash
el italiano Italian
izquierdo/a left

j

jadear to gasp, to pant
el jadeo gasping, panting
jamás never
el japonés Japanese
la jaqueca migraine, headache
el jarabe syrup (medicine)
el jengibre ginger
la jeringa, la jeringuilla syringe
el jitomate tomato
joven young
el jueves Thursday
el jugo juice
   —de naranja orange juice
   —de manzana apple juice
   —de ciruela prune juice
julio July
junio June

k

el kilogramo kilogram

l

la the
el labio lip
la laceración laceration
el lado side
la lágrima tear (secretion)
la laparoscopia laparoscopy
largo/a long

el láser laser
lastimar to injure, to wound
latente pulsating
el látex latex
lavar(se) to wash
el laxante laxative
la leche milk
leer to read
lejos far
la lengua tongue, language
el lenguaje language
los lentes eyeglasses
lento/a slow
la leptospirosis leptospirosis
la leucemia leukemia
levantar(se) to get up, to arise, to raise
leve light, slight, minor
la libra pound
el libro book
el limón lemon, lime
la limpieza cleaning
limpio/a clean
líquido liquid
el litio lithium
la llamada call
llamar to call
llamar(se) to be named, to call oneself
el llanto crying jag, weeping
la llegada arrival
llegar to arrive
llevar to carry, wear
llorar to cry
loco/a crazy
la lombriz intestinal intestinal worm
luego later
el lugar place
la lumpectomía lumpectomy
el lunar mole
el lunes Monday
la luz light

m

la madrastra stepmother
la madre mother
la madrina godmother
majado/a mashed
majar to mash
mal badly

el malestar general malaise
malo/a bad
la mancha stain
manchar to stain
la mandíbula jaw
manejar to drive, to manage
la manía mania
el/la maníacodepresivo/a manic-
  depressive
la mano hand
la manteca lard; heroin (*slang*)
**la manteca de cacahuate, la manteca
  de maní** peanut butter
la mantequilla butter
la manzana apple
la mañana morning
mañana tomorrow
la máquina machine
el marcapasos pacemaker
mareado/a dizzy
el mareo dizziness
la marijuana marijuana
el martes Tuesday
marzo March
más o menos more or less
matar to kill
matarse to commit suicide
materno/a maternal
la matriz womb
mayo May
el medicamento medication
la medicina medicine
el/la médico/a doctor
  —de cabecera general practitioner
  —general general practitioner
  —generalista general practitioner
  —internista internist
la mejilla cheek
mejor better
mejorar to get better
la meningitis meningitis
la menopausia menopause
la menstruación menstruation
menstruar to menstruate
mensual, mensualmente monthly
la merienda snack
el mes month
el metástasis metastasis
el miedo fear

la miel de abeja honey
el miembro penis
el miércoles Wednesday
la migraña migraine
el miligramo milligram
el mililitro millilitre
mirar to look
el moco mucus
el moho mold
moler (o-ue) to grind
molestar to bother, to annoy
la molestia bother, annoyance
molesto/a uncomfortable, annoyed
molido/a ground
la monga common cold, flu (*slang*)
el monitor monitor
la mononucleosis mononucleosis
moreno/a dark, brunette
el moretón bruise
morir (o-ue) to die
mortificado/a tormented
mover(se) (o-ue) to move
el/la muchacho/a child
la muela molar
la muela del juicio wisdom tooth
la muerte death
la muestra sample
la mujer woman
la muleta crutch
la muñeca wrist, doll
el músculo muscle
el muslo thigh
muy very

n

nacer (*irregular*) to be born
el nacimiento birth
nada nothing
nadie nobody, no one
la nalga buttock
la nariz nose
natural natural
la náusea nausea
nebulizar to nebulize
el nebulizador nebulizer
la necesidad need
necesitar to need
la nefrectomía nephrectomy

la nefritis nephritis
negativo/a negative
el nervio nerve
nervioso/a nervous
la neumonectomía pneumonectomy
la neumonía pneumonia
el/la neumonólogo/a pulmonologist
la neurología neurology
el/la neurólogo/a neurologist
la nevera refrigerator
ningún, ninguno/a none, not any
el/la niño/a child
la nitroglicerina nitroglycerine
la noche night
nombrar to name
el nombre name
la norsa nurse (*slang*)
nosocomial nosocomial
nosotros/as we, us
noveno/a ninth
noviembre November
el nudillo knuckle
la nuera daughter-in-law
nuestro/a our, ours
nunca never

o

o or
la obesidad obesity
obeso/a obese
el/la obstetra obstetrician
la obstetricia obstetrics
obstétrico/a obstetric
octavo/a eighth
octubre October
la odontología dentistry
el/la odontólogo/a dentist
ofender to offend
ofendido/a offended
ofrecer to offer
la ofrenda offering
la oftalmología ophthalmology
el/la oftalmólogo/a ophthalmologist
el oído ear (inner), hearing
oír to hear
¡Ojalá! I hope so!
ojalá que . . . I wish that . . .
el ojo eye

oler (*irregular*) to smell
el olfato smell
el olor odor, smell
olvidar to forget
el omóplato scapula
la oncología oncology
el/la oncólogo/a oncologist
oprimir to press
oral oral
el orégano oregano
la oreja ear (outer)
orgulloso/a proud
la orina urine
orinar to urinate
el oro gold
la ortopedia orthopedics
ortopédico/a orthopedic
el/la ortopedista orthopedist
oscuro/a dark
la osteoporosis osteoporosis
el ovario ovary
la ovulación ovulation
ovular to ovulate
el oxígeno oxygen

p

el/la paciente patient
padecer (*irregular*) to suffer (from an illness)
el padecimiento ailment, illness; suffering
el padrastro stepfather
el padre father
los padres parents
el padrino godfather
pálido/a pale
el palo pole, stick
palpar to palpate
la palpitación palpitation
el paludismo malaria
el pan bread
 —**tostado** toast
el páncreas pancreas
la pandemia pandemic
pandémico/a pandemic
la papa potato
las papas fritas French fries
la paperas mumps
la papiloma papilloma

la parálisis paralysis, palsy
  —**cerebral** cerebral palsy
el/la paramédico/a paramedic
la paranoia paranoia
paranoico/a paranoid
el parche patch
la pareja partner, couple
parir to give birth
el/la partero/a midwife
el parto birth
pasar to happen, to pass
el pasillo hallway
la pastilla pill
la patela kneecap
paterno/a paternal
el pato de cama bedpan
el pecho chest
el pedazo piece
el/la pediatra pediatrician
la pediatría pediatrics
pediátrico/a pediatric
pedir (e-i) to ask for, to beg
peinar(se) to comb
el peine comb
pelear to argue, to fight
el peligro danger
peligroso/a dangerous
el pelo hair
la pelotita lump
el pene penis
peor worse
pequeño/a small
percutir to percuss
perder (e-ie) to lose
el perico cocaine (*slang*)
el período period
el permiso permission
el peroné fibula
persistente persistent
persistir to persist
personal personal
pesado/a crushing, heavy
pesar to weigh
el pescado fish
pescar to fish
el peso weight
el pían yaws

picar to itch
la picazón itch, itching
el pie foot
la piel skin
la pierna leg
la píldora pill
la pinta pinta
los piojos lice
la pirámide pyramid
el piso floor
la placa film, plaque, x-ray
la placenta placenta
el placer pleasure
el plan de alimentación diet
el plan médico health insurance
la plata silver, money
pobre poor
poder (o-ue) to be able
el polen pollen
la polio polio
el pólipo polyp
el pollo chicken
el polvo dust
polvorizar to crush
la pompa inhaler (*slang*)
la pompis buttock
el pómulo cheekbone
poner (*irregular*) to put
¿por qué? why?
la porcelana porcelain
la porción portion
porque because
el portador (sano) (asymptomatic) carrier
el portugués Portuguese
positivo/a positive
el postre dessert
la precaución precaution
la pregunta question
preguntar to ask a question
la presión pressure
  —**arterial** blood pressure
  —**de la sangre** blood pressure
  —**sanguínea** blood pressure
presionar to press
la prevención prevention
prevenir to prevent
preventivo/a preventive

primero/a first
el/la primo/a cousin
privado/a private
probar (o-ue) to test, taste, try
el procedimiento procedure
profundo/a deep
el pronóstico prognosis
la próstata prostate
la prostatitis prostatitis
la proteína protein
provocar to provoke
la prueba test
la prueba de Pap Pap smear
la psicología psychology
el/la psicólogo/a psychologist
la psicosis psychosis
psicótico/a psychotic
el/la psiquiatra psychiatrist
la psiquiatría psychiatry
psiquiátrico/a psychiatric
la psoriasis psoriasis
el pueblo town
la puerta door
la pulgada inch
el pulmón lung
la pulmonía pneumonia
el/la pulmonólogo/a pulmonologist
el pulso pulse
el punto stitch; period, dot, point
puntual punctual
punzante stabbing
el puré puree

q

que that
qué what, how
quebrado/a broken
quedar(se) to remain
quemado/a burned
la quemadura burn
quemar(se) to burn
querer (e-ie) to want, to like
el queso cheese
quién who, whom
la quinina quinine
quinto/a fifth
el quirófano operating room

el quiste cyst
quitar(se) to remove

r

el radio radio, radius
la radiografía x-ray
la radiología radiology
el/la radiólogo/a radiologist
rápido/a quick
la raquiña itch, itching (*slang*)
la reacción reaction
la reanimación cardiopulmonar CPR
el/la recepcionista receptionist
la receta prescription
recetar to prescribe
rechazado/a rejected
rechazar to reject
el rechazo rejection
recibir to receive
el recibo receipt
recordar (o-ue) to remind, to remember
el recto rectum
el reemplazo replacement
el reflujo esofágico esophageal reflux
el refresco soda pop
el refrigerador refrigerator
la regla period, menstruation
regular regular; okay
el remedio cure
  —**casero** home remedy
repentino/a sudden
la res, la carne de res beef
el resfriado common cold
el resfrío common cold
resistente resistant
la respiración respiration
respirar to breathe
la resucitación resuscitation
resucitar to resuscitate
el resultado result
retirar to withdraw
el retraso mental mental retardation
rico/a rich
el riesgo risk
la rigidez stiffness
el riñón kidney
rociar to spray

la rodilla knee
romper to break
  —fuente to break water
el ron rum
las ronchas hives
la ropa clothes, clothing
la rubéola rubella, German measles
rubio/a blond, blonde, fair

S

el sábado Saturday
la sábana sheet
saber (*irregular*) to know
sacar to take out
el sacro sacrum
la sal salt
la sala de
  —emergencia emergency room
  —espera waiting room
  —operaciones operating room
  —recuperación recovery room
  —urgencias emergency room
la salchicha sausage
la salud health
sanar to heal
sangrar to bleed
la sangre blood
sano/a healthy, healed
el sarampión measles
la sarna scabies
el sarpullido hives, rash
el sarro plaque (dental)
satisfecho/a satisfied
la secreción secretion
el/la secretario/a secretary
la sed thirst
el sedante sedative
seguir (e-i) to follow
segundo/a second
el seguro insurance
seguro/a safe, sure
el sellante sealant
la semana week
sencillo/a plain, easy
el seno breast; sinus
  —frontal frontal sinus
  —paranasal paranasal sinus

la sensación sensation
sentar(se) (e-ie) to sit
sentir(se) (e-ie) to feel
septiembre September
séptimo/a seventh
ser (*irregular*) to be
severo/a severe
sexto/a sixth
el shock anafiláctico anaphylactic
  shock
la sicosis psychosis
sicótico/a psychotic
siempre always
la sífilis syphilis
el silbido wheeze
la silla chair
la silla de ruedas wheelchair
la silleta bedpan
simpático/a kind
el SIDA AIDS
el síndrome syndrome
el síntoma symptom
sobre on, about, around
la sobredosis overdose
sobrepeso/a overweight
sobrio/a sober
solitario/a alone
la sonda catheter
la sonografía ultrasound
la sopa soup
el soplo bruit
  —cardíaco heart murmur
sordo/a deaf; dull (ache)
sorprendido/a surprised
su your, his, her, their
sudar to sweat
el sudor sweat
los sudores nocturnos night sweats
la suegra mother-in-law
el suegro father-in-law
el sueño dream, sleep
el suero IV fluid
la suerte luck
suicidarse to commit suicide
el suicidio suicide
el supositorio suppository
la suspensión suspension
el susto fright
suyo/a yours, his, hers, theirs

t

la tabla board
el tacto touch
el tajo cut
también also, too
tampoco neither
la taquicardia tachycardia
tarde late
la tarde afternoon
la tarjeta card
el té tea
el/la técnico/a technician
el teléfono telephone
la temperatura temperature
temprano early
tener (*irregular*) to have
la tensión arterial blood pressure
el/la terapeuta therapist
  —**físico/a** physical therapist
  —**de lenguaje** speech therapist
  —**del habla** speech therapist
  —**respiratorio/a** respiratory therapist
tercero/a third
el termómetro thermometer
el testículo testicle
el tétano, el tétanos tetanus
la tía aunt
la tía abuela great-aunt
la tibia tibia
tibio/a lukewarm
el tiempo time, weather
tímido/a shy
el tío uncle
el tío abuelo great-uncle
la tirita small bandage
el tiroides thyroid
la tisana infusion (drink), tea
la toalla towel
el tobillo ankle
tocar to touch
tomar to take
el tomate tomato
la tomografía computarizada CT scan
la tonsilectomía tonsillectomy
tópico/a topical
la torcedura sprain
torcer(se) (o-ue) to sprain
torcido/a sprained

la toronja grapefruit
la torta cake
la tos cough
la tos ferina pertussis, whooping cough
toser to cough
la tostada toast
el/la trabajador/a social social worker
trabajar to work
el trabajo job
  —**social** social work
el trabalengua tongue twister
la tradición tradition
tragar to swallow
el trago swallow
traicionado/a betrayed
trasnochar to stay up all night
trasplantar to transplant
el trasplante transplant
el trastorno disorder
el tratamiento treatment
  —**de canal** root canal
tratar to treat
los triglicéridos triglycerides
triste sad
la tristeza sadness
la trombosis thrombosis
la trompa de Falopio Fallopian tube
tu your
tú you
la tuberculosis tuberculosis
el tumor tumor
el/la tutor/a custodian
tuyo/a yours

u

la úlcera ulcer
el ungüento ointment
la unidad unit
la uña fingernail
la urgencia urgency, emergency
la urticaria urticaria
usted you
el útero uterus
útil useful
la uva grape

v

la vacuna vaccination
vacunar to vaccinate

la vagina vagina
la varicela chicken pox
el varón male
el vaso glass
el vegetal vegetable
la vejiga bladder
la vena vein
el vendaje bandage
venir (*irregular*) to come
la ventana window
el ventilador fan, ventilator
ver to see
la verdad truth
verdadero/a true
verde green
verdoso/a greenish
la verdura vegetable (green)
la vergüenza shame
la verruga venérea genital warts
la vertebra vertebra
la vesícula biliar gallbladder
la vez time (occurrence, occasion)
la víctima victim
viejo/a old
el viernes Friday
el VIH HIV
el vino wine
virar(se) to roll over
la viruela smallpox
las viruelas locas chicken pox

el virus virus
la visita visit
el/la visitante visitor
visitar to visit
la vista sight
la vitamina vitamin
la viuda widow
el viudo widower
vivir to live
vivo/a alive
volver (o-ue) to return
vomitar to vomit
el vómito vomit
la voz voice

y

y and
ya already, at last, right now
el/la yerno/a son-in-law, daughter-in-law
el yeso cast
yo I
el yogur yogurt

z

la zanahoria carrot
el zapato shoe

Answer Key to *Ejercicios*

Chapter 1

1.3 Ejercicio

A. tú   B. tú   C. usted   D. usted   E. tú   F. usted

1.4 Ejercicio

Soy Juan.	I am Juan.
Soy norteamericano.	I am North American.
Soy enfermero.	I am a nurse.
¿Es usted estudiante?	Are you a student?
Él es el señor Soto.	He is Señor Soto.
Él es norteamericano.	He is North American.
Ella es la doctora Jerez.	She is Doctor Jerez.
Ella es mexicana.	She is Mexican.

1.6 Ejercicio

A. Necesito una inyección.	Usted necesita una enfermera.
B. Sufro de problemas cardíacos.	Usted necesita un cardiólogo.
C. Sufro de diabetes.	Usted necesita un endocrinólogo, nutricionista, dietista, oftalmólogo.
D. Necesito una operación.	Usted necesita un cirujano.
E. Sufro de cáncer de los pulmones.	Usted necesita un oncólogo, cirujano.
F. Sufro de cataratas.	Usted necesita un oftalmólogo.
G. Necesito una dieta especial.	Usted necesita un dietista, nutricionista.
H. Sufro de problemas emocionales.	Usted necesita un psicólogo, psiquiatra, trabajador social.
I. Sufro de artritis.	Usted necesita un reumatólogo.

J. Tengo la clavícula fracturada.   Usted necesita un ortopedista.
K. Sufro de psoriasis.   Usted necesita un dermatólogo.
L. Mi bebé tiene fiebre.   Usted necesita un pediatra.

1.9 Ejercicio

A. El doctor Colón es neurólogo.   La doctora Palma es neuróloga.
B. El doctor Aquino es odontólogo.   La doctora Valenzuela es odontóloga.
C. Ana es trabajadora social.   Tomás es trabajador social.
D. El señor García es consejero.   La señora Marques es consejera.
E. Leomara es farmacéutica.   Alfredo es farmacéutico.
F. La doctora López es cardióloga.   El doctor López es cardiólogo.
G. La doctora Negrón es dentista.   El doctor Losada Gutiérrez es dentista.

1.10 Ejercicio

A. la clínica   las clínicas
B. la puerta   las puertas
C. el monitor   los monitores
D. la cama   las camas
E. la sábana   las sábanas
F. la frazada   las frazadas
G. la almohada   las almohadas
H. el doctor   los doctores

1.11 Ejercicio

A. El Sr. Romero   él es
B. Juan y yo   nosotros somos
C. Sergio y Ana   ellos son
D. las enfermeras   ellas son
E. la familia   (la familia) es
F. la clase y yo   nosotros somos
G. los doctores   ellos son
H. el doctor y el enfermero   ellos son
I. la clínica   (la clínica) es
J. usted, usted y usted   ustedes son

1.12 Ejercicio

A. Juan and Marco are nurses.   Juan y Marco son enfermeros.
B. Ana and María are doctors.   Ana y María son doctores.
C. We are students.   Somos estudiantes.
D. Pablo and I are social workers.   Pablo y yo somos trabajadores sociales.
E. Héctor and I are neurologists.   Héctor y yo somos neurólogos.

F. The (female) nurses are Mexican.	Las enfermeras son mexicanas.
G. The (mixed gender) nurses are Spanish.	Los enfermeros son mexicanos.
H. Daniel and Patricia are psychologists.	Daniel y Patricia son psicólogos.

1.17 Ejercicio

A. La esposa del Sr. Flores se llama (b. Marisol).
B. El doctor Vargas es de (a. Puerto Rico).
C. La familia Flores es de (b. La República Dominicana).
D. El doctor Vargas es (c. médico generalista).
E. El cardiólogo trabaja con problemas (a. del corazón).
F. Necesitas un urólogo si tienes problema con (b. la próstata).
G. Si te duele el oído, necesitas consultar con un (a. otorrinolaringólogo).

1.19 Ejercicio

A. alto	bajo
B. delgado	gordo
C. bajo	alto
D. viejo	joven
E. grande	pequeño
F. corto	largo
G. largo	corto
H. feo	bonito, guapo
I. gordo	delgado, flaco

1.20 Ejercicio

A. La doctora es inteligente.	Sí, es una doctora inteligente.
B. Los estudiantes son interesantes.	Sí, son unos estudiantes interesantes.
C. La enfermera es joven.	Sí, es una enfermera joven.
D. El profesor es guapo.	Sí, es un profesor guapo.
E. El médico es alto.	Sí, es un médico alto.
F. Los pacientes son delgados.	Sí, son unos pacientes delgados.
G. Los doctores son viejos.	Sí, son unos doctores viejos.
H. El neurólogo es simpático.	Sí, es un neurólogo simpático.

1.21 Ejercicio

A. Pedro es feo. ¿Cómo es Estrella?	Estrella no es fea. Es bonita.
B. Marta es gorda. ¿Cómo es Juan?	Juan no es gordo. Es delgado.
C. Miguel es alto. ¿Cómo es Rosa?	Rosa no es alta. Es baja.
D. Ana es baja. ¿Cómo es Marco?	Marco no es bajo. Es alto.
E. María es vieja. ¿Cómo es José?	José no es viejo. Es joven.
F. Carlos es guapo. ¿Cómo es Ana?	Ana no es guapa. Es fea.

G. Luis es delgado. ¿Cómo es Estrella?   Estrella no es delgada. Es gorda.
H. Juana es joven. ¿Cómo es Timoteo?   Timoteo no es joven. Es viejo.

Chapter 2

2.1 Ejercicio

Estoy enfermo.   I am ill.
¿Estás bien?   Are you well?
Juan está regular.   Juan is okay.
Mi bebé está enfermo.   My baby is sick.
Rosa y yo estamos enfermos.   Rosa and I are ill.
Los pacientes están mejores.   The patients are better.

2.5 Ejercicio

¿Dónde está usted?   Where are you?
Estoy en casa.   I am at home.
Estoy en el hospital.   I am at the hospital.
¿Dónde está el cirujano?   Where is the surgeon?
El cirujano está en el hospital.   The surgeon is at the hospital.

2.6 Ejercicio

A. las sábanas de Elsa   sus sábanas
B. la cama de usted   su cama
C. las frazadas de nosotros   nuestras frazadas
D. las camas de José y Rosa   sus camas
E. la silla de la doctora   su silla

2.13 Ejercicio

Buenos días. Me llamo Hilda Rodríguez Portocarrero. *Soy* enfermera en el
hospital Nuestra Señora de la Altagracia. El hospital *es* grande y famoso. El
hospital *está* en Lima, Perú. Trabajo con la doctora Kathy Collins. La doctora
Collins *es* norteamericana. Ella *está* en el hospital todos los días, pero yo no.
Los sábados *está* en la clínica y los domingos *está* en casa. Los domingos la
clínica *está* cerrada. La doctora *es* alta y delgada. Yo *soy* baja y no muy delgada.
La doctora y yo *estamos* muy contentas.

Chapter 3

3.8 Ejercicio

A. Una cama es buenísima cuando tengo sueño.
B. Un carro deportivo es buenísimo cuando tengo prisa.
C. Una frazada es buenísima cuando tengo sueño.
D. Un osito de peluche es buenísimo cuando tengo miedo.
E. Una hamburguesa es buenísima cuando tengo hambre.
F. Un abanico es buenísimo cuando tengo calor.
G. Un vaso de agua es buenísimo cuando tengo sed.
H. Una discusión es buenísima cuando tengo razón.

3.21 Ejercicio

A. Usted tiene el dedo quebrado. El dedo está quebrado.
B. Usted tiene la pierna quebrada. La pierna está quebrada.
C. Usted tiene el pie quebrado. El pie está quebrado.
D. Usted tiene las rodillas quebradas. Las rodillas están quebradas.
E. Usted tiene dos costillas quebradas. Dos costillas están quebradas.
F. Usted tiene tres dedos quebrados. Tres dedos están quebrados.
G. Usted tiene el tobillo izquierdo quebrado. El tobillo izquierdo está quebrado.
H. Usted tiene la muñeca derecha quebrada. La muñeca derecha está quebrada.

3.22 Ejercicio

A. La rodilla no está quebrada, gracias a Dios; está torcida.
B. Los tobillos no están quebrados, gracias a Dios; están torcidos.
C. El cuello no está quebrado, gracias a Dios; está torcido.
D. Las muñecas no están quebradas, gracias a Dios; están torcidas.
E. El dedo no está quebrado, gracias a Dios; está torcido.
F. La espalda no está quebrada, gracias a Dios; está torcida.
G. El tobillo izquierdo no está quebrado, gracias a Dios; está torcido.
H. La muñeca derecha no está quebrada, gracias a Dios; está torcida.

3.23 Ejercicio

A. La encía está hinchada, pero no está infectada.
B. Los labios están hinchados, pero no están infectados.
C. La rodilla está hinchada, pero no está infectada.
D. Los tobillos están hinchados, pero no están infectados.
E. El dedo del pie está hinchado, pero no está infectado.
F. El codo está hinchado, pero no está infectado.
G. La lengua está hinchada, pero no está infectada.
H. El ojo derecho está hinchado, pero no está infectado.

Chapter 4

4.4 Ejercicio

A. Su temperatura está en noventa y ocho grados.
B. Su temperatura está en ciento punto ocho grados.
C. Su temperatura está en noventa y siete punto cuatro grados.
D. Su temperatura está en ciento tres grados.
E. Su temperatura está en ciento cuatro punto dos grados.
F. Su temperatura está en noventa y ocho punto nueve grados.
G. Su temperatura está en ciento uno punto dos grados.
H. Su temperatura está en ciento punto tres grados.

4.5 Ejercicio

A. Ciento diez sobre sesenta y ocho.
B. Ciento sesenta y seis sobre ciento diez.
C. Ciento treinta y cuatro sobre ochenta.
D. Ciento veintiocho sobre setenta.
E. Ciento veintidós sobre ochenta y cuatro.
F. Ciento dieciocho sobre noventa y dos.
G. Ciento seis sobre setenta y cuatro.
H. Ciento veinte sobre ochenta.

4.16 Ejercicio

A. Son las tres.
B. Son las doce y quince. Son las doce y cuarto. Son las doce quince.
C. Son las diez y media. Son las diez treinta.
D. Es la una menos veinticinco. Son las doce treinta y cinco.

4.18 Ejercicio

A. Son las once menos quince de la mañana.
    Son las once menos cuarto de la mañana.
    Son las diez cuarenta y cinco de la mañana.
B. Son las seis y quince de la mañana.
    Son las seis y cuarto de la mañana.
    Son las seis quince de la mañana.
C. Son las ocho y media de la noche.
    Son las ocho treinta de la noche.
D. Son las doce menos cinco de la noche.
    Son las once cincuenta y cinco de la noche.
E. Son las cuatro menos cuatro de la tarde.
    Son las tres cincuenta y seis de la tarde.

F.   Son las seis y cinco de la tarde.
    Son las seis cinco de la tarde.

4.20 Ejercicio

A.   Usted tiene una cita con el dentista (el odontólogo) el jueves catorce de diciembre a las tres y media de la tarde.
B.   Usted tiene una cita en la clínica el martes veintidós de enero a las diez y quince (cuarto) de la mañana.
C.   Usted tiene una cita con el doctor Leicasch el viernes veintiocho de febrero a las siete menos quince de la tarde.
D.   Usted tiene una cita con el neurólogo, el Dr. Solano, el miércoles 30 de mayo a la una de la tarde.

Chapter 5

5.2 Ejercicio

A.   los padres de usted   sus padres
B.   la madre de usted   su madre
C.   el abuelo de Pedro   su abuelo
D.   los abuelos de Pedro   sus abuelos
E.   los hijos de nosotros   nuestros hijos
F.   las hermanas de nosotros   nuestras hermanas
G.   la familia de ustedes   su familia

5.3 Ejercicio

A.   La esposa de mi hermano es mi cuñada.
B.   El hijo de mi hijo es mi nieto.
C.   El hijo de mi padrastro es mi hermanastro.
D.   La hermana de mi madre es mi tía.
E.   El hijo de mi tía es mi primo.
F.   La hermana de mi primo es mi prima.
G.   La madre de mi esposa es mi suegra.
H.   El hijo de mi esposa y su ex esposo es mi hijastro.

5.4 Ejercicio

Hola. Me llamo Marta. Soy la primera hija de mis padres. Mi madre tiene una hermana. Ella es mi tía y su nombre es Linda. Yo soy sobrina de mi tía Linda. Ella tiene un hijo. Él es mi primo. Tengo otra tía. Ella es hermana de mi padre. Los hijos de ella son mis primos también. El padre de mi padre es mi abuelo. El hermano de mi abuelo es mi tío abuelo.

5.25 Ejercicio

A. Les receto un medicamento para sus hijos.
B. Le escribo una carta a usted.
C. Le llamo una ambulancia para la paciente.
D. Les enseño español a los estudiantes.
E. Le contesto el teléfono por la secretaria.
F. Le leo el libro a usted.
G. La doctora nos contesta la pregunta.

Chapter 6

6.1 Ejercicio

A. ¿Toma usted antiácidos por la noche?
B. ¿Toma doña Violeta una aspirina todos los días?
C. ¿Tomas medicamento para los ataques epilépticos?
D. ¿Toma el señor Altamirano un diurético para quitar el agua?
E. ¿Toman los padres de Juan medicamento para la hipertensión?
F. ¿Toman los pacientes antibióticos para curar las infecciones bacterianas?

6.3 Ejercicio

A. Favor de llamar al doctor mañana.
B. Favor de esperar por cinco minutos.
C. Favor de ir a la farmacia hoy.
D. Favor de tomar el medicamento todos los días.
E. Favor de tomar dos acetaminofén cuando le duele la cabeza.
F. Favor de usar la nitroglicerina cuando tiene dolor del pecho. / Favor de usar la nitroglicerina cuando le duele el pecho.
G. Favor de hacer una cita en la clínica.

6.5 Ejercicio

A. Hay que (tiene que) tomar una pastilla cada cuatro horas.
B. Hay que (tiene que) tomar una cucharadita por la mañana y dos al acostarse.
C. Hay que (tiene que) tomar el medicamento con leche.
D. Hay que (tiene que) tomar una pastilla cuatro veces al día por diez días.
E. Hay que (tiene que) tomar mucha agua con el medicamento.
F. Hay que (tiene que) tomar una cucharadita por la mañana.
G. Hay que (tiene que) tomar dos pastillas cada cuatro horas si es necesario para el dolor.
H. Hay que (tiene que) poner dos gotas en cada ojo dos veces al día.
I. Hay que (tiene que) aplicarse la crema por la mañana y por la noche.

6.6 Ejercicio

A. Acetaminofén, tome 2 tabletas cada 4 a 6 horas cuando es necesario para el dolor.
B. Mylanta®, tome 2 cucharadas al acostarse.
C. Omeprazole, tome 1 cápsula a las 8 de la mañana.
D. Isoniazid, tome 1 tableta todos los días por la mañana.
E. Fluoxetine 20 mg, tome 1 cápsula por la mañana.
F. Phenytoin 100 mg, tome 1 cápsula 3 veces al día.
G. Loperamide, tome 1 cápsula cada 2 a 3 horas cuando es necesario para la diarrea.

6.9 Ejercicio

A. Advil® es un antiinflamatorio no esteroide.
B. Proventil® es un broncodilatador.
C. Bactrim® es un antibiótico.
D. Coumadin® es un anticoagulante.
E. Lasix® es un diurético.
F. Ex-Lax® es un laxante.
G. Benadryl® es un antihistamínico (antialérgico).
H. Prozac® es un antidepresivo.
I. One-a-Day® es una vitamina.
J. Sudafed® es un descongestionante.

6.11 Ejercicio

A. Tome el medicamento (la medicina) todos los días sin falta.
B. Amoxicilina (250 mg/5 ml), tome 1 cucharadita 3 veces al día por 5 días.
C. Guaifenesina, tome 1 cucharada 4 veces al día para la congestión (constipación).
D. Salbutamol, tome 1 inhalación cada 4 a 6 horas cuando es necesario para la falta de aire.
E. Donepezilo, tome 10 mg por la boca (por vía oral) 1 vez al día (1 vez diario) por la mañana.
F. Ginkgo, tome 160 mg por la boca (por vía oral) a las 8 AM y las 8:00 PM.

6.12 Ejercicio

Quiero enseñarles cómo usar el inhalador para recibir el máximo beneficio del medicamento. Primero, *agite* bien el inhalador. Así. *Quite* la tapa protectora. *Exhale* completamente a través de su nariz y *mantenga* la boca cerrada. *Abra* la boca completamente y *ponga* la boquilla a una o dos pulgadas de su boca. Así. *Inhale* lentamente y profundamente y, al mismo tiempo, *oprima* la parte de abajo del envase para rociar el medicamento en la boca. Así. *Contenga* el aliento durante cinco a diez segundos, *retire* el inhalador y *exhale* lentamente a través de la nariz o boca. Así. *Ponga* la tapa protectora en el inhalador. Después de cada tratamiento, *enjuague* su boca con agua o enjuague bucal.

6.13 Ejercicio

Don Ignacio, es muy importante usar *estos* medicamentos en la manera indicada. *Esta* crema es para aliviar el dolor de la quemadura. En caso de fiebre, *estas* pastillas son para quitar la fiebre. Si tiene mucho dolor, *estas* pastillas son para el dolor. *Este* jarabe es para la tos. Si está peor mañana, favor de llamar a *este* número de teléfono. Finalmente, *estas* recetas son para comprar más medicamentos.

6.14 Ejercicio

A. Esta crema es para quitar la picazón (la comezón).
B. Esta medicina (Este medicamento) es para bajar el colesterol.
C. Este jarabe es para quitar la diarrea.
D. Este suero es para quitar (eliminar) la infección.
E. Esta pastilla es para bajar la presión arterial.
F. Esta inyección es para quitar el dolor.
G. Esta medicina (Este medicamento) es para quitar (bajar) la hinchazón.
H. Estas pastillas son para eliminar el agua.

Chapter 7

7.8 Ejercicio

A. No, no debe cocinar con manteca.
B. Sí, debe comer pollo y pescado.
C. No, no debe comer mucho coco.
D. Sí, debe tomar leche baja en grasa.
E. Sí, debe comer queso bajo en grasa.
F. No, no debe comer papas fritas.
G. Sí, debe usar aceite de maíz.
H. En vez de la carne de res, debe comer (*answers will vary*).

7.9 Ejercicio

A. No, no debe usar mucha azúcar cuando cocina.
B. Sí, debe comer ensalada.
C. No, no debe beber vino.
D. No, no debe comer muchos dulces.
E. Sí, debe comer frijoles.

F. No, no debe usar leche condensada.

G. Sí, debe tomar refrescos dietéticos.

H. Sí, debe usar azúcar artificial.

Chapter 8

8.5 Ejercicio

El señor Flores está *enfermo.* El problema es que hace tres o cuatro días que le duele *el pecho* cuando tose. Cuando *tose* hay *flema* y el pobre don Francisco tiene *fiebre.* El doctor Vargas dice que el señor Flores tiene *pulmonía* y que necesita *antibióticos y una radiografía del pecho.* Tiene que tomar los antibióticos *por vía oral.* Pronto el señor Flores va a estar *mejor.*

8.14 Ejercicio

A. ¿Qué es un angiograma?

B. ¿Qué es una supervisión Holter?

C. ¿Qué son las imágenes por resonancia magnética?

D. ¿Qué es una broncoscopia?

E. ¿Qué es una biopsia?

F. ¿Qué es un mamograma?

G. ¿Qué es la espirometría?

H. ¿Qué es una colonoscopia?

Chapter 9

9.11 Ejercicio

El tres de enero el doctor Aquino y Ana comieron en la casa de Javier.

El cinco de enero el doctor Aquino visitó a doña Mercedes en Boston.

El once de enero el doctor Aquino trabajó en la clínica desde las ocho hasta las cinco.

El trece de enero el doctor Aquino y don Máximo fueron a la clase de inglés.

El catorce de enero el doctor Aquino consultó con el anestesiólogo.

El quince de enero el doctor Aquino no comió o bebió nada después de la medianoche.

El dieciséis de enero el doctor Aquino tuvo una colonoscopia.

El diecisiete de enero el doctor Aquino fue donde la doctora Muñoz Domínguez para un examen físico.

El treinta de enero el doctor Aquino fue de vacaciones a Venezuela.

9.13 Ejercicio

A. La prueba de embarazo fue positiva.
B. El análisis de sangre fue negativo.
C. La prueba del SIDA fue negativa.
D. El sonograma de la vesícula fue negativo.
E. La biopsia fue positiva.
F. La tomografía computarizada fue negativa.
G. La prueba de tuberculosis fue positiva.

9.20 Ejercicio

Cuando *era* niño, *vivía* en Puerto Rico. Mis abuelos *vivían* con nosotros. Abuela *sabía* mucho de las plantas medicinales. Cuando *tenía* gripe, me *hacía* té de hojas de limón y naranja. Cuando *tenía* gases en la barriga, me *preparaba* té de anís. Mis padres no me *daban* remedios caseros. Ellos me *llevaban* a la farmacia, y el farmacéutico nos *vendía* un jarabe o una pastilla. No me *gustaban* los jarabes. *Prefería* las tisanas de mi abuelita.

Chapter 10

10.11 Ejercicio

Dra. Ávila:	¿Sufre usted de alguna enfermedad?
Doña Rosa:	No, no sufro de *ninguna* enfermedad.
Dra. Ávila:	*¿Toma algún medicamento?*
Doña Rosa:	No tomo *ningún* medicamento.
Dra. Ávila:	¿Es usted alérgica a *algún* alimento?
Doña Rosa:	No *soy alérgica a ningún alimento.*
Dra. Ávila:	En su familia, *¿alguien* ha tenido cáncer?
Doña Rosa:	No, en mi familia *nadie* ha padecido de cáncer.
Dra. Ávila:	¿Hay *alguien* en la casa para ayudarla?
Doña Rosa:	Vivo sola. No hay más *nadie* en casa.

10.17 Ejercicio

A. La artroscopia
B. La cirugía ambulatoria
C. La nefrectomía
D. La laparoscopia
E. La cirugía exploratoria

Chapter 11

11.12 Ejercicio

A. Se me rompió un hueso.
B. Se me olvidó ponerme la insulina.
C. Se me fracturó el dedo.
D. Se me quemó la mano.
E. ¿Se le perdió la receta?

Chapter 12

12.7 Ejercicio

A. *No hagas* la cita para hoy. *Haz* la cita para mañana.
B. *Sal* temprano de la casa. *No salgas* tarde.
C. *Ve* al consultorio. No *vayas* al hospital.
D. No *bañes* al bebé hoy. *Baña* al bebé mañana.
E. No *te bañes* hoy. *Báñate* mañana.
F. *Ponte* la bata del hospital. No *te pongas* ropa interior.
G. No *comas* nada después de las once. *Come* bien mañana.

12.8 Ejercicio

A. ¡Muévete!
B. ¡No te levantes!
C. ¡Vírate!
D. ¡Báñate hoy!
E. ¡No comas!
F. ¡No te acuestes!
G. ¡Levanta el brazo!
H. ¡No respires profundamente!

12.9 Ejercicio

A. ¡No te preocupes!
B. ¡Relájate!
C. ¡No comas nada!
D. ¡Si tienes sed, ¡no tomes (bebas) nada; come pedacitos de hielo!
E. ¡Empuja!
F. ¡No empujes!
G. ¡Respira!
H. ¡No respires!

Illustration Credits

The Food Pyramid that appears on page 158 is a public domain resource courtesy of the United States Department of Agriculture. DartZ Business Solutions LLC of New Britain, Connecticut, adapted it slightly. Truth-Function of Aiken, South Carolina, provided the companion video still shots that appear throughout the book. Robert O. Chase shot the remaining black-and-white photographs.

DartZ provided the icons that distinguish classroom activites, including the DVD, bicyclist, drama masks, and recycling arrows. DartZ also provided the following drawings: nurses, pages 5 and 11; specialists, page 9; clinic, page 13; body forms, page 21; hot water bottle, page 32; bedside, page 33; elevator bank, page 36; fever, page 53; headache, page 55; head, page 63; body, page 64; skeleton views, pages 66 and 67; telephone conversation, page 83; clocks, page 89; family trees, pages 102 and 105; medication forms, page 138; hives, page 145; pill reminder, page 150; dietitian, page 160; breakfast, page 162; fruits and vegetables, page 163; physical exam, page 191; emergency room patients, page 216; gallbladder, 217; cardiac rehabilitation, page 221; measles and mumps, page 237; various internal organs, pages 247 and 248; morning routine, page 268; teeth, page 273; dental hygiene, page 274; dental conditions and treatments, page 275; and feeling states, page 278. Robert O. Chase created the remaining drawing and illustrations.

Index